The Village Players

A Narrative History of the Village of Fenton
1937-1941

Robert G. Harris

The Village Players

A Narrative History of the Village of Fenton
1937-1941

Copyright © 2006
Robert G. Harris, Fenton, Michigan

ISBN: 1-59872-702-8

Printed in USA by InstantPublisher.com

Table of Contents

Foreword...In the Beginning

All the world's a stage,
And all the men and women merely players,
They have their exits and their entrances,
And one man in his time plays may parts.

William Shakespeare

It was the spring of 2005 and I had returned home from a winter stay in Florida to find my friend Robert Dery had been hospitalized and was now at home in recuperation. Bob's condition required periodic returns to the hospital to remove fluid that was causing considerable swelling of his abdomen and legs. His visits to the hospital were becoming more frequent and the prognosis for his recovery was not good.

I visited with Bob about every other day and usually found him sitting in his "lazy boy" chair with his swollen legs elevated. His physical condition did not diminish his mental capacity and he was always talkative and upbeat...he was not complaining although he had much about which to complain.

Robert J. Dery

Although he was a few years younger, we found our conversation generally drifted to the "old days"...high school, Michigan State, our military service and of people and things as they once were in Fenton, when we were much younger, before World War II. I started making a list of the people we could remember from the "old days"...the merchants, the teachers, the village leaders, the community center, the high school football games, the girls, the boys, the stores, Kelly's, Mickey's... the movies at the Rowena Theater.

Both of us enjoyed the reminiscing and I saw the exercise as one that provided a diversion for Bob that kept his mind occupied with some pleasant thoughts and an escape from thinking of his dispiriting situation.

I told Bob that we needed to write about the old town, the old days, so those who followed us would have some "memory" of the way things were in the pre-War II Village of Fenton. I told Bob we would call our book "The Village Players"…citing the elegant words of William Shakespeare quoted above. Bob's immediate reaction was…"No, we can't do that…the Village Players (*a local theater group*) already have the name". My reply is now more than apparent!

Not long after, Bob Dery died. He left a large void in the lives of his family and friends…and the community, the City Of Fenton, which he served so well, in many capacities, for over sixty years. This book is dedicated to his memory.

* * *

This book could not have been written without the generous assistance given by Ken Seger and his wife Donna. Ken Seger is the Curator of the Fenton Museum and Donna Seger serves as the President of the Fenton Historical Society. Mr. and Mrs. Seger have devoted hours of every day, every month, every year for years to the collection and preservation of the writings, photographs, artifacts…any and all evidence of our past…for the people of Fenton. They have done all this with the help of a few volunteers and nominal financial support Consequently, any profits derived from the sale of this book will be directed to the Fenton Historical Society in appreciation of and in support of their efforts to preserve the history of our community.

The Prologue

During the decade of the 1930s, the United States and the rest of the world found themselves in a state of economic depression. Following the "crash" of the stock market in October 1929, the United States government took a number of ill-advised actions, such as increasing the tariffs, which only made the situation worse. Their actions were intended to protect the nation's workers and businesses, however what they did further depressed international trade and the economic conditions worsened.

Not unlike the rest of the country, Fenton experienced the effects of the "Great Depression". With the election of Franklin D. Roosevelt in 1932, the "New Deal" began. The "New Deal" was Roosevelt's program to stimulate the economy by providing jobs for the people and financial assistance to State and local governments and businesses, primarily through massive government spending programs.

Throughout the nation, as the number of unemployed citizens increased to an unacceptable level, government assistance to the needy became necessary. County programs were set up to provide the basic foods and necessities. Many of the families in Fenton found the head of the household unemployed and they required assistance from the County. The terms used in the 30s were not those used today; "welfare" was not a common word to describe the "help for the needy" programs. Those who received assistance then were said to be "on relief".

Those "on relief" would visit specified distribution points, such as the Fenton Fire Hall, to pick up their allotment of food. Those who participated in this program received generous amounts of corn meal, butter, lard, flour and California navel oranges as part of their ration. Most of the food products distributed came from Federal surplus food banks. In the early 30s, California navel oranges were not generally available in the town markets, so the school children sporting a California Navel Orange in their school lunch box were usually from a family "on relief".

Unfortunately, there was a bit of a stigma associated with accepting "relief", however there weren't many "rich uncles" around to help out in these times. Everyone needed to feed and cloth their family and most people were grateful for the help in a time of need. Your friends,

2 The Village Players

your neighbors and your relatives all seemed to be struggling. Although some didn't know it, in one way or another, everyone was "poor".

At the beginning of the depression, Fenton had two banks in town. The Commercial Savings Bank, located on the southwest corner of Leroy and Caroline Streets and the Fenton Savings Bank positioned on the northwest corner of the intersection. As the depression worsened and depositors became alarmed by an increasing number of bank failures, the Commercial Savings Bank, fearing a "run" on their bank, closed their operations and attempted to restore their solvency. While they were closed an agreement was made with the Fenton Savings Bank and in 1931 they merged with the more solvent Fenton Savings Bank and the bank was renamed the State Savings Bank of Fenton. The State Savings Bank of Fenton had closed briefly, but being in a much better financial position, reopened and stayed open throughout the depression except for the mandatory "bank holiday" proclaimed for the banks of the entire nation by President Roosevelt in 1933.

In Southeastern Michigan, the economy had marginally improved by the mid-thirties as the automobile industry gained some momentum. A recession in 1935 was a setback and the "Sit Down" strike of 1937 didn't do much to help the return of prosperity. At the depth of the depression in 1933, about one-third of the nation's workers were unemployed and while unemployment was a serious problem in Fenton it never was as severe as in other parts of the country. To say it was not a "serious problem" reminds one of the oft-used distinctions between a "recession" and a "depression". It was said if your neighbor was unemployed it was a recession. However, if you were unemployed it was a depression!

The farmers in the area found the prices for their crops at an all time low, and while many farmers were forced off their farm, in general they were survivors. The farmers were producing products of value, and while the market price for their products was depressed, the products still had value and could be sold or bartered in the local economy. There's a myriad of stories of the farmer paying his Doctor's bill with a couple chickens and a few dozen eggs

Throughout the bad years most of the retailers of the community prevailed and provided the products and the services required by the people of Fenton and the surrounding area.

Paul Bottecelli tells of an incident related to him by his father. It was during the darkest days of the depression when the merchants in town were having a very difficult time keeping their businesses open   Late one afternoon, his father Joseph, then the proprietor of an ice cream parlor on North Leroy Street met Walter Hillman, the owner of a men's clothing store across the street.   Joe was lamenting to Walter that he had been open since noon and he had only 35 cents to show for his efforts.   Walter then told Joe that he should not feel so bad since he hadn't made one sale...not one penny...in the past two days.

For the better part of the decade it is estimated about 15 percent of the residents of Fenton were employed outside of the town, mostly in the automobile manufacturing factories of Flint.   The health of the automobile industry was not only important to the well being of Flint, Michigan it was also important to the economic welfare of all of Genesee County.

While farming and retailing were principal occupations in the Fenton area, the Industrial Machine Tool Company and later the Genesee Tool Company were two employers who provided employment for both skilled and unskilled industrial workers.   With the beginning of the war in Europe in 1939 and especially with the military buildup in the United States just prior to our entry into World War II, these two companies expanded their operations and employed a larger number of both men and women.   Similarly, the automotive industries employed increasing numbers as the war approached and many of the area residents found employment in Flint, as well as the more distant cities of Pontiac, Lansing and Detroit.

Most of the married women in town were not employed outside of the home. Those with children were, for the most part, "stay at home Moms". However, several women were quite prominent in the village businesses. Julia Sweeny, who officed with Attorney Maurice Matthews, was active in real estate and served as Justice of Peace for a period of time.   Maude Hunt had a Millinery store downtown and later Suzanne Luther and Ruth Smith opened Suzanne's Hat Shop.   Dorothy McBroom ran the ice cream parlor for Mickey's Dairy where almost everyone in the region came for malts, milkshakes and five-cent ice cream cones piled high.   Dorothy was a large woman who also excelled in skeet shooting, winning many championships in the State.

Julia Sweeney

Several businesswomen, while not owners or the principals in their respective businesses, were well known to most of the townsfolk. Women such as Mary Hill of the A & P and later a familiar face at the State Savings Bank was a delightful woman who in her quiet way represented her employer in the very best manner.

The Rowena was the only movie theatre and unless you "snuck in" you had to buy your ticket from Mrs. Emily O'Berry. The ten-cent ticket price for children under twelve years of age presented a challenge for some youngsters. It seemed that as hard as one would try to "shrink" as you purchased your ticket, Mrs.O'Berry was certain to find you out. She probably not only knew most of the children in town, but most likely the parents and the birth dates of all their children.

Mary Hill

The "stay at home Moms" faced the daily chores of maintaining a household and family. However, these were the days of radio dramas, the "soap operas", and doing the family wash was made more pleasant while listening to "The Romance of Helen Trent", a program that proposed "that because a woman is 35, or older, romance in life need not be over…that the romance of youth can be extended into middle life and even beyond…"

"Our Gal Sunday" was the story of an orphan girl named Sunday from the little mining town of Silver Creek, Colorado who in young womanhood married England's richest most handsome lord, Lord Henry Brinthrope…the story that asks the question, "Can this girl from a mining town in the West find happiness as the wife of a wealthy and titled Englishman?"

Then there was "Ma Perkins", "The Guiding Light", "Just Plain Bill", "Young Widder Brown", Life Can Be Beautiful", "Hilltop House", "Mary Noble, Backstage Wife" and many other daytime serial stories produced for the American housewife.

Soap Opera characters experienced emotional depths and heights far beyond the experience of most listeners. They came at a time when all Americans, perhaps American women most of all, needed some entertainment and an escape from their immediate problems. They learned how others, even though they were fictional characters, overcame their difficulties, generally more troublesome and complex than theirs.

Outside the home, the Fenton housewife found many opportunities to socialize through a myriad of clubs. Several Child Study groups were active as well as many clubs for playing Bridge or Pedro and other card games. "Bunco", a dice game, was very popular and there were clubs organized to play the game. In addition, it appears as if all the churches had active women's organizations.

In the 1930s, two of the more prominent women's clubs were the Bayview Club and Entre Nous. Both of these clubs were organized in the 1800s and surprisingly, both clubs continue to be active in the community to this day.

The Bayview Club was started in Fenton in 1897 and was related to a movement in Michigan's Methodist Church traceable to 1875. In October of 1897, Mrs. Roe, a field secretary for the Bayview association, met with 15 ladies in Fenton and formed a Womens club, the Bayview Reading Circle of Fenton.

The Entre Nous Club celebrates its origin in Fenton in the year 1878 and attributes it's founding to Miss Helen L. Wood. Miss Wood lived with her brothers Frank and Will and her sister Abbie, all of whom remained unmarried. There residence was the house on the corner of Roberts and Oak Streets that in later years became the home of the American Legion post. Miss Wood became the Principal of the Fenton High School and enjoyed an excellent reputation as a teacher, administrator and a disciplinarian.

All the research on Entre Nous strongly indicates the club was an independent local organization and not part of a larger club organization, however in 1938 there is a report in *The Fenton Independent* newspaper that suggests the club is to send two members to a "convention in Traverse City". In the absence of any other evidence to the contrary, the Entre Nous of yesterday was, as it is today, a local unaffiliated Womens club.

It was the "heyday" for lodges and other fraternal organizations for both men and women. Several of the fraternal organizations owned their own buildings and meeting halls. For example, the Mason's owned a three story brick building on the northwest corner of the intersection of Leroy and Caroline Streets. The Masons used the top two floors of their building while the State Savings Bank and Tamlyn's Camera store occupied the ground floor.

The I.O.O.F. (Independent Order of Oddfellows) and their partners, the Rebekahs owned a building in the first block of South Leroy Street. Their meeting hall was on the second floor .The street level space in the building was occupied by the Fenton (Bowling) Alleys and until late in 1940, the U.S. Post Office

Sandwiched (no pun intended) in between the entrance to the Odd Fellow's hall and the Post Office was a small restaurant. The restaurant, often called "The Hole in the Wall", had its own doorway just next to the Odd Fellows entrance to the stairs to the second floor. Diners would come through the doorway and move to the rear where the lunchroom was located beneath the stairway to the second floor. During its existence, several different persons operated the lunchroom and many others worked there over the years. Hazel Merrill, who had previously operated the restaurant then owned by John Hoskins, had "Merrill's Lunch" in the space in 1939.

The Odd Fellows had instituted their Lodge in Fenton in June of 1899 and through the years had played a significant role in the community. However, the Lodge became defunct in June of 1967. The Rebekahs, named the Favorite Rebekahs, who had served Fenton women for most of the period, also left the scene at that time.

The Isaac Walton League never owned a downtown building, during this period, but they were very active, especially with the hunters and other "outdoorsmen" in the community. While not as prominent in the public eye, the Fenton club has continued to survive to the present day.

The American Legion and the Veterans of Foreign Wars were very energetic and their activities helped develop and maintain a very strong sense of patriotism..."Americanism"…among the citizens. These veteran organizations were obviously concerned about the rise of Communism in Russia and the activities of some Americans disenchanted with American "capitalism" and advocating socialistic and communistic solutions to America's economic problems.

The American Legion and Veterans of Foreign Wars organizations were both populated with veterans of the First World War. Most of the veterans were in their mid to late thirties and had the energy and the interest to do work for the general welfare of the community.

The James DeWitt Post of the American Legion was established in 1919 and immediately took an active role in community affairs. For years, the American Legion hall was at the northwest corner of East Caroline and Walnut Streets on the second floor of the building referred to as the "Macabee Building". Years later, the Legion Post purchased the residence of Bert Rollins at the corner of Roberts and Walnut, behind the Macabee building, to use as their meeting hall

In 1935 there were still three Union veterans of the Civil War living in Fenton. They were Andrew Bly, Isaac Lawrence and Charles Bentley. Mr. Bly's son, Andrew Jr. was a World War I veteran and one of the founders of the Curtis-Wolverton Post of the V.F.W. in Fenton. The V.F.W was organized in 1935 and chartered on July 5, 1936. The V.F.W. had no regular meeting hall until 1938 when it leased the second floor of the building just north of the Mason's building on North Leroy Street.

The three remaining Union veterans of the Civil War living in Fenton were: L-R Andrew Bly, Charles Bentley and Isaac H. Lawrence. This picture was taken on September 7, 1935,. Their ages at that time were 91, 92 and 93 respectively.

The V.F.W. began when, on March 12, 1935, a group of World War I overseas veterans held an organizational meeting at the home of Joseph Bottecelli and formed what has become known as the Curtis-Wolverton Post. At that meeting they elected the following persons as their officers: Commander Walter Stiff; Senior Vice Commander Jesse D. Straugh; Junior Vice Commander Floyd Lee; Chaplain Joe Franks; Officer of the Day R. L Walker; Quartermaster Joe Oberlin; Adjutant Hoyt Glaspie; Guard Henry English and Trustees: Calvin Stiff, Fred Slover and George Pellett.

The V.F. W. post was named the Curtis-Wolverton Post after Leal Curtis and Howard Wolverton. Leal Curtis was the first soldier from Genesee County to lose his life in World War I. Howard Wolverton was the first man from Fenton to die in the conflict.

Jesse Straugh played a large role in both the V.F.W and the American Legion in the 1930s. Jesse had a large family and very little money, and

Jesse Straugh

One would suspect from his general circumstances that he was not well educated. His income was derived from various odd jobs that came his way. He managed the Fenton (Bowling) Alleys for several years until Clarence "Bud" Edinger purchased the business and took over the management himself.

In the late 1930s, Jesse wrote a weekly report on the V.F.W. for *The Fenton Independent*. It was not just a sketchy outline, but a lengthy exposition of the new Post's activities, plans and philosophy. On occasion, he wrote excellent articles on topics related to patriotism or veteran affairs. His writings demonstrate intelligence, writing skill and an insight often masked by his physical appearance and his obviously poor economic condition.

The Daughters of Union Veterans and Women's Relief Corps were active patriotic organizations active during this period and often held joint meetings and cosponsored patriotic events. Both organizations were connected with the Grand Army of the Republic, the GAR. The national organization, Womens Relief Corps, was formed to serve the then unmet needs of the Union veterans and their families. Sometime in the 1940s both organizations disappeared from the village scene.

One of the men's clubs, which was organized in the early part of the century and continues to exist in the present, was the XX Club. The XX Club is a very unusual organization. It has no goals, no agenda, and no fund raising projects, none of the trappings of clubs like Kiwanis or Rotary. They have a dinner meeting monthly…purely social. Interestingly, today's members have little institutional memory and consequently have little to contribute to its history or records of the club.

Consequently, what is reported here is the most prevalent and accepted "myth". As the story goes, Fenton men had organized an

EXchange club, as part of a national organization. As such, part of their local dues and fees were passed on to the District and National headquarters of the organization. This is a standard and accepted practice in national and international organizations

But, then comes the "great depression". Money was tight and the local club members questioned the practice of sending "their" money to an enigmatic distant group when they needed the money at home. Consequently, they decided to become a "local" club and sever their relationship with this national organization. Since they had to rename their "new" club, they chose name "XX Club", which bore some relationship to the old …E " X " change Club name.

Fentonites were very active with club activities, but they still exercised the many other opportunities for recreation and entertainment available. They devoted considerable time and efforts to play production, going to the movies, fishing, skating, swimming and other outdoor sports.

While some young people were very active in team sports, opportunities for participation in individual sports were not readily available. Tennis, skiing and golf were not as attractive as they are today. There were no public tennis courts in Fenton and the only golf course in the area was on the west side of Lake Fenton, (generally referred to as Long Lake) on Torrey Road. The hills of Tyrone Township provided an opportunity for snow skiing and those that may have had a set of skis did try the sport in this hilly terrain, however, there were no winter sports facilities with structured ski slopes in the area.

With all the lakes within a few miles of Fenton, the summer provided lots of opportunity for swimming, sailing, fishing and boating. There were only a couple powerboats on the lakes, so water skiing had not yet made a presence. The winter sports on the lakes included skating, ice boating, and fishing. During the winter months, the lakes were dotted with small shanties, which sheltered those who enjoyed spearing fish.

However, a principal source of entertainment for most families was the wide selection of radio programs. These were the radio days of "The Lone Ranger", "Jack Armstrong-The All American Boy", "The Aldrich Family" "Fibber McGee and Molly", "Gang Busters", "The Green Hornet", Fanny Brice's "Baby Snooks", Edgar Bergen and Charlie McCarthy, "Mercury Theatre" with Orson Welles, Jimmy Allen and Speed Robertson, "Little Orphan Annie" and many others.

The youngsters would hurry home to catch the latest episode of the Lone Ranger and Tonto, or other favorite adventure stories and later huddle around the radio with their family to laugh with Charlie McCarthy and Edgar Bergen. At the end the day, many would be lying in bed and scaring themselves to sleep listening to "Inner Sanctum" or the "Green Hornet" or some creepy murder mystery.

President Roosevelt would have the nation sitting close to their radios to hear his "Fireside" talks. Joe Louis, "the Brown Bomber" had most of the villagers anxiously following every round, every blow of his fights with the likes of Max Schmeling and others.

The teenagers and young adults listened to the "Big Bands" of Benny Goodman, Tommy Dorsey, Artie Shaw and others, even "royals" like "Duke" Ellington and "Count" Basie. While the older citizens were convinced the end of "good music" had arrived, most enjoyed the singing of Frank Sinatra, Dick Haymes, Ella Fitzgerald, "Lilting" Martha Tilton or Helen Forrest. For the "older" folks, the Saturday and Sunday programming of national radio networks often included opera performances and some serious theatre dramas.

The people of Fenton actually created much of their own entertainment. Hardly a week went by without one of the theater groups at the community center, the churches or the high school presenting a play, musical or choral or band concert. The City Band presented a weekly outdoor concert throughout the summer months and several shows during the winter.

Most of the townsfolk found a myriad of "things to do" with their clubs, dances, plays, sports and shopping. Yes, shopping! It was not unusual for a group of young ladies to catch a Short Lines bus in front of the Fenton Drug store at Leroy and Caroline Streets and travel to Flint for a shopping tour. The bus stop in Flint was at the Milner Hotel on South Saginaw Street just a few blocks from Smith Bridgman's and a host of other stores in downtown Flint, Michigan.

Smith Bridgeman's was a typical upscale city department store of the time. Operator-controlled elevators served the many departments on several floors. The uniformed operators would announce the floor and the various products to be found at that level as the elevator doors were being opened.

Flint, Michigan offered many other attractions to the people of Fenton, both young and old. Flint had many large movie theatres, and the Capitol with its organ playing between the screen presentations was always a special treat. And then there was the IMA Auditorium. The IMA was the place to go to dance to the music of the "big bands" on tour. Most of the time the "dancers" were "standers" crowded near the bandstand to watch the singers and musicians. For many, nothing was more thrilling than to be only a few feet away from young Frank Sinatra as he sang with the Tommy Dorsey orchestra.

A trip to Flint, especially for the younger crowd, was not complete without a stop at "Kewpies" for a very special hamburger or a "Vernors" at the their store on South Saginaw. . The Vernors people had a parking lot immediately adjacent to their establishment and the wall of the building bordering one side of the parking area had a very colorful painting of a group of gnomes doing what they needed to do to produce this very special ginger ale called "Vernors". However, it wasn't all fun and games; there was work to be done!

Fenton was the center of a significant farm community and where one of the State's leading agribusinesses, the Michigan Bean Company, had chosen to locate a grain elevator. Country elevators were an essential part of the agriculture business at this time. They were the tall, round, grain silos that stood in rural towns next to railroad sidings. While Fenton's elevator lacked the "round silo" it was an impressively large wooden structure, which dominated the area and would continue its domination for years after the elevator business was terminated.

Local farmers would bring their beans, grains, and other produce to the nearest elevator to trade goods and sell their crops. Louis A. Reidel "was" the Michigan Bean Company in Fenton and, in addition to managing the elevator; he played a constructive role in community organizations and activities

Not far from the Michigan Bean elevator across the railroad tracks and a bit to the east stood Fenton's railroad depot. Fenton was one of the many stops along the Grand Trunk's Muskegon to Detroit rail line.

The person most identified with the depot during the early part of the century was George Anglen. Mr. Anglen had become the baggage man at the depot in 1912 and continued to serve throughout the decade and beyond. Besides handling and storing the baggage, he was responsible for receiving the U.S. Mail and delivering it to the Fenton Post Office. While celebrating his 25th year on the job in 1939, George reported he hadn't taken a vacation for eleven years and had never failed to deliver the mail. In earlier years, when the cement plants west of town at Silver and Ponemah (better known as "Mud" Lake) lakes were in production, George had a crew of nine men working with him at the depot. By the 1930's it had become a one-man show.

The older Leo Miner was the Grand Trunk's general agent and during the 30's his office and work area was across the tracks from the passenger depot.   Here he handled the freight that flowed into and out of this active town.

The third individual in the depot was John Weidman who was the telegrapher and doubled as the Ticket Agent. Upon entering the depot, one would generally hear the click of the telegraphy equipment and soon John would leave his telegraphy room and become a "ticket agent".

While the rail line was still important to the business and well being of the citizenry of Fenton, automobile and truck traffic was very evident and began to assume a dominant role in the town's commerce.

Highway route US 23 ran directly through the town from north to south before veering to the southwest and becoming the road to Hartland.   There was a flow of vehicles moving through downtown most of the time.   It seemed to only become a "problem" on football Saturdays at the University of Michigan in Ann Arbor, some forty miles to the south. On these fall Saturdays, the vehicular traffic through town was "bumper to bumper" for several hours before game time and for several hours after the end of the game.

No one prospered more from this heavy traffic moving through town than Art Dumanois, proprietor the historic Fenton Hotel. Many of the football fans either stopped at the Hotel on the way to the game or on their way home. The Fenton Hotel became a popular place to stop for a pre-game lunch or for dinner following the game.   Since Art Dumanois held the only "liquor by the bottle" license in town, those who were interested in having a "nip or two" during the game found the hotel a convenient place to purchase their 'liquid" refreshments. Some jokesters suggested that half of the empty bottles which littered the UM stadium following a game came from the Fenton Hotel.

The blacktopped US 23 only extended to the south just beyond the village limits before it turned into a gravel road. By 1937 the hard surfacing of the highway had only reached Brighton and it was late in the decade before the stretch of road from there to Fenton was completely a hard surface road.

The Fenton Hotel was the premiere establishment in the "pecking order" of the   town's "watering holes". Several other establishments were well attended by the "ordinary" folks of the town. Rightly or wrongly, the Fenton Hotel's clientele were looked upon as the town's "upper crust". Perhaps it was because the Hotel was the only place in town that served liquor by the glass. All the other vendors had only beer and wine to offer. It wasn't until 1936 when Joe Bottecelli was granted a license to sell liquor by the glass at his Virginia Tavern.

A fellow having just finished a day's work at the Buick factory in Flint was unlikely to stop at the Fenton Hotel for drink on his way home. The same fellow would, however, feel quite comfortable having a few mixed drinks or dinner and drinks at the Hotel in the evening with his wife. But, after work, he would more likely "have a beer" at the Virginia Tavern, John Turco's Central Tavern or Beck's Tavern, all in the same block on North Leroy Street, or stopping at Walden's Cobblestone on Fenton Road (Leroy Street) just north of the village limits.

Before they closed in May of 1937, he may have stopped at the Wander Inn, especially if he was interested in eating as well as drinking. The Wander Inn was more of a restaurant that served beer, unlike the others, which were taverns with a limited food menu.

A couple of "out-of-town" favorites were Mickey Allen's tavern on Mud Lake (now Lake Ponemah) and the Green Lantern on Torrey Road. Only trouble with going to Mickey Allen's was the steep and dangerous railroad crossing, where, on occasion someone would unexpectedly meet one of the Grand Trunk's finest. Another proprietor now operates a tavern at the location and the dangerous crossing still exists.

Joe Bottecelli was the proprietor of an ice cream and confectionary shop in the 100 block of North Leroy, when in 1934 he purchased the corner building and leased it to Leah Marr. She opened a beer garden called Leah's Rendezvous. In a year or so, after the business failed, Joe Bottecelli took over the tavern and renamed it the Virginia Tavern after his oldest daughter.

Joe Bottecelli

On a nice day, especially if business was slow, one could observe John Turco, wearing a large white apron, standing in front of his tavern. Occasionally, Ed Gould his next-door neighbor would be taking a break and standing in front of his market. Ed wore a large white apron also; however, while John Turco's was a brilliant white, Ed Gould would generally have some blood staining from his butcher shop activities.

Of all the downtown taverns, undoubtedly Beck's tavern was the rowdiest and had the worst reputation. Beck's Tavern was owned and operated by Thomas. M. "Beck" Carmer. Carmer was a decent enough fellow, a law-abiding citizen; however some of his "regulars" were marginal to say the least. "Beck" enjoyed playing cards at the pool hall across the street from his tavern where he smoked his notorious 'black devil" cigars

It was not uncommon for the downtown storeowners to live with their families in an apartment above their place of business. At one time or another, the Bottecelli, Piccinni and Turco families lived in these downtown apartments. Martin Piccinni, whose wife was the sister of Agnes Bottecelli, was a shoemaker and ran the "Up to Date" Shoe Repair shop next to Bottecelli's Ice Cream Parlor.

On some of the hot summer nights, the conditions in the apartments were not very conducive to sleeping. Paul Bottecelli, Joe's oldest son, tells of how he and his siblings would often sleep on the back porch of their upstairs apartment on those hot nights. Their back porch over-looked the alley running behind the businesses on North Leroy Street and Bottecelli's store was only two doors south of the notorious Beck's Tavern. It is told that on frequent occasions, some of Beck's customers would take their disputes to the alley behind the tavern and in view of the Bottecelli children on their back porch. The fights became part of their summer entertainment.

The second floors of the downtown buildings were not only used as apartments. There were several meeting halls and some businesses. Dr. Kochenderfer, and later Dr Noble Peckham, had their dental offices above Harry Lemen's grocery store. This second floor office had a very large window facing Leroy Street. The dental chair was placed in this area, so one could sit in the chair and observe the activities along the 100 block of South Leroy Street, as the Dentist did his work...

The *Rowena* theatre building housed several other businesses. Upstairs were the insurance office of Horace H. Hitchcock and the law office of George McNeal. In addition to the theatre the ground floor had a barbershop and a jeweler's store. John A. Johnson advertised his professions as "Jeweler and Optometrist". In June 1938, Harvey W. Walters and Arlene Pilmore purchased the Lobdell Barber and Beauty Shop from Howard Lobdell. They renamed the business The Fenton Barber and Beauty Shop. Howard Lobdell and Theda Brooks former operators would assist the new owners on a part-time basis. Later, in 1940, J. C. Peck, owner and operator of the theatre and building, did an extensive remodeling of the theater front. The Rowena remodeling eliminated the barbershop, but the second floor offices remained as well as Johnson's Jewelry Store.

One time there was a rumor of some outside persons investigating the possibility of opening a new movie house in Fenton. Whether or not, "Jaycee" Peck heard the same rumor or not, it wasn't long before he purchased the McCracken building directly across the street from the Rowena. He redid the front of the building in the style of a theatre and built a projection booth inside. That was the extent of the remodeling for theatre use, but the basic changes had been made, so a rapid conversion from an "ordinary store" to a theatre could be made expeditiously. There were no further rumors or evidence of a new theatre coming to Fenton. In actuality there probably was no need for a second theatre. J.C. Peck brought first run movies to the Rowena, which had three programs changes a week and he kept the place clean, orderly and with a reasonable admission charge.

J. C. Peck was one of the most interesting persons in the town during the 1930s and beyond until his death in 1988. "Jayce" was well known to all the villagers, both young and old, and he was very friendly, witty and talkative as he moved about the town. He was a "man on the go" as it seemed he was always crossing Leroy Street on his way to John Turco's Central Tavern, Kelley's Ice Cream parlor (formerly Joe's) or some other place where he had business or a person to visit.

J. C. Peck was very proud of the fact he was a descendent of Clark Dibble, one of the early settlers who founded "Dibbleville" on the south bank of the Shiawassee in the early 1800s.

JC's father Marc, who once was a tavern owner, started the first movie theatre in town. He took an ordinary store on South Leroy Street, set up a. white cloth for a screen, a piano, some seats and a projector. Since it was silent movies, the pianist, Mrs.Olive Parker, would play music that would support the action or emotion being displayed on the screen. At the end of each reel of film, the audience would have to wait as a new reel was placed upon the projector. At the end of a showing, each of the reels would need to be rewound. Consequently the next group of theatre-goers would be required to wait until the reels were rewound and first reel was on the projector and ready to go again.

As the movie industry developed, Mr. Peck built a new theatre in the middle of the 100 block of North Leroy Street. Previously there had been a cigar store at that location, however after a fire, the lot stood vacant until the theatre was built. The new theatre was named after his daughter and JC's sister, Rowena.

In 1925, upon the death of his father, and at the age of 19, "J.C" dropped out of the University of Michigan and assumed management of the *Rowena*.

There were just a few "ice cream" parlors in town during the Thirties They really were the only places you could purchase ice cream. The grocery stores did not have frozen foods, including ice cream, or the capability to keep them frozen.

Unless you made ice cream at home, which some people did on occasion, and you had the "taste" for some ice cream you needed to drop in at Joe Bottecelli's (later Kelly's), or across the street at the Oakland Dairy (which closed in the winter!), English's Confectionary, the counter at O'Dell's drug store (all on North Leroy Street) or Chris Gunis' shop in the "south side" business district.. But more likely you went to Mickey's Dairy on South Leroy Street.

During the summer, people would drive from miles around to buy one of Mickey's Malted Milks, served in a tall metal container and so thick it was difficult to draw the frosty mixture through a straw…all for 15 cents! A piled high cone of ice cream was available for 5 cents. Besides, if the store's counter was crowded, you could have "curb service" and enjoy your treats in the comfort of your car. Many of the young men seemed to prefer "curb service" since then they had the opportunity to talk to the pretty young girls who served the customers in their cars.

Marie Durant at Mickey's "Curb Service" with new Community Center in background

There was an abundance of grocery stores in "downtown" Fenton at the time. Grant Whitman's and Ed Gould's markets were on the east side of the first block on Leroy Street north of Caroline Street. On the other side of the 100 block of North Leroy, one would find Byerly's, which was managed by C.A. "Bud" Leech. On the west side of South Leroy Street, the first block south had Moffett's (later Alchins) which was managed by Don Alchin, J.E. "Fritz" Judevine's (later Harry Lemen's market), the A & P store managed by Elton Austin and the Kroger Store, which had several managers during the period, including Bill Weideman, Jim Townes and John Millington.

Again, the "south side" had its own grocery stores. Arthur Dubord was the proprietor of the South Side Grocery. Most of his customers lived on the "south side" and traded with him in lieu of walking "downtown" where the majority of the grocery stores were located. Arthur Dubord was the sole grocer for years before Charles Truchan opened the Sanitary Market just a few doors north of Dubord's.

Most stores had small, separate meat departments. In a way the butchers were like celebrities. Many shoppers traded at the store where their favorite butcher worked. If the butcher would move to another store, the shopper was likely to follow him to his new store. Some of the "stars" were Nelson Curtis of Moffett's, Willard "Butch" Hatfield of the A & P, Kroger's Fred Carroll and Lemen's Burt Burrows.

Ed Gould did his own butchering and his persistently bloody apron was evidence of the fact. Duane Theisen, the oldest son of Hugo Theisen, the town's Ford dealer, tells the story of his dealings with Mr. Gould.

About once a week, Duane's mother would give him 25 cents and on his way home from school, he would stop at Gould's market and ask Mr. Gould for 25 cents worth of fresh pork shoulder. Ed Gould would proceed to cut a piece of pork, wrap it and Duane would take it home where his mother would prepare it for dinner that evening. In those days, the 25-cent piece of meat was more than enough to feed the family of four

Most of the time during the Thirties, there was angle parking on Leroy Street. On Saturday nights, especially during the summer months, the downtown parking was very crowded, and one would generally find groups of three of four men, obviously farmers, dressed in clean bib overalls, with red sun baked faces and a freshly scrubbed appearance, visiting with their friends and neighbors while their wives did the shopping.

All of the stores had "clerks" to fill your order. Most of the part-time clerks were young high school age boys and girls. The stores had a counter that ran the length of the store a few feet from the wall. Along the wall, behind the counter, were shelves, which were loaded with canned goods and other products.

The customer would usually present the clerk with a list of the items desired, although many held tight to the list and ordered one item at a time. The clerk would leave the customer, who stood on the other side of the counter, and move down behind the counter to the location of the desired item, remove it from the shelf, return and place it on the counter before the customer.

As each item was delivered, the price of the item was written in pencil on the side of a large brown paper bag, "27, 18, 31, 33, 25..." Then when the shopping was completed, adding the long list of numbers..."7...15...16...19...24... write down 4...carry the 2..." There were no adding machines or calculators available, so if you had trouble with addition, you could not do the job!

When the clerk had possession of the list, he/she could reduce the number of trips by picking several items on the list on one trip. However, many times the clerk found himself running from one end to the other chasing down the items as the customer read them one by one from the shopping list.

The fresh vegetables were displayed in one area and were occasionally sprinkled with fresh, cold water to improve their appearance. At closing time, the vegetables were packed in cracked ice in a large 55-gallon drum. A layer of carrots, more ice, a layer of head lettuce, more ice ...etc. On the following day, the vegetables were removed from the drum, the unsightly wilted or rotting parts were pared away and the vegetables placed in the most attractive display possible. There were no packaged vegetables available. No cellophane bags of carrots or any other vegetable.

Up until the late 1930s, most of the celery sold in Fenton came from the farms around Kalamazoo. These farms were known for a rich black soil that was very well suited for the growing of celery. Then all at once, California grown celery called "Pascal Celery" hit the market. Most agreed that it was greener, tenderer with larger stalks and much better than the pale; small stringy stalks of Michigan celery. It wasn't many years before the "Pascal" celery took over the market (even to this day) and the farms in Southwest Michigan were growing something other than celery.

The A & P store was one of the few stores that had large sacks of flour available. These 100-pound sacks were made of cotton cloth and each had a different printed pattern. When the lady shopper came to the flour item, she would accompany the clerk to the back storage room to look over the stack of flour sacks. Invariably, the lady's choice of pattern was on the sack at the bottom of the pile. Once the pile was "unstacked" the selected bag of flour would be hoisted on the clerk's shoulder and delivered to the customer's auto...parked somewhere along Leroy Street.

Most all the customers expected and received "carry-out" service without needing to request it. Many clerks looked forward to a "carry-out", especially during hot days or nights, which provided an opportunity to get out of the store for a "breather".

Home delivery of groceries was not usually available especially at the larger stores such as A & P, Kroger's or Byerly's, however some stores such as Lemen's and Dubord's would make a home delivery for certain customers.   Perhaps home delivery was akin to "charge accounts". During the depression, small groceries, such as Dubords and Lemens, extended credit to regular customers. As the grocery purchases were made, they were recorded in a book kept for each customer, and at the end of the week (hopefully ending in a payday); the customer was expected to pay all or part of his account.   Most of the larger stores, especially the "chain" stores, could not operate in this manner. Those stores that did conduct "credit" business were often left holding accounts that were non-collectible.   However, both Dubords and Lemens didn't appear to have this experience.

Harry Lemen did experience some political problems because of his policy of providing credit to individuals who were Village employees. As Village President, some of his detractors, of which there were relatively few, circulated a rumor just before an election, saying that one of Harry's conditions for employment for Village employees was that they had to purchase their groceries at his store.   Harry Lemen faced this accusation squarely and publicly and silenced his critics by winning an overwhelmingly victory at the election

At the time, Fenton was blessed with some of the best retail stores in the county. It seemed as if Don McGuire's Hardware store in the 100 block of North Leroy had a few of every bolt or nut ever manufactured. That is probably a gross exaggeration, however one could only dream of a hardware store so well equipped to meet the many and diverse needs of the people in the environs of the Village of Fenton in the late 1930s. Affable John Dooley, who ran the store with his uncle, Don McGuire, was very knowledgeable and extremely helpful.

Newcomer Lewis Gage opened his hardware store in the old Commercial Savings Bank building and he did a remarkable job serving his customers. However, "Lewie" Gage will be remembered more as a "fiddler" than as a proprietor of a hardware store. "Lewie" Gage, his violin and his orchestra played for hundreds of dances at the Community Center and all around the area.

The Granger Hardware, operated by Frank Granger was also in the 100 block of North Leroy Street and his ability to meet the needs of the community and its people is evidenced by his many years in business.

The largest retail stores in Fenton in the late 1930s were the D & C Store, Pellett's Department Store, Rolland's Dry Goods Company and Becker's Federated store.

The D & C store was managed by Carl Tisch and was in the tradition of the "Five and Dime" stores of the era. The "D" in D & C represented the name of the chain store owner, Mr. Dancer of Mason, Michigan. Long after the D & C store disappeared, "Dancer's Department Store" continued to serve the people of the community.

Before 1937, the D & C store was located on the east side of South Leroy Street in the second building from Caroline Street. In 1937, they purchased the corner building and expanded their store to Caroline Street. The new store was very "spacious" for a store in Fenton and typical of "dime stores" of the time, it displayed a large assortment of goods on tables throughout the store.

One of the features of the "new D & C" was a large two-sided candy counter with glass display cases full of tempting candies. Jean (Gordon) Weigant, one of the schoolgirls employed at the D & C recalls the candy counter position was only entrusted to older, more experienced employees. Mr. Tisch was aware of how candy could mysteriously disappear!

The store employed a good number of women, both school age "kids" and older ladies, during a time when jobs were difficult to find. The D & C was an important integral part of the downtown business community and it's manager, Carl Tisch, was personally involved in many of the village activities

A visit to Rolland's Dry Goods store was rather like a "step back in time" even in the 1930s. The store was one of the largest in town and was shaped like a backward "L". It had its main entrance on the eastside of North Leroy Street, just two doors north of the intersection of Leroy and Caroline Streets. A "rear" entrance was located behind the corner drug store on the north side of East Caroline Street.

The merchandise was displayed on an array of tables throughout the store, as was the customary way of displaying merchandise in that period. What everyone who ever entered the store is most likely to remember was the "trolley" system " which ran throughout the store. It was used to transport the money and receipts to and from Mr. Rolland's "office".

As a customer, once you had selected the item you wished to purchase, and presented your cash payment to the clerk, he/she would place the sales slip and your money in a small "casket-like" box and attach this box to a vertical track that led to an overhead trolley system. The box would move overhead through the store to the raised office location where Mr. Rolland would be there to receive it. He would proceed to empty the "box", place any change that was due, along with a receipt of purchase, into the box and return the box to the trolley line. The box would then make a return trip to the clerk's location and the clerk would deliver the contents to you, the customer, to complete the transaction.

Mr. Rolland's "office" was quite unique. The office was raised about three feet above the floor and provided a vantage point from which he could observe the comings and goings throughout the store.

From appearances alone one could make an intelligent judgment about the man. Charles Rolland was always dressed to the "T". When searching for adjectives that would best describe him, these come to mind: urbane, sophisticated, cultured, and refined. His contemporaries had great respect for him and his wife Grace and both played very influential roles in the affairs of the community. Charles Rolland was the first Chairman of the Board of Governors for the Fenton Community Center.

Charles and Grace Rolland at home

In the thirties, Pelletts Department Store was the principal "department" store in town. Their brick three-story building was built in 1875 and had been in continuous use as a retail store since its completion. The owner, George W. Pellett served as an Army artillery officer in World War I and following the conclusion of the war he returned to his home county, Genesee County. He entered business in Mt. Morris but after two years there, he came to Fenton in 1921 to open Pelletts Department Store.

Pelletts Department Store and the D & C store had larger street frontages than any of the other businesses on Leroy Street, each with the equivalent of the width of three lots.

Pelletts had a complete offering in men's furnishings as well as a large women's department. Mrs. Grace Wright had worked for George Pellett since the first days of the business and she headed the "Corset and Domestics" department. Young Neal Woodward, who graduated from Fenton High School in 1937 was in charge of the "Men's Clothing and Furnishings". Although he was still a student, young George Pellett, the owner's oldest son, spent many hours in the store and was very knowledgeable of the retail clothing business.

George W. Pellett

Art Becker's Federated Department Store was a smaller operation compared to Pelletts, but had a strong customer base and provided the community with a varied selection in both men and women's clothing. Art Becker had operated the shoe department at the Rolland's store, before opening up his own store on East Caroline Street. Later Becker's moved to South Leroy only a door away from Pelletts.

Fenton enjoyed one very unique store…"Tamlyn the Camera Man". George Tamlyn served most the photographic needs of the town. He photographed the graduating seniors at the High School, all the athletic teams and did hundreds of individual portraits for both the young and the old people. George Tamlyn's store and studio was next door and directly north of the State Savings Bank which was on the corner of Leroy and Adelaide Streets. George generally had a few selected pictures positioned in his display window. Everyone walking past Tamlyn's seemed to stop and view his display of pictures. When someone's portrait appeared in the window, a new "town celebrity" was born!

Significantly, George Tamlyn performed another very valuable service for the community. George Tamlyn literally created a photographic history for the Village for over three decades. His photos of Fenton's downtown mill burning in 1921 are graphic recordings of one of the more momentous events to occur in Fenton during the early part of the Twentieth Century. About the same time, he took to the sky and produced aerial photos of the town. These aerial photos of the community were probably the first of their kind.

In general, George Tamlyn's name appeared in white lettering on his photos. If they were photos of buildings, street scenes, celebrations, parades or news worthy events, one would generally find an inscription identifying the subject and the date the photo was taken. Of the thousands of "Tamlyn" photos that were printed and distributed, several hundred have been collected and placed in the Fenton Museum.

Residents of small towns are more likely to remember town "characters" than the people in the larger cities. Each era undoubtedly have their own eccentrics, and for most of the 1930s Fenton had Herb Dutton and his bass drum and his long time associate, snare drummer William H. "Billy" Thompson.

In those days, Herb and Billy would often stand in front a store and perform a "drum duet". After a time, the merchant would come out of the store and suggest they move to another location...perhaps near the entrance of his competitor? The pair would willingly accept a cash offering for their efforts and following the merchant's suggestion move to another location before continuing to play their "music".

In the early thirties, Marge Kelly worked as a waitress at John Hoskins Restaurant. She tells of the pair, Dutton and Thompson coming into the restaurant, sitting at prime table near the window and, with paper and pencil in hand, start working on their "music".

On at least one occasion, they brought with them a fresh jar of honey with bees still swarming around the gooey mass. She reports they never bought anything and after a time would return to the streets, perhaps to try out the new tune they had written?

"Billy" died in April of 1937 and subsequently Herb seemed to play his drum less than in prior years

It is interesting to note, that no one seemed to get too upset with the shenanigans of the two drummers. Herb and Billy were accepted, no one called the police, they were just part of the village scene and in a way they brought a smile to everyone's face.

Herb Dutton & Billy Thompson

Actually, the town was filled with "interesting" persons. One such "interesting" person was Allen Gunning. Mr. Gunning was in the real estate business. He not only brokered the sale of real estate, but also on occasion bought and sold property on his own. His sales activities were not limited to the immediate Fenton area and neither were his clients. It was not unusual for him to negotiate the sale of a farm in Montrose to a resident of Detroit.

Those who remember Mr. Gunning recall he was always dressed in a suit, not necessary well pressed, for he was a man on the street. Frequently, he would take a well-worn uncashed check for $10,000 from his wallet and show it to his associate at the time, as if to show he was a man of some means.

Since he seemed to be on the village streets most of the day, he was often looking for an available toilet to satisfy his needs. After using the facility at one location for a while, he would often "wear out his welcome" at that location and have to cultivate another rest stop in the downtown area.

He would visit Faye Beach, the editor and publisher of *The Fenton Independent* quite frequently and Mr. Beach would often report the subject of their conversation in his newspaper. On one occasion, Mr. Gunning came to Mr. Beach with what he claimed to be the "oldest cigar in Fenton". It seems that many years ago, a satisfied client gave a cigar to Mr. Gunning and he had kept it in its original wrapper since that time. Once his claim had been published in the newspaper, Mr. Beach had several visitors who disputed the Gunning claim. It provided some interesting and unusual copy that undoubtedly helped Mr. Beach fill some space in his weekly issue.

A common sign around Fenton…and the whole area…proclaimed "5 Gals $1". No it wasn't an advertisement for a dance hall or anything more sordid, it was proclaiming the going price for gasoline! In the late thirties, the gasoline at almost all stations was selling for twenty cents a gallon, and the price rarely varied, hence the almost permanent sign…"5 Gals $1".

Fenton did not lack in the number of "gas stations". There were many located all around town with the full range of brands available. Some of those were: Kenny Robbins with a nice new Standard Oil station at the corner of Leroy and Ellen; A newly built station at Shiawassee and Leroy for Floyd Lee and later Russell Carmer; Guy Merrick's Super Service sold Buick automobiles, Firestone tires and Hi-Speed gasoline at the corner of Roberts (now Silver Lake Road) and North Leroy Streets; Floyd Hartley's had his station only one block away, west on Roberts; Joe Pasco had a Shell station at the corner of Shiawassee and Adelaide Streets; and there was Aldrich Locke's Mobilgas station on Fenton Road (now North Leroy) just north of the village limits.

Many of the youthful drivers of the period can remember the single gas pump located at Ray Hagerman's store one block east of the Fenton Hotel on Main Street. Occasionally, a young driver would note that the family car, which he had been allowed to drive that evening, was dangerously low on fuel. It was generally after midnight when this occurred and all of the gas stations were closed. What to do? At this time one remembered that Mr. Hagerman would sell you gas at almost any hour; after all other stations were closed.

One only needed to drive up to the pump and honk the horn. Shortly, Mr. Hagerman, usually in a robe, would emerge from his store and deliver the needed gasoline. It was somewhat embarrassing since one generally had only enough money for a few gallons, even though his prices were very low, at one time only thirteen cents a gallon.

It was an exceptional service and many teenagers escaped the wrath of their parents by putting gasoline in the family car before returning home. It was well known, that nothing upsets a father more than to find his car registering "empty" on the fuel gage, as he prepares to drive to Flint to work at 6 AM in the morning!

Another vendor of gasoline, who stands out in the minds of the impressionable youth of yesterday, is Aldrich Locke. Aldrich later became Mayor of Fenton (the city), owned and operated Locke's Dry Goods (formerly Rolland's Dry Goods) and later developed a shopping mall on North Leroy (then within the expanded "city" limits), which featured Locke's Party store.

When Aldrich Locke was the owner/operator of a gasoline station, a young Harold Barden remembers being in

Aldrich Locke

the front seat of his father's automobile while "gassing up" at Locke's station. Invariably Aldrich would come to the car and lean in and exchange some pleasantries with Harold's father. When Aldrich would place his forearms on the window opening on the passenger side, his hand would be very close to young Harold's face. Harold remembers being attracted by the gold Masonic ring Mr. Locke wore.

For many years, Aldrich Locke was the best "Santa Claus" in town. He had a very handsome costume and an especially well made set of "whiskers". Not just the ordinary "fake looking" ones, but a set that looked very, very real. "Santa" would set up in the Community Center and the town's young children would line up for the opportunity to tell "Santa" exactly what they wanted for Christmas.

Young Harold Barden was one of those youngsters and when his turn arrived, he mounted "Santa's" knee. As he was about to answer "Santa's" inquiry as to his wishes, he noticed "Santa" was wearing a beautiful gold ring...just like Mr. Locke's. He knew then who this "Santa" really was!

Most of the young men and boys in town, may not have known who "Santa" was, but they knew their barber! The barbers in town were somewhat like celebrities; everyone knew them and they seemed to know everyone in the surrounding territory. Each of the barbers had a committed clientele who would follow them from one barbershop to another in the event they changed location, as some were disposed to do.

Surprisingly to some of the young men of today, the young men of the thirties, including the teenagers, visited their barbers quite often. .

While the "crew cuts" of the later decades had not yet come into vogue, the use of electric clippers was only beginning to become the "instrument of choice" for some barbers. Most of the barbers in Fenton during this time had been performing their trade for many years and they continued to use of the scissors and comb. There were no long sideburns, or long hair in general, but some of the high schoolers favored a "pompadour" look kept in shape by a liberal use of some product like "Wild Root Crème Oil".

Glen Carpenter had his shop on East Caroline in the new D & C building. Basil Chappelle was usually found in Glen Carpenter's shop when he was not assisting Leon Durkee policing the town.

When the *Rowena* Theater was remodeled in 1940, Harvey Walters was forced to move to the basement shop, formerly used by William Eddy, where his assistant was Ed Bretzke. This basement shop was under the corner drug store, The Fenton Drug store, on the northeast corner of Leroy and Caroline Streets. The stairs leading down to the shop were on the Caroline Street side of the building. Young Leo Helmboldt began his career working a second chair in this basement shop.

Later Harvey Walters moved again, this time to a house on the corner of Roberts and Walnut Streets.

The American Legion owned the house, the former residence of Bert Rollins, and the main portion of the house was used as their meeting hall after the Post moved from the Macabee Building.

William "Bill" Marshall had a shop on the west side of South Leroy and just north of the new Community Center. Bill also sold a line of hunting and fishing equipment from his shop. His building was just outside the "demolition" zone, where the building of John L. Rohm and his "Golden Rule" barbershop fell to the wrecking ball as they cleared the area for the new Community Center

George Giles, shared a building with Maurice Hinkley's Jewelry Shop, two doors from Roberts Street on the west side of North Leroy Street. Each of the businesses had there own doorway and the resulting shops were ½ the width of the building.

While most of the barbershops were "downtown", some, such as the shop of Hayes Harris, were on the "south side". Hayes' shop was on West Shiawassee just off South Leroy Street. Guy Gillem spent a lot of time in Bill Marshall's shop, but moved around to other shops on occasion.

Ray Pillen had his shop set up in his home on Orchard Street. Ray was deaf and mute. He only charged ten or fifteen cents for a haircut while the other barbers going rate was twenty-five cents. Because Ray Pillen had difficulty communicating many of the young men came to him with some fear and trepidation. In his efforts to communicate, he would make some throaty sounds that were "scary" to some young fellows. He worked quickly and was heavy with the clippers and some said they could recognize a "Pillen Haircut". However the urge to save ten cents, which then could be spent surreptitiously on "other things", sometimes overcame all fears.

The main building of the Fenton High School was a three-story, red brick structure on the west side of Adelaide Street between West Caroline and West Ellen Streets. The three-story structure had been placed in front of some older existing structures and with the attached buildings the complex provided the required spaces.

The three-story building was relatively narrow, with only one classroom and a hallway in depth. The older part of the complex housed the gymnasium/auditorium on the ground floor, with the Study Hall/Library and two classrooms on the second floor directly above. Another older two-story section was attached on the west and could be entered from the study hall. It contained a classroom on the second floor with music rooms below.

Those who have memories of attending Fenton High School during this period are most likely to recall many unusual and distinctive characteristics of these buildings:

Probably the most memorable was the fire escape in the Study Hall. There was a circular steel tube, which sloped from its second floor Study Hall entrance to the ground below. It was at about a 45-degree angle and was attached closely to the side of the building. The tube was about 3 to 4 feet in diameter, which allowed a person to enter and slide to the ground level at a fairly rapid speed. While most everyone disliked the fire drills, most of the boys and some of the girls didn't really mind if the drill occurred while they were in the Study Hall.

Another "unforgettable" may be the "cracker box" gymnasium. The gym was a rectangular room with the main entrance at one end and a raised stage at the other.

One would enter the gym from the ground floor hallway of the three-story building. There was a short concrete hallway from this hallway that sloped down to the entrance doors of the gymnasium.

During a basketball game the double doors at this entrance were left open during the game. This was done to prevent possible injury to a player. When a player was driving to the basket, his momentum would often carry him beyond the end of the court. With the doors open, the player could go off the court, through the entrance and stop somewhere along the sloping hallway. If the doors were closed, the player would likely crash into the closed doors.

There was only space along the sidelines of the court for one row of folding chairs. In addition, there were two small bleachers, one on each side of the entrance doors for spectators. A larger bleacher placed upon the raised stage was also used for spectators.

When a player would need to "inbound" the ball, he would need to find room out of bounds by standing between the seated spectators.

Yes, it was a "cracker box"! However, small it was, it was well used by both the school and the general community.

Several events during the year used the stage and the "auditorium". Several hundred folding chairs would be placed in rows and a theatre would be created. The presidium type stage was raised about four feet above the floor, which provided an acceptable line of sight for even the occupants of the "back row" seats

The school used the gymnasium for its various stage events…plays, band or orchestra concerts, and glee club and chorus performances. It was also the venue for dances.

During the school year there were many Friday night dances, either with a live "band" or recorded music. "Sock Hops" were very popular with the students. When a live "band" was playing they would set up on the stage and not unlike their more professional counterparts at the IMA, they would attract a number of dancers who preferred standing by the stage and listening.

The schools athletic fields were on the west side, directly behind the school buildings. The area was one large rectangular field extending the length of Ellen Street to West Street. During the football season, the goal posts and the chalk lines delineated the playing area. Portable wooden benches were provided for each of the two competing teams on opposite side of the playing field. Portions of the field were usually bare of grass, since the "game" field was also the "practice" field.

A four-lane cinder track circled the football field and during the spring of the year, the track and field athletes used the facility…however, they did not have exclusive use of the area.

The baseball diamond was positioned in the southeast corner of the large field, with the backstop closest to the school buildings and Ellen Street. The center fielder would be positioned around the fifty-yard line and a trackman would find his way around the track just beyond second base. The available outdoor space was well utilized and while there was some overlapping, no one complained.

During the summer months, other groups used the fields and once in a while, the city attempted to create a skating rink on the grounds during the winter months.

There were only two busses used to transport students to and from school. The smaller bus, orange with black lettering, was used for students residing in and around Long Lake (Lake Fenton). The larger bus of the two, painted red, white and blue, was used to pick up other students living in the rural areas. The busses would load and unload at the side of the school building on West Ellen Street.

There were no lunch facilities available at the school. Consequently, the students desiring food at the midday break needed to bring their own lunch, go home for lunch or walk the short distance to "downtown" and purchase something to eat. There was no discussion of a "closed;' or "open" campus. The students were free to move anywhere they chose during the lunch period. Most of them returned for afternoon classes and there was none or little trouble as a result of all this "freedom". Occasionally, some mischief occurred. One such incident occurred which is worth mentioning.

The railroad crossing at North Leroy near Roberts Street (now Silver Lake Road) was a busy one and on more than one occasion, the motorists where inconvenienced as a train maneuvered to and fro while moving a boxcar of lumber onto a siding near the intersection.

George W. Pellett, son of one of the town's leading merchandisers, recalls one time when he and a group of youngsters were making their way home from school during the lunch period. Their path took a shortcut across the tracks, through the lumberyard and up Main Street a short distance east of the rail intersection.

On this particular day, the switchman was busy maneuvering the train as it was moving a boxcar onto a siding. As the group of youngsters passed through the area, one of them noticed a partially open, unlocked switch and without considering the possible consequences, he threw the switch the other way and continued on his way home for lunch.

George recalls that when he was making his way back to school after lunch, reversing his earlier path, he came upon a scene of utter consternation. It seems that while he was having lunch, one of the rail cars had jumped the tracks near the intersection and both rail and automobile traffic had been severely interrupted. No one seemed to know how such an accident could have happened, but George had his suspicions.

Some of those who lived in Fenton during the late Thirties recall the town had some young men who deservedly earned reputations for being "fast drivers". The *Fenton Courier,* on more than one occasion reported on young D.A. O'Dell, son of L.M. O'Dell, the proprietor of the drug store bearing his name. On one occasion the *Fenton Courier* referred to D.A. (reportedly short for Diogenes Augustus) as "the slick haired boy who minds the soda fountain for his daddy". (In truth, D.A. was a registered pharmacist)

In 1937, the young man was caught by Roma Bly, then acting in the capacity of a Deputy, going 45 miles per hour on East Street. Judge E. M. Beckwith fined him $5 for this violation. The *Fenton Courier* article reported, "He had been previously warned".

Jerome Dumanois, son of the proprietor of the Fenton Hotel, or Hotel Dumanois as he preferred, was also one who had a "reputation' for exceeding the speed limits. Paul Bottecelli tells of a time when he was riding with Jerome and they were in Flint. They came upon another fellow from Fenton and before long Jerome had accepted his challenge as to who could get back to Fenton in the shortest time. Paul says he still remembers careening south on Fenton Road, even though he can't remember who won the race.

Probably the one young man who most all will agree was the wildest driver in Fenton in the late 1930s was Don Clark. Don was the son of Mr. and Mrs. Wilbur Clark and his mother ran the office that sold the automobile license plates. Don was not only a fast driver he was one that didn't mind traveling great distances. Most of those who attended the high school J-Hop would travel to some out-of-town location after the dance. Some of the students would end up in Flint or some nearby town. Occasionally, some would even make it to Detroit. However, following one J-Hop, Don and his party drove all the way to Toronto!

On one occasion, Jim Frew, Bob Harris, Ron Butler and Don Clark traveled to Chicago together. Don's father had just purchased a brand new Chevrolet four door sedan. For whatever reason, he allowed his son Don to take this new car on the trip to Chicago.

Upon arriving in Chicago's downtown area, "the loop", Don decided to take a short cut down one of the alleys behind the Marshall Fields store. The alley was full of trucks unloading their cargoes

Once in the alley, Don found a large truck coming towards him and he pulled the car over as close as possible to a building to allow the truck to pass through the alley. As it turned out Don didn't leave enough room for the truck to pass without striking the car. As the truck passed, one could hear the metal on the side of the new Chevrolet crunching and tearing away.

The truck continued down the alley and disappeared around the corner. How Don ever explained all this to his father God only knows!

Another young man who was considered a "fast driver" was Arnold "Sonny" Westman. "Sonny" was the son of Arnold Westman, the President of the Industrial Machine Tool Company. Sonny was probably the only one in Fenton High School who drove a flashy new convertible. Perhaps, he was unjustly accused of being a fast driver because of his automobile. When he was sitting at the wheel of his new convertible, it looked as if he was speeding even when he was parked!

Lee "Red" Gordon tells of the time he and his passenger Lyle Pratt, one of his high school friends, were speeding down Main Street in the early hours when Deputy Basil Chappelle stopped them. Basil read the "riot act" to the young fellows and ordered them to follow behind his car as he led them to the Village "lock-up". Obediently, they fell in line behind Basil's car as it turned south on Leroy Street in the direction of the town jail. After a few moments, the Deputy stopped his car, whereupon, Gordon stopped directly behind him. Basil Chappelle, who had apparently "cooled off", left his car and walked back to the driver's window and told the young men "let this be a warning". "Red" and Lyle breathed a sigh of relief...and "Red" has a vivid memory of the incident some sixty years later.

In spite of conditions at home or abroad, the late Thirties was a good time to be living in Fenton. Times were "tough", but "everyone was in the same boat"...everyone was "poor"...and those who were "better off" weren't of the type to "flaunt" their affluence. Some of the best examples of this were to be found in the membership of organizations like the Men's Fellowship, the American Legion and the Veterans of Foreign Wars and their Auxiliaries. In those organizations men and women who were known to be "better off" worked side-by-side with those who were, in today's terminology, below the "poverty line".

After the war, World War II, the village changed. The men and women, who had served in the armed forces or worked in the defense plants, were now much more sophisticated and demanding. The Village became a City in more ways than one, many of the citizens had seen "the other side of the mountain" and their innocence was lost.

Old Fire Hall with volunteer firemen standing by their fire trucks.
L-R Fred Williams, Tom Woodworth, John Bacon, Fred Horrell, Robert Beach,
Tom Rector, Merle Chappell, Harry Moore, Shull Woodworth and Howard Craft.
Note the newly constructed Fenton Community Center to the left rear of the Fire
Hall. Also, white building to the right is Walcott's Mill.. Both the Fire hall and
Walcott's Mill would be razed shortly after this picture was taken in late 1937.

Act One...The Year 1937

Scene One...Good News...Great News!

Mr. Sol F. "Faye" Beach, Editor and Publisher of Fenton's weekly newspaper *The Fenton Independent* ran a banner headline on December 17, 1936 that read...

RACKHAM FUND APPROVES GRANT OF $200,000
FOR ERECTION AND MAINTENANCE OF LOCAL COMMUNITY CENTER

"The Community House is to be erected on Leroy Street on the property now occupied by the Woodworth Brothers, the Wander Inn and John L. Rohm's Barber Shop. Following acceptance of the grant, action was started immediately for the purchase of the property ...some work will begin to tear down the buildings ...in preparation for the construction of the Community House."

The townsfolk were elated to learn of this unexpected bequest. The Village Council and all parties involved moved very quickly to get the project underway. There were no major problems, no seemingly endless negotiations, no court challenges and no never-ending delays that one would probably encounter in the present day. It was a "simpler time".

In a period of less than six months, the officials completed the legal work, purchased the buildings and property required, started the process of clearing the area and began the construction of the "community house".

The Village President Harry Lemen and the Village Council composed of William Stocken, Gustav "Gus" Lutz, Floyd Poppy, John Hoskins, Shull Woodworth and J.E. "Fritz" Judevine had entered into an agreement with the Horace H. and Mary A.. Rackham Foundation on January 20th to build a "community house".

The new "community house" would also require the removal of the "old" Fire Hall in addition to four buildings along South Leroy Street. The *Fenton Courier* reported there was controversy in town about the destruction of the old hall. Some people wanted to move the old hall to a new location, but there was no money on hand to make it happen. Others were in agreement with demolishing the old hall and building a new one, but here again, the Village didn't have the money to build a new hall. .

But the controversy was short lived when soon after the original announcement of the grant; The Rackham Fund also provided the funds to build a new Municipal Building to replace the "old Fire Hall". Consequently, the old Water Works plant on the southeast corner of Ellen and South Leroy streets would be demolished to make way for this new municipal building, aka the "new" Fire Hall

The building housing the plumbing business of Tom and Shull Woodworth was to be razed as well as the Wander Inn, owned and operated by Mrs. Martha Lamareaux and Mrs. Grace Faint.

The flourmill owned by Frank and Anson "Ed" Walcott would be torn down at an early date, while the building where John L. Rohm had his barbershop was temporarily spared when the W.W.Wood Construction Company of Detroit set up their "on site" office there.

The fifth building and last to be razed, was that housing the Fenton Odorless Cleaning Company owned by Mrs. W.J. Foster. The lot was leveled and prepared for parking to relieve the shortage of downtown parking caused by the new construction. .

Thanks to the tireless efforts of the Village President, the members of the Village Council, Village Clerk Robert L. Beach, Village Treasurer Horace W. Hitchcock, Village Attorney Maurice R. Matthews and a special committee appointed to work closely with the Rackham Foundation people, the project moved along exceptionally well.

The special committee composed of Charles E. Rolland, George Green and Roma Bly was charged with working on matters pertaining to the Rackham Fund. Charles Rolland was the owner of the Rolland Dry Goods Company; George Green, was the Chairman of Board of Directors of the State Savings Bank; and Roma Bly was the head of the Village's Public Works. They performed their responsibilities in an excellent manner and their contribution to the successful completion of the project cannot be underestimated.

By mid June, the construction company had begun razing the buildings (Wolcott's Mill was first to go!) and, having moved a large steam shovel on the site, the work of excavating began.

In preparation for the razing of the Fire Hall, the clock and bell that served the village since 1875 were to be removed. The town's pride and joy was the clock in the old Fire Hall and the bell that marked the arrival of each hour. At the time, Earnest Fuller had maintained the clock and bell in the fireman's hall for the past twenty-five years.

One of his last duties was to remove the clock and bell and store them pending their installation in the tower of the new to-be-built municipal building, aka "the new fire hall". Even today, many of the older Fenton residents believe the clock in the "new" fire hall is the same one that was in the "old" fire hall. That may have been the original intention, but actually the Village Council purchased a "new" Seth Thomas clock with an illuminated face for the "new" hall. However, Ernie did have the "old" bell installed. It was said the people were used to the sound of the old bell and it should be reinstalled. His son "Ernie", Will Collins and David Klinger, assisted Mr. Fuller in removing the old clock and bell.

After the clock was removed and before the Fire Hall was leveled, it was reported that the townsfolk were having a difficult time being without a clock. The people were so accustomed to the clock they caught themselves glancing toward the tower to ascertain the time, only to find the clock missing.

While the Fire Hall had a limited space for assemblage many of the town's groups used the hall for their meetings and other activities. For example, the fledgling V.F.W. Post held their January meeting in the Fire Hall. In February, the annual Fireman's banquet and social meeting was held on schedule. That event and the Citizens Party caucus were the very last meetings in the hall.

At the Citizens Party Caucus meeting, Floyd Chapin rose to point out there were three people present in the hall at that time who were in attendance at the very first meeting in the hall, some sixty-three years before: Mr. Joe Mount (a former village trustee), Mrs. Edith Davis and himself. Floyd A. Chapin had served as Village President and Council Member in past years and at this time was the Village Assessor.

The fire siren was removed from the roof of the old building and along with the fire trucks, transported to a garage owned by Arthur Dubord on the south side of town, an area now referred to as "Dibbleville".

Arthur Dubord was the proprietor of the South Side Grocery. Most of his customers lived on the "south side" and in lieu of walking "downtown", where the majority of the grocery stores were located, they shopped as Dubord's.. During the depression years, Mr. Dubord allowed his customers to purchase their groceries "on credit" from payday to payday. Each of the patrons using the "credit" had a small book held in a large metal cabinet with each book held in place by a spring-loaded clamp.

Dubord's garage, which was immediately south of his grocery store, also served as a temporary meeting place for the Village Council as they awaited the construction of a "new" fire hall at the corner of Ellen and South Leroy streets.

While these changes were happening, the village leaders continued to be active in their pursuit of funds for a number of public works. They had received WPA funds to build storm and sanitary sewers in sections of the town where none had previously existed. The storm sewers relieved many of the problems of annual flooding in the most susceptible areas of the village.

The primary purpose of the Works Progress Administration (WPA) was to provide job opportunities for the nation's unemployed by funding public works projects proposed by local governments. In February, the WPA funded storm sewer project employed 23 local men for three months.   The WPA was a part of President Franklin D. Roosevelt's "New Deal" program.

It is interesting to note that the building of the sanitary sewers was done a couple years before the proposal to build a sewage disposal plant was addressed by the Council.

Some of the land owners "downstream" had complained about the pollution of the Shiawassee River. The Wilbert H. Keddy family lived on Remington Road (now North Road) and downstream on the river. They were complaining about the river pollution damaging their property and they were seeking redress from the council for this damage.   It was a real concern since the Village Dump sat on the riverbank near the center of the village. Because the "dump" was now the site of the new community center, the dump was to be moved, which was expected to reduce the pollution of the river.

Finally, in December, W. H. Keddy sued the Village and asked $12,000 in damages. The Village Council delayed a hearing on the issue until the following year. The *Fenton Courier* wrote the following: "The unpleasantness of using the river for a sewage disposal bed has long been a source of complaint by people down the river and a thorn in the side of Fenton. State examination of the river, however, does not show nearly as much pollution as in many other sections of Michigan."

It wasn't until October of 1941 before the sewage treatment facility was built near the junction of North Leroy Street and North Road (then Fenton Road and Remington Road, respectively) just inside of the northern village limits   Building sanitary sewers with WPA money in 1937 either demonstrated the foresight of the village leaders or more of the present day attitude toward federal funds, which seems to be..."get it while you can".

However, from the 1937 writings of Harry Lemen in his review of village affairs, he clearly states, "...all this is being done with the expectation that in the future Fenton will be called upon to build a plant for disposal of its sewage."

For years, the property donated to the village by Dexter Horton for a park was used as the "dump". Now, this property was to be the site of the new "community house" and the Council ordered "no more dumping of rubbish on the premises" and closed the old dump and opened a new dump south of town.

Previously, the Council had authorized Richard Adams to operate a "garbage collection" business in the village for those residents who agreed to pay fifteen cents a week for the service. However, many chose to dispose of their own garbage and take it to the village "dump".

Advertisement in *Fenton Independent* on April 15, 1937

Moffett's Food Market	
Butter	35c lb
Sugar 10lb	53c
Curtis Meats	
Ground Beef	15c lb
Smoked Picnics	19c lb

From same edition....

Grand Trunk Train Schedule		
Eastbound	6:20 AM Daily 11:21 AM Weekdays Only	
	3:53 PM Daily	
Westbound	11:21 AM Week days only	
	3:02 PM Daily 12:45 AM Daily	

The following pictures of Fenton High School athletic teams of 1937-1938 were copied from the Fenton High School Annual for 1938 entitled the "Twin Pines".

FHS Football 1937: 1st Row L-R Dick Avery, Dave Black, Don Herman, Ralph Ellsworth, Bob Black. 2nd Row L-R Mgr. Bob Dode, Bob Searight, Harold Bradley, Jack Lea, Sid Smale, Chauncie Lucke. 3rd Row L-R Brad Hoffman, Jack Hartley, Roy Goodrich, Robert Atkins, Donald "Bud" Lemen

FHS Basketball 1937-38: L-R Joe Craft, Jack Lea, Jack Hartley, Garwood Marshall, Roy Goodrich, Robert Atkins, Don Herman, Bud Lemen

Scene Two... Building Frenzy?

While the construction of storm and sanitary sewers was very important to the village, the real "Jewel in the Crown" of all the WPA projects for the Village was the building of a new dam on the Shiawassee River.

Building the new dam was of considerable interest to the townsfolk during its construction. The construction began soon after the funding was approved in May 1936 and the work was completed on June 4, 1937.

As evidence of the "magnitude" of this effort, Mr. Charles J. Furlong (who will be best remembered as the longtime secretary for the Fenton School Board) reported on the material used in the construction of the dam.

He reported the following materials had been used: Lumber-7,040 feet; Cement-480 Barrels; Steel Reinforcing bars- 5,000 lineal feet; Wire Mesh- 4,800 square feet; Expansion joints-100 square feet; Sand-100 cubic yards; Gravel-500 cubic yards; and Fill dirt (Top)- 200 cubic yards.

Mr. Furlong, who also served as an auditor for the village, reported the total cost for the dam was $13,422.21 of which the Village's portion was $2,239.55. This left the bulk of the cost, $11,182.66, paid by the Federal government's WPA.

One would not have thought the economic depression continued to plague the nation by witnessing the building and remodeling activity in downtown Fenton

The D & C Store bought the Damon Building on the southeast corner of Adelaide and Leroy streets. They extended their store from its former location, the second store from the intersection, to include the corner store. This development displaced the Housewife Equipment store (MacFaydeyn and Sons), and threatened to displace the insurance office of D.R Stiles and Glen Carpenter's Barbershop. Accommodations were made for the businesses of Mssrs Stiles and Carpenter in the new building with entrances on Caroline Street, however the MacFayden's Housewife Equipment store moved to North Leroy and operated a short time before going out of business.

These weren't the only businesses to be dislocated by the D & C expansion. While only a seasonal business, Bob Gill's popcorn wagon had to move "kitty-corner" across the street to the Bank corner. The editor of the *Fenton Courier* remarked. "...Bob's corn and baseball season always come in simultaneously". And just as it was at his former corner location, Bob Gill had a drinking fountain nearby.

At this time there were two downtown fountains maintained by the village, one on northwest corner of the intersection of Leroy and Caroline Streets and a second diagonally opposite on the southeast corner of the intersection. These fountains were made of concrete with small stones in the aggregate. A pipe of about an inch in diameter was in the center of the bowl shaped top from which a continuous stream of fresh cold water flowed. These water fountains were used and enjoyed by all comers…man or beast! In the summer time, for several years, a large shaggy St. Bernard dog would come by several times in the day and, with his paws on the rim of the bowl, spend several minutes lapping the flowing water.

As Leo Weigant related in his book *Fenton Remembers When*, the fountains provided an opportunity to play a favorite schoolboy trick. It would occur as the town's youngsters were making there way to school. A group of schoolboys would loiter on the corner until some unsuspecting fellow would approach. At the proper moment, two or more youngsters would grab the innocent fellow and set him squarely on top of the fountain.

Mickey's Dairy on South Leroy, directly across the street from the "Community House" site, had just completed a new addition to their dairy, which provided an ice cream parlor and a facility to make their own ice cream, cottage cheese and a variety of new dairy products.

The Industrial Machine Tool Company, immediately south of the "Community House" site, added over 27,000 square feet of space to accommodate their expanding manufacturing and tool making business.

The Fenton schools received a $34,363 grant from the Public Works Administration (PWA) to add a two-story, ten room addition to the north of the high school building on Adelaide Street for the use of the elementary grades.

While both the efforts of the WPA and the PWA were both directed at reducing unemployment, the PWA was primarily concerned with the financing the construction of large public works projects. But in addition to dams and highways, between 1933 and 1939, the PWA funded seventy percent of the new schools built in the nation.

Other smaller private building projects such as Kenny Robbins's new Standard Oil station on northeast corner of Ellen and South Leroy Streets and Dr. Kochendorfer new dental office on South Leroy Street directly across the street from the A.J. Phillips Library, also added to the building "frenzy" during the year.

Perhaps the building "frenzy" was stimulated by the unusually mild weather. The winter of 1936-37 was unseasonably warm and pleasant and William Kirkdale, one of Fenton's old-timers remarked, "never seen anything like it". Kirkdale recalled the last winter this warm was 47 years before when he was working a farm near Clarkston. Charles Stewart reported the tulips in his garden were up an inch on February 7th. The snow had disappeared from the ground and some reported the Robins had returned. In the first week of January, Mrs. Claude Cheney reported the Pussy Willows were in bloom and it was like "June in January". There was no doubt; the warm rain and early thaw gave indications of a premature arrival of spring.

Not only Fenton and Lower Michigan was affected by the early thaw, but also this early thaw caused severe flooding along the Ohio and Mississippi rivers. There was considerable concern about the situation throughout the nation and the Red Cross appealed to the citizens for help.

The people of Fenton responded by raising funds and supplies for the flood victims. Cash donations were made at the State Savings Bank, and the American Legion collected and delivered a truckload of clothing, bedding and food to the distressed area.

The millpond in the center of town had frozen over early that winter, but with the temperate weather, the ice had begun to weaken and was no longer safe for skating or walking

One day in February, young Dick Hiscox was on his way to his home on East Street when he saw seven-year-old Howard Bowman fall through the thawing ice. He immediately went to the rescue of the boy but soon found himself through the ice and in the water and in distress. Fortunately, two men, Messrs. Copeland and Jack Sweet, who resided near the millpond, had witnessed the incident and rushed to help the boys. Members of the Fire Department arrived and attempted a rescue, but despite the valiant efforts of all involved, they were only successful in saving Dick Hiscox. Seven-year-old Howard Bowman lost his life that day. .

This accidental drowning sparked a general concern about the safety of skating on the millpond and the provision of an outdoors skating rink was a subject of considerable discussion.

In the following winter, the newly formed Veterans of Foreign Wars Post obtained an area owned by the Grand Trunk railroad near its depot for use as an outdoor skating rink. The Veterans flooded the area and attempted to keep it ready for skating. However, frequent thawing and heavy rains made it practically impossible to maintain a decent ice surface The V.F.W. finally gave up on the project. As the city was to find out in later years, when they created another outdoor rink, the maintenance of an outdoor skating facility is not always possible.

Earlier in the year before the big thaw, the frozen surfaces presented a lot of pleasure for many skaters, but on occasion "ice" presented some serious problems. In late January, the Fenton area was hit by an "ice storm". The *Fenton Independent* wrote extensively about the many locals who were injured on the ice.

The paper reported" Many Fenton people were injured in falls on icy walks or skating rinks and traffic was seriously congested in several areas when the temperature dropped suddenly and ice blanketed the walks and roads".

Miss Dorothy Gould, eighth grade student, cut the tendon and chipper the kneecap of her right leg while skating. Miss Doris Lobdell, FHS student, broke her arm when she fell while skating on Lake Fenton. Bobby Godard, six hear old, fell on the ice on his sidewalk and broke his shoulder. Lloyd Kelley fell on the ice outside the Fenton Hotel and fractured his right ankle. Drs. William Rynearson and Carl H. White set the broken bone. Lloyd was confined for three months before he could navigate with the aid of crutches. All in all quite a casualty list!

The *Fenton Independent* further reported the "Traffic has been moving very slowly because of the danger of the icy pavements". The traffic moving on US 23, had trouble negotiating a steep hill south of town. Several minor crashes resulted from skidding on the hill.

Scene Three…"Not in our town!"

However, it wasn't the floods or weather that was the "talk of the town", when a very unusual occurrence attracted everyone's attention.

It was the morning of February 2nd 1937. The stores and shops were open and the townsfolk were moving about in a very normal manner. That is until shortly before noon, when two strangers, both wearing "colored' glasses, parked their Ford V8 car on Leroy Street directly in front of the State Saving Bank of Fenton. As they entered the Bank, one was carrying a long deer rifle and the other a nickel-plated revolver and a black leather bag. Apparently, they made no attempt to conceal what they were carrying.

J. C. Peck happened to be on the street and he observed the men entering the bank and he headed directly for the Fenton Drug Company on the corner directly across the street from the Bank.

The two strangers entered the bank and moved to the rear of the building where they encountered the bank manager, Mr. E.C. Reid, holding a meeting with E.C. McGugan, a Bank Examiner and three employees: Robert Smith, George Warner and Margaret Barnum.

At the point of a gun, Mr. Reid and the others were kept in position as the men entered the "cage" and approached the tellers, Otis Furman and Miss Gertrude Berryman.

Otis Furman, who was nearest to the money drawer, opened the drawer and put his hand in the cash drawer. It was then that one of the robbers, evidently fearing he was reaching for a gun or an alarm button, struck Otis over the head several times with the butt of his revolver. He then forced the bleeding teller and Miss Gertrude Berryman into the bank vault. After scooping all the money from the drawer into the bag, the two bandits left the building, ran to their car and drove south out of town with $2,700 of the Bank's money.

Bill Weideman, manager of the Kroger grocery store, was just entering the Bank as the robbers were making their exit. Bill had an envelope with $250 of his store's money he intended to deposit. The robbers ordered him to lie down, which he did immediately and on top of his deposit envelope. Luckily he was not hurt or robbed, however, poor Otis Furman, his shirt, tie and suit covered with blood, had to be taken to a Doctor's office where he required four stitches to close the wounds on his scalp.

While all this was going on, J.C. Peck told George Atherton and Clifford J. Phillips, who were customers at the Fenton Drug Company of what he had observed.

Leonard Limpach, the store's proprietor, also noticed some "suspicious" actions and when the robbers came running out of the bank, Mr. Limpach rushed to the phone and called the State Police. About the same time, Mr. Reid realizing the bandits had left the bank, called for the police.

It so happened that a State Trooper on patrol had just left Fenton and was heading north toward Flint on the Fenton Road. When he received the radio message about the robbery he was about seven miles north of Fenton. He turned and sped back to Fenton, where J.C. Peck was able to provide the license number of the robber's car which he had observantly copied as they sped away.

By then a small crowd had gathered in front of the Bank. Many of those assembled had been listening to the Flint radio for news about the ongoing "sitdown" strike at the General Motors plants, when the news bulletin about the bank robbery in Fenton was announced. In spite of the public interest and the actions of the lone State Trooper, the robbers made their escape. Some reported they had observed the bandits car speeding from Fenton in an easterly direction over the South Holly Road. It turned out that the license plates had been stolen from another car in Detroit the month before and therefore did not belong on the getaway car.

In those sensitive times for banks, it is interesting to note that the Bank's insurance company delivered a check for the exact amount of the loss, $2,671.25, within 24 hours of the robbery.

An even more interesting event was triggered by the holdup. Two of Fenton's young men, Clifford Crystal and Jack Hutchins got the idea they could track the robbers and began following their reported escape route. While they were "tracking" in the town of Milford, the State Police noticed their unusual behavior. They were arrested as suspects in the robbery, handcuffed and returned to Fenton. They were not released until the Bank employees established their innocence

The now infamous "sit down" strike, which began on December 30, 1936 at the General Motors factories in Flint, Michigan, involved several Fenton men as active participants. Clark Thompson was a Deputy Sheriff of Genesee County and he was wounded during the police's attempt to control the rioting during the strike. He was shot through the right leg during the January upheaval at the Chevrolet plant where most of the violence occurred.

Those village residents who were employed at the General Motors plants involved, principally the Chevrolet and Fisher Body facilities, but were not among those "locked in" were strong supporters of the strikers. Others not directly involved were more concerned with the issues of public disorder and the seizure of private property by the strikers.

The wives of the strikers and fellow workers not "inside" brought food and refreshments, newspapers and magazines to the plant windows in support of those inside. Even one of Fenton's "characters", bass drummer Herb Dutton made several appearances at the plants and serenaded the men with some drum solos.

The town's people had by and large recovered from the bank robbery…a real rarity for Fenton…when the news of a much more tragic event hit them head on! It was the most shocking crime ever committed in Fenton and at the time the most brutal in this section of the state.

Dr. C. H. White was making a house call on Mrs. Eleanor Davis at her farm home on State Road, just south of the county line. When no one appeared to answer his call, he returned to Fenton to the home of Mrs. Davis' son, Jay Davis. Accompanied by Mrs. Jay Davis, they returned to the farmhouse, where Mrs. Jay Davis found entry to the house through an unlocked window. After entering the house she discovered the dead body of her father-in-law, Jehiel Davis lying on a bed. Eleanor Davis and her sister-in-law, Mrs. Lydia Hilderbrandt, who had been visiting her, were not to be found in the house. They immediately called for help.

When the officers from Livingston County and Fenton arrived, they conducted a search of all the farm buildings and found both women in the barn. They had been stuffed into a grain box, which had the top nailed shut. Mrs. Hilderbrandt was dead, but Eleanor Davis was still living. Mrs. Davis was rushed to Hurley Hospital in Flint, Michigan where she died four days later.

In reconstructing the crime, it appeared as if Ray Larsen, a farm hand employed by the Davises, had lured the two women to the barn where they were attacked and thrown into the grain box. Larsen then returned to the house where he murdered Mr. Davis. After killing Mr. Davis, he took his clothes and all the cash in the house and escaped in the Davis'

Ford truck. Later that night, the truck was found abandoned in Flint, Michigan, but Ray Larsen had disappeared and was never captured.

The family of Mr. and Mrs. Sheridan Foust suffered a tragic loss when their nine-year-old son Lyle Foust was killed when he darted in front of an oncoming automobile. Your Lyle was walking with his older brother Kenneth and his friend, Philip Pettis, on their way to his grandparent's home on east of Fenton. As they approached the home of Mr. and Mrs. Charles Lee, young Lyle broke away from the older boys and ran into the road and was fatally injured.

In just a few months the people of Fenton had experienced four horrific events…an accidental drowning, a bank robbery, the death of a young boy and, worst of all, a brutal triple murder …things like that "just didn't happen in our town". Some folks were wondering, "What's going to happen next"? In spite of these tragic events life went on as usual for most of the villagers.

And while the outbreak of measles in the schools was not as horrific, at one time in February as many as one-fourth of the students were absent because of measles, mumps or chicken pox. Even the teachers were susceptible, and Miss Thelma Barker and Miss Zelma Oole missed several days of class.

Fenton High School as seen from Adelaide Street

Scene Four…Keepin' On Doing!

But for others, things were "looking up". Anson "Ed" and Frank Walcott's Mill was scheduled for the wrecking ball, but they were fortunate to find the mill in Argentine empty and available. They began moving their machinery to their new location where the Walcotts mill would operate for another sixty years.

In spite of the confusion, in early February, the Wolcott's Mill hosted their "last supper"…a Pancake Supper… in the old Fire Hall on Leroy Street. The Walcotts had made this supper an annual event for the Kroger Company as a show of "appreciation" for Kroger purchasing their products. 147 people, many from Kroger's Detroit office as well as all Kroger employees in the Fenton store attended this year's event. The "Fire Boys" served the "supper".

"The Fire Boys", the men of Fenton's volunteer Fire Department, were very experienced in cooking pancakes since they traditionally served a Pancake Breakfast at the Fire Hall on St Patrick's Day. This annual St. Pat's event was held on schedule even though the "old" Fire Hall was scheduled to be demolished and the "new" Hall was still on the drawing boards. Over 595 villagers showed up for breakfast, which were more people than show up for elections! Some wag suggested they serve pancakes on election days.

Not to be out done, the fellows of the Isaac Walton League held their annual Smelt Fry in the old hall. Led by Nelson Curtis and Don Alchin, the club served over 200 diners at their supper. While "dining out" was enjoyable, real live "singing and dancing" was more to the liking of many of the townsfolk and the Fenton High School Glee Club was prepared to deliver!

The Glee Club produced the operetta "Hollywood Bound" in early February and over 350 crowded the high school auditorium to see the show. The production involved dancing, singing and the school orchestra. Virginia Barnard and Jim DeVoght had the leads in the production but there was a large cast including: Jean Reidel, Doris Hubert, Eileen Minock, Jeanette Dery, Edwin Norton, James Bachus, Glenn Hull, Robert Baker, Robert Dode. Deforest McKinley, Arnold Westman, Harold Bristol, Gordon Jenison, Donald Rowley, Howard Cronk, Arthur Barnard, Francis Anible and Jack Brooks.

In addition to Miss Barker, the faculty members participating as Assistant Directors were: Ellen Wicklund (Dances), Phyllis Lenzner (Piano Accompanist) and Clarence Wilder (Orchestra).

There were many other activities in town besides "suppers" and "operettas" and bowling was one of the favorites for the winter days, for both the female and the male population.

The Fenton Recreation was the principal bowling establishment in town (all two lanes of it). It was located on the east side of South Leroy Street next to the U.S. Post Office and immediately north of the Methodist Episcopal Church. Jesse D. Straugh managed the alleys for a couple of years until "Bud" Edinger bought the business and assumed control of the operation.

The other bowling establishment, the Packard Bowling Alley, closed in April and moved out of the Carmer Building. In the

FENTON BOWLING ALLEYS
Next to Post Office
Where you bowl with pleasure
And have a good time

Public Bowling every
Afternoon and
Tues., Wed., Thurs. and Sat.
Evenings

J. D. STRAUGH,
Manager

couple months they were in operation this year there were men and women leagues in operation. Some of the leaders for the men were: Eugene Chappelle, Don Swartz, Al Gray, C. Crystal, Sax Dawson, Keith Burdick, Jack Hutchins, Tac Lyons, Bob Woodward and Bill Irish. The women were very active and their leaders were: Jean Brooks, June Tamlyn, Esther Jepson, Grace Brooks, Dorothy Long, Blanche Parker and Helen Brooks.

The Fenton Recreation, had leagues for both men and women during the season and each team was sponsored by a local business or organization. In the 1937 season the teams were sponsored by Mickey's Dairy, The Fenton Independent, Butcher's Garage, the Industrial Machine Tool Company, the I.O.O.F., the American Legion, the Fenton Courier, Fenton Hardware, the Cobblestone Tavern, St. John Church, the Masons and an independent group, the Boosters.

The limited number of lanes resulted in men's league bowling taking up the "prime" time on the alleys. Even so, the women did get their bowling done, mostly during the days, and many of the female bowlers posted very good scores.

Guy Simmons, an employee of *The Fenton Independent* wrote a weekly column for both bowling and softball during their respective seasons. On one occasion, he wrote that "some (most)" of the women bowlers could beat the "gentlemen". That seemed to be a bold statement for the 1930s, and he undoubtedly heard from many of the men who were bowling.

Womens bowling teams were formed in different ways, probably not much different than the men, except one never heard of men having matches with the "Married vs. Single"! The top women bowlers were: Miss Mary Asman, Virginia Hoskins, Mrs. Mabel Tamlyn, Mrs. Dorothy McBroom, Miss Alice Pasco, Mrs. Alice Butcher, Mrs. Dorothy Craft. Dorothy Long and Verna Hoskins.

On one occasion, some of the "boys" participated in a more physical activity to raise some money for the school athletic program. The businessmen from the "East side" of Leroy Street challenged their counterparts from the "West side" in a Donkey Basketball game to be held the high school gym.

The "boys" representing the West side were Hoyt Glaspie, George Tamlyn, Horace Hitchcock, Herb McKinley, Myron McGlynn, and M. Richmond. All were of early middle age and active businessmen in town.   A younger group represented the East side: Bob Hunt, Bob Woodward, Bernard Webber, Francis Marshall, Harold Dode and Bob Beach. The teams mounted twelve Mexican burros and someone threw up a basketball and the game was on! To add to the excitement and entertainment young Charley Case wrestled a brown bear during the half-time intermission

As the year moved along, bowling gave way to softball. For the most part, the softballers were a younger group of men then the bowlers. The "boys of summer" had some of the same businesses or organizations as sponsors of their summer fun. However, there were more teams organized and other sponsors such as Attorney Maurice Matthews, Hagedorn's Dairy, Aldrich Locke's Service Station, Gambles store and Gould's Grocery joined in the action.

A hundred or so villagers participated in these athletic activities and many gained recognition for their excellence. George Hall, Hugo Theisen, Tom Woodworth, Jerry Pasco, Morris "Mickey" McBroom, Jim McKinley and Ralph Richmond topped the bowlers while Elmer and Bob Hunt were among the "stars" in softball.

Guy Simmons, the erstwhile "sports reporter" for *The Fenton Independent* took a more active role in the summer serving as an umpire for softball. Simmons along with Basil Bowman and John Dery officiated the softball playoff games.

The business people in town were strong supporters of all the Fenton High School teams. George Tamlyn, "The Camera Man", offered a traveling trophy for the basketball competition between the Fenton and Holly High Schools. After three years, the school with the winning record would retain the Tamlyn Trophy.

In the 1936-1937-basketball season, Fenton prevailed 29-14 for its third consecutive winning season and the "Tamlyn" was placed in the school's trophy case. Harold O'Grady, Don Lemen, Garwood Marshall and Don Herman led the winning team.

In this modern era of basketball, where scoring often exceeds 100 points per game, a final score of 29-14 would be very low and very unusual. However, it should be known that in 1937, after each made basket, the teams would return to center court for a "toss-up". It was a much slower game in "the old days"!

A Recreational Basketball League had been organized for the "older young" men in the community. There were six teams sponsored by Hoffman's, Swingle's, Joe's, Kroger's, Moffett's and Locke's in the league. Hoffman's had the two high school coaches, Lester Miller and Roger Leestma on their team and unsurprisingly Hoffman's were the league champions. Ed Bretzke led the Locke's team and Herb Walters, Bill Dode and Neal Woodward played for Joe's. Moffett's top players were Bill Lanning and Don Alchin.

Despite the presence of a Men's League, the sports program at the Fenton High School *was* the town's sports program. Just as the City of Detroit identifies with the Detroit Tigers as *their* team, so did the village associate with the Fenton High School sports teams. The town's people followed the football team very closely and the "stars" of the team were treated like celebrities in the town.

1937 was a very good year for FHS football...Fenton was the undefeated County Champions. The Genesee County League included the high school teams from Clio, Flushing, Mt. Morris, Davison, Grand Blanc and two Flint schools, Bendle and the newly founded Beecher.

Lester Miller coached the team and Roger Leestma assisted him. Both coaches were very well liked and worked together for the other varsity sports at the high school: basketball, baseball and track.

The football team boasted 17 letterman: Don Herman (Honorary Captain), Donald "Bud" Lemen, Robert "Junie" Atkins, Robert Searight, Brad Hoffman, Sidney Smale, Don Black, Robert Black, Jack Lea, Ralph Ellsworth, Harold Bradley, Chauncie Lucke, Richard Avery, Ronald Covert and Roy Goodrich

1937 FHS Football Squad: First Row: Bob Runyan, Bob Harris, Jim Frew, Ron Longworth, Bob Morea, Bob Zoll, Dick Smale, Bill Rynearson, Unkown. Second Row: Harold Bradley, Bob Searight, Junie Atkins, Paul Botticelli, Don Herman, Bud Lemen, Jack Hartley, Sid Smale. Third Row: Asst Coach Roger Leestma, Bob Black, Dave Black, Rolly Covert, Ralph Ellsworth, Roy Goodrich, Dick Avery, Chauncey Lucke, Jack Lea, Al Turco, Don Hunt, Coach Lester Miller. Top Row: Llewelyn Crystal, Lem Sarosky, Earl Robinson, Jim Rash, Dave Dawson, Larry Sugden, Art Barnard, Bob Dode

. Herman, Smale and Covert earned 1st Team All-County recognition and Goodrich and Robert Black were 2nd team selections. Don Herman was one of the best athletes ever to attend FHS. He earned letters in football, basketball, baseball and track in each of his four years in high school. He went on to Hillsdale College where he starred for their football team

About the same time the German airship *The Hindenburg* was exploding and burning in Lakehurst, New Jersey, Coach Lester Miller was organizing the high school baseball team for another season. The team had a good season placing high in the county league standings.

Some of the stellar athletes that played baseball in 1937 were Don Herman, Don Walters, Bill Dode, Robert "Junie" Atkins and Paul Bottecelli. On one occasion in May, Paul Bottecelli came into the game as a replacement for Don Herman. Don Herman left the game to join

Coach Roger Leestma's track team practice, where his event was the pole vault. The next day at the County track meet at Flint Central's field, Don set a new conference record in the pole vault at 10' 6".

The High School girl's track team was very good in 1937, led by an outstanding athlete in Mary Thompson. In the County Track Meet this year Mary won 1st Place in the Baseball Throw and placed in three other events. Eugenia Buckingham, Dorothy Milliken, Helen Weigant won events and the Fenton team won the County Meet.

In addition to the town's softball leagues, the American Legion recruited a baseball team of high school age players for competition in the American Legion program. Roy Goodrich and Paul Bottecelli pitched and George Paine and Bill Silver coached the Legion teams.

Not all of the Legion's interest in baseball was devoted to *playing* the game. With Nelson Curtis in charge, they sponsored a "Baseball Excursion" to Detroit's Navin Field to attend the Detroit Tigers game with the New York Yankees.

For $3.00 (the price of the game ticket included) you could travel with the group by train to Detroit and return. If you didn't want to attend the game, you could make the round trip to Detroit for $1.50. The train left Fenton at 11:30 AM, arriving in Detroit at 1:00 PM. Returning, the train left Detroit at 7:30 PM and arrived back in Fenton at 9:00 PM.

"Baseball Excursions", similar to the American Legion trip of 1937, were also sponsored by other organizations and occurred once or twice a year. They were well attended especially when the trip was made by chartered bus and a keg of beer was placed in the aisle to address the thirst of the passengers aboard.

Although golf was not as popular as it is today, several men and women played the game. The only local course was on Torrey Road to the west of Long Lake (the name had been officially changed to Lake Fenton, but the natives still used the Long Lake name).

Those who played found the fees at the Long Lake Golf Club to be quite reasonable. The charge for nine holes of play was 40 cents and for 18 holes 70 cents. The all day golf pass, which included a Buffet lunch, was $1.00.

The Industrial Tool and Die Golf Tournament was held in July at the Long Lake Golf Club and the *Fenton Courier* reported the winners: Charles Robinson, Evar Strom, R.P. Smith, John Martin, Bud Walker, Frank Bachus and George Hall.

The Fenton Independent reported that Father Daniel Tighe of St John Catholic Church had a "hole in one" while playing that course. His witnesses, as if any were required, were the members of his foursome Dr. M.B. Smith, Ray Brownell and Fred J. Cornell, all of Flint, Michigan.

In reference to the name change of Long Lake-to-Lake Fenton, it should be known that the older Charley Case, who lived on the island bearing his name, was publicly calling for a return to the Long Lake name. In his letter to *The Fenton Independent*, he wrote "I think we have worn out the name Lake Fenton and that it is time to change back to that glorious old name, Long Lake...I hope this will take place before long". Sorry Charley, it never happened!

He also was asking for the redirecting of the Shiawassee River, back to its original course, which passed through the southern tip of Long Lake. It seems that in the mid 1800's an ambitious mill owner had the river diverted in order to provide waterpower to his mill. The mill has been long abandoned, but the river was never returned to its original course. Sorry Charley, it never happened!

Around Thanksgiving Day, Charley Case wrote the *Fenton Courier* about those living on the Lake Fenton Island bearing his name. He said Pete Hunter and his wife, William Otes and his family and he..."the hard case" would be "the population on the island this winter."

Living on Case's Island through the winter could present some very difficult problems for the inhabitants. During the summer months, when the water is open, the inhabitants could come to the "mainland" with their boats. When the lake had frozen, they could walk or sled to the shore. However, there is always that period in the early winter and the early spring when the transit cannot be made by boat...or sled.

While it is likely that electricity had come to the island, probably some of the inhabitants, especially during the summer months, were continuing to use kerosene lamps and stoves.

In the present day, one year long resident of the island found a hovercraft to travel to and from the mainland shore. The hovercraft had no difficulty traveling over water or ice or whatever nature presented. I wonder what ol' Charley Case would have had to say about something like that?

Of the other notable occurrences along Torrey Road during this year was the opening of "The Green Lantern" opposite Black's Landing on Mud Lake (now Lake Ponemah). This tavern would prove to be a very popular "watering hole" for many years to come

The April 29, 1937 edition of the *Fenton Independent* advertised one of the newest "labor-saving" machines for the nation's housewives!

Scene Five…Who's in charge?

Back "downtown" the Village government stood for another election and one of the long serving members, J.E. "Fritz" Judevine resigned from the council because of his ill health and a short time after his resignation he succumbed. Mr. Judevine had operated a grocery store in the 100 block on South Leroy prior to his death. William "Bill" Marshall was appointed to fill his seat on the council.

In the following election, when a total of 48 votes were cast, all of the incumbents, including Bill Marshall, were reelected.

The area's Representative in Congress at the time was A.J. Transue of Flint. Congressman Transue, like many others, had a "letter" published in each of the weekly editions of *The Fenton Independent.* A number of his reports dealt with the issue of President Roosevelt's proposal to expand the membership of the U.S. Supreme Court. Those opposed to the proposition, which included Chief Justice Charles Evans Hughes and most everyone else in the nation, succeeded in forestalling this attempt to "pack the court". In one report, the Congressman told of the efforts to line up more support for an Anti-Lynching bill. He reported the proponents of the bill had 200 votes committed but needed 218 to pass the legislation.

More important issues, closer to home, were the efforts of Fenton and other US 23 communities to obtain a commitment from the State to extend the paved highway from Brighton to Fenton. It was disturbing to know that US 23 was paved all the way from the Straits of Mackinaw in northern Michigan to the airport in Miami, Florida, *except* for the stretch from the southern limits of Fenton to a point just north of Brighton.

At a meeting with the State's Highway Commissioner Murray "Pat" Van Wagoner they learned there was now 15 to 20 miles between Brighton and Fenton to be paved and this would be done at a rate of five miles per year. By early September, work on the first 5 mile stretch extending from Brighton northwest to Hartland had begun. Murray D. "Pat" Van Waggoner later became Governor of Michigan. (1941-43)

Whether the roads were paved or not, Leon Durkee traveled them each night making his rounds. Leon Durkee's title was "Nightwatch" and he patrolled the downtown businesses and checked on whether the doors were locked and the properties secured for the night. Leon was paid a modest salary and he was the village's only full-time policeman. Basil Chappelle served as a part-time assistant to Durkee. The "police team" of Durkee and Chappelle was rewarded at a Council meeting in March, when Durkee's salary was raised to $50 per week with an automobile maintenance allowance of $104 per year. His assistant, Basil Chappelle's allowance was increased to $5 per night.

In a column in *The Fenton Independent*, Leon Durkee enumerated some of the services he provided for the citizens of the village:

All stores patrolled at night
Highways patrolled in Business and Residence district at night
Police car meets train at night and will take you anywhere in town, or come and get you for train.
Going away for a night, week, or month? We will watch your home.   A small fee will be charged for this service.
Want a wrecker, storage for your car, battery, tires, Doctor, ambulance, drug supplies, rooms, gasoline or Police?
Yes, we will drive you home, if you get too much to drink at the party.
DON'T DRIVE DRUNK, or you will go to jail.
Call telephone operator for Police connection, between 8 at night and 4 in the morning for this service.

It was the accepted practice in Fenton and other small towns to allow the town "Nightwatch" to accept fees for other services to complement the "salary" paid by the Village.   Each of the merchants would contribute 25 or 50 cents a week to the Nightwatch "in appreciation" of the Nightwatch checking their establishment for unlocked doors or open windows after closing. As the town grew and the need for police protection changed, this practice would become a matter of discussion in the town and the Village Council.

Sometimes the Nightwatch found more than an unlocked door. In November, while Basil Chappelle was on duty and making his rounds of the downtown businesses, he returned to his car to find an inebriated stranger sound asleep in the front seat of the car. It was an easy call for Basil; he drove to the town jail and deposited the stranger in a cell where he could sleep more comfortably.

Scene Six… School Days… Golden Rule Days!

In June 1937, Fenton High School graduated forty-six young people with Earl Alberts as their Valedictorian and June Duby as the Salutatorian (See Appendix One for a list of all graduates for the years 1937 through 1941.)

The enrollment in the Fenton Schools in the fall of 1937 was the largest in the history of the schools. A total of 906 students were enrolled at the beginning of school in September. The average number of students in each of the K-12 grades was about sixty. With the highest enrollment in the 9th grade with 88 students and the lowest class sizes of 54 and 58 were in the 4th grade and Kindergarten respectively. The enrollment in the four high school grades was 318, which exceeded the cutoff number of 300 and moved Fenton High School from Class "C" to Class "B" in interscholastic athletics.   The schools in the Genesee County League had enrollments abut the same as Fenton. Moving to Class "B' would determine where Fenton would play in post season tournaments.

In their July meeting, the Board of Education approved the hiring of 24 full time teachers and expected both the Superintendent Clarence R. Heemstra and the Principal Charles D. Arrand to teach several classes. Mr. Arrand and nine other teachers would carry the instructional load for the four high school grades.

The School Board held their elections in July and with 55 votes cast the incumbents President Harry A. Lowe, John A. Cox, William J. Rynearson, Morris G. Sanders, and Clyde J. Furlong were retained. Messrs. John Cox and Clyde Furlong were the only board members standing for election at this time and Horace Hitchcock and D.R. Stiles unsuccessfully challenged them. In August, Morris Sanders resigned his position and John J. Weidman, a former Board member, was appointed to take his place.

In our present world of education, the perpetual mantra is that teachers' salaries are too low. Even if one recognizes the value of the dollar has changed greatly from 1937 to today, one cannot help but be astounded at the salaries of full time teachers in the late 1930s. It is interesting to note that well-known, well-liked, experienced, competent and, in most cases, remarkable teachers at the Fenton High School in 1937 were paid some very unremarkable salaries.

Lester Miller who taught Biology and was Head Coach for Football, Basketball and Baseball was paid $1,551 for the year. His Assistant Coach in three sports and the Head Track Coach, Roger Leestma taught Geography for an annual wage of $1,193.50. August Arndt, an outstanding Mathematics teacher, who later became the High School Principal, earned $1,403.50. Gordon Thomas taught English, Literature and coached Dramatics and later became Mayor of East Lansing and a Professor of Communication Arts at Michigan State University, worked for $1,037 even! The future Mrs. Gordon Thomas, Phyllis Lenzner taught English and Latin for $1.033.50. Bessie Cramer, a 1910 graduate of Fenton High School and a one-woman Commercial Arts department, taught Bookkeeping, Typing and all business courses for $1,384. Thelma Barker, the Vocal Music lady, received $1,184 for her work Martha Wagbo taught Home Economics. Many young girls learned sewing, cooking and other domestic skills in her classroom, and she was paid $1,232.50 for the year. C.D. Arrand was the high school principal and also taught Chemistry and Physics. His combined salary for both Principal and Teacher amounted to $1,709.12. Similarly, the Superintendent C.R. Heemstra was paid the "big bucks", a total of $2,696

Two of the student's most favorite persons, custodians Odie Wilhoit and John Chapman were not overlooked and they were paid $1,114 and $1,104 respectively. From the student's perspective, Odie and John kept them warm in the winter, provided a clean environment and while not "buddies"; they were friendly and treated everyone with respect.

The salaries paid to the Fenton administrators and teachers were probably very typical of the salaries paid throughout the schools in Michigan. Most of the Fenton Teachers worked during the summer months when school was not in session. Mr. Miller worked in a local service station and later ran a summer recreational program for the Fenton Community Center.

Mr. Raymond Lee, who taught History and Civics at Fenton High School, was qualified as a merchant seaman and spent his summers sailing the Great Lakes on the ships carrying iron ore from the ports on Lake Superior. Even with two jobs, Mr. Lee was obviously not a wealthy man. He generally wore a blue serge suit, which had been cleaned and pressed so often the cloth had a mirror-like finish.

These were the depression years and money was "tight" for everyone, including the Fenton Schools. The Board's operational budget for the 1936-1937 school year, ending on July 1st, was a little over $60,000.

They had receipts of about $75,000   which along with a carry over balance from the proceeding year allowed them to put $20,000 into the building fund and still have $20,000 to carry forward for the next year. They finished the year with no outstanding Bills Payable and about $20,000 in accounts receivable.

It is interesting to note that one of the school's most successful graduates, Mr. Bryson D. Horton, Class of 1890, continued to make his annual gift of $250 to support the teaching of Geography. Mr. Horton was the brother of Mary A. Rackham. The Horace H. and Mary A. Rackham Foundation provided the funds for the building of the new "Community House".

The Board of Education had a building program of their own "in the works". Having received $34,363 from the Federal Government's PWA, they were ready to build a two-story addition to the high school building to provide ten more classrooms.

The Board had demonstrated excellent planning in establishing a building fund for use with the project. However, since the building construction cost would be about $70,000 the Board concluded it would be necessary to sell $16,000 in bonds to supplement the money in the building fund and the PWA grant. In the November election the voters overwhelmingly approved the sale of the bonds. The tally was 189 Yes to only 18 No votes.

The classroom space was sorely needed, since for the last year they had used classrooms in the Methodist Episcopal church   They would continue to use the church classrooms and the old South Ward school, until the addition was completed.

The only "government" in the community with a smaller budget than the Village or the Board of Education was undoubtedly Fenton High School's "Student Government". The President of the Student Council was Donald "Bud" Lemen. Bud Lemen was one of the most popular persons at Fenton High School and like his father, the Village President Harry Lemen; he won his election "going away".

The Student Council was comprised the four class Presidents and 2 to 4 other representatives from each class. In the 1937-1938 school year the following students were members of the council: Seniors: Mary Thompson, Don Herman, Nellie Davis, Robert Atkins, Donald Lemen, Blanche McLenna, Burton McGarry, Jack Hartley and Class President Garwood Marshall   Juniors: Richard Riedel, Doris Lobdell, Jeanne Copp, Donald Bell, Jean Gordon and President Paul Bottecelli. Sophomores: Dorothy Milliken, David Dawson, James Frew and

President Gorton Milliken.   Freshmen: June Hartley, Robert Zoll, Robert Harris, Virginia Joslin and President George Pellett.

The students planned and conducted many successful events during the school year such as the two plays, the junior class play, the All-Hi Banquet and the J-Hop. They were most proud of producing a yearbook entitled "The Twin Pines". They said this yearbook was only the second such publication in the last seventeen years. Little did they know at the time, but it would be the last yearbook published at Fenton High School until 1947 when the "Fentonian" made its appearance as the school annual.

The name of the yearbook was taken from the pair of tall pine trees that at the time stood in the front of the high school building on Adelaide Street. The pages were mimeographed on a soft paper and about 23 black and white, glossy photographic prints were glued into their respective positions throughout the book. The book included photos of each class, athletic teams, and faculty and school organizations. Those who did the work were rightfully proud of their efforts to assemble the people for the taking of the photos, the mass production of the photos, the artwork, the writings and the painstakingly difficult job of constructing over 200 books. Copies of the "Twin Pines" are to be found in the Fenton Museum collection.

The "Twin Pines" staff was comprised of the following students: Jeanne Copp (Editor), Mary Simmons, Ann Walters, Nellie Davis, Mary Thompson, May Thompson, Better Alexander, Marguerite Lee, Leone Doane, Cecilia Kucharski, Paul Bottecelli, Dee Marshall, Justin Ruckel and Dorothy Milliken. The faculty advisor was the Art teacher, Charlotte Holbrook. Other teachers such as C.D. Arrand, Zelma Cole, Gordon Thomas, and Bessie Cramer made substantial contributions.

The annual J-Hop was as "big" as ever for the students at FHS. This year the committee had engaged the "Michigan Ramblers" Orchestra that had a very excellent reputation around the area. A plus for the "Ramblers" was that three Fenton men were members of the group. John Hoskins (Village Councilman doubling at piano), Robert Lutz and Carl Ives.

As was the custom, the Class President Garwood "Fuzz" Marshall led the Grand March. Those primarily responsible for the "good time had by all" were: Dorothy Jones, Mary Thompson, May Thompson (who was selected as "Miss Genesee County" for the Romeo Peach Festival), Jean Richmond, Marianna Garner, Nellie Davis, Yvonne Stein, Betty

Merrill, Don Herman, Donald "Bud" Lemen, Burton McGarry, Bruce Cox, James DeVoght and Arnold "Sonny" Westman.

One of the new organizations in the High School was the Hi-Y club. The club advisor was Mr. Roger Leestma and the club was one of many in the county high schools sponsored by the Flint YMCA.

James Frew and Harold Schupbach represented the club at the National Hi-Y Congress at Berea, Kentucky.

FHS Hi-Y Club; 1st Row L-R: Brad Hoffman, Bob Searight, Bob Harris, Bob Dode, Don Bell, Francis Trimmer. 2nd Row L-R: Don Rasmussen, Rex Wood, Harold Bristol, Mr. Roger Leestma, Art Barnard, Dick Reidel, Dick Smale 3rd Row L-R: Ron Longworth, Harold Schupbach, Jim Frew, Don Clark, Bob Zoll, Walter Conrad.

While the Hi-Y membership was "all boys", but the "girls" were not without their own exclusive club. The Girl Reserves was an active group participating in the school functions   At Christmas time they moved beyond the school walls and presented decorated Christmas trees to two elderly women who would otherwise been without a tree.

In May, the Girl Reserves held their annual Mother-Daughter Banquet. Later they showed their domestic skills by making fifty baby garments for a charitable organization in Flint.

Girl Reserves: 1st Row L-R: Pauline Stiff, Marie Dery, Violet Bachus, Sponsor Miss Lorina Goerz, Sponsor Miss Bessie Cramer, Betty Merrill, Eileen McKeon, Marion Evert. 2nd Row L-R: Harriet Abbey, Marion Morgan, Geraldine Stedman, Doris Hubert, Cecelia Kucharski, Irene Schoemaker, Rose Nakovic, Marguerite Lee, Frances Irvine. 3rd Row L-R: Kathryn Trollman, Helen Weigant, Pearl Alpaugh, Jacqueline Reed, Ruth Durkee, Ann Walter, Onalee Brown, Hazel Karshner, Eugenia Buckingham. Absent: Marianna Garner, Hilda Wortman.

It wasn't only the students who had their clubs and found many interesting "things to do". During this time, many of the townsfolk found membership in one or more of the many clubs and church organizations an excellent way to socialize with their fellow villagers, and at the same time provide valuable community service.

Scene Seven…Club (*klub*)(n)

There was a plethora of clubs in the community. The fraternal lodges, women's clubs and the patriotic/veterans organizations attracted a large number of the residents. As one reviews the membership lists of the many organizations, one finds many men and women belonged to two or more organizations. They were not only members but, they were active in these organizations, with several serving as officers.

Probably the most visible and active organizations in the community were the patriotic/ veterans groups.

The Daughters of Union Veterans and the Womens Relief Corps, both organized in support of the Union veterans of the Civil War were surprisingly active in the late 1930s. Etta Poppy and Marie Steward of the D.U.V. and Kate Hempstead, Clara French, Ida Barden and Myrtle Dode of the W.R.C. were a few of those most active.

Commander Frank B. Mytinger led the American Legion Post and the following men were officers: 1st Vice Commander Basil Bowman, 2nd Vice Commander Joe Bottecelli and Adjutant Hollis Winn. Others in leadership roles were: Roy Goodrich, Sam Casazza, Elton Austin, J.C. White, Nelson Curtis and Harry Reed

The American Legion Ladies Auxiliary was as active as their male counterparts during the year. Their officers were: President Mrs. Hollis (Florence) Winn, 1st Vice President Mrs. Walter Conrad and 2nd Vice President Mrs. Joe Franks.

The Colonel Fenton Post of the Grand Old Army of the Republic, the G.A.R., still had three members living in Fenton. One of the three, Andrew Bly, a veteran of the Union Army, while in his mid-90s, attended the G.A.R. State Conventions in Detroit and was the only Civil War veteran that actually marched in their parade! Jesse Straugh, who was active in both the American Legion and Veterans of Foreign Wars posts, marched behind Mr. Bly carrying the flag of the Colonel Fenton G.A.R. post.

One must remember that in 1937 the nation had a very vibrant memory of the First World War. Many of the men in the community had served in the Armed Forces during that conflict and when they returned home to Fenton in 1919, they formed the James DeWitt Post of the American Legion.

It wasn't until March of 1935, before a group of overseas veterans of that war founded the Curtis-Wolverton Post of the Veterans of

Foreign Wars. The top officers of the V.F.W for most of the year were: Commander Jesse D. Straugh, Sr. Vice Commander Glen Palmer and Jr. Vice Commander Emanuel Boilore. Other officers were: Walter Stiff, Fred Slover, Sam Casazza, Joe Bottecelli, Dr. W.J. Rynearson and Claude Tice.

Many of the men were members of both the American Legion and the V.F.W. and many of them served as officers in both organizations. The women were also active in the Ladies Auxiliaries of both the American Legion and the V.F.W. However, the opportunity for women to become "clubbers" was not limited to those two organizations. There were many other Womens clubs active in the community and here again many women belonged to more than one club.

Mrs. Louis (Irma) Riedel was President of Entre Nous for the year 1937 and their club met regularly throughout the year at the home of one of their members. Each meeting featured a presentation of one or two papers researched by a member. At the January meeting at the home of Mrs. Mark (Alice) Gordon, Mrs. McKeon presented a paper on the "History of Michigan" and she was followed by Mrs. Ida Conrad's talk about the "Isle Royale".

Other hostesses and presenters during the year included Mrs. George (Carolyn) Pellett, Mrs. Frank (Jean) Mytinger, Mrs. Don Morehouse, and Mrs. A.T.F. Butt, all members. On occasion, a guest presenter, such as Miss Wagbo, the Home Economics teacher at the Fenton High School would address the members. On October 8, 1937, Entre Nous celebrated its 41st anniversary.

The February meeting of Entre Nous was their "Colonial Costume Party". Members came dressed in the fashion of the colonial period in our country. The costumes ranged from the dress of the Negro slave "Mammy" to accouterments and trappings of the most aristocratic lady in colonial Philadelphia. Mrs. George (Carolyn) Pellett hosted this year's Colonial party. Mesdames Butt and Cooley sang two numbers which seemed appropriate to the theme: "Listen to the Mocking Bird" and "Drink to me only with thine eyes".

The Bayview Club was led this year by Mrs. John (Doris) Hoffman. Similar to the Entre Nous, the Bayview meetings were characterized by an informative presentation by a member. For example, in February, Mrs. Myron (Hazel) McGlynn and Mrs. E. C. (Dessah) Reid offered a review of the book " Drums Along The Mohawk"

Their meeting in October was a very special meeting. It was held at the Long Lake Golf and Country Club on Torrey Road. The meeting was special since the honored guests were: Mrs. A.F. Phillips, a Charter Member; Mrs. Charles L. Bussey (the former Myra Horton, sister of Mary Horton Rackham) of Detroit, formerly of Fenton; and Mrs. L.F. Becker who had been a member of the club for 39 years. Also attending, as guests were three former members: Mrs. J.R. Winglemire, Mrs. John Dalrymple, and Mrs. Warren Richards.   Edith E. Crane hosted the meeting.

There were three active "Child Study" clubs in Fenton in 1937. They were named: The Child Study Club, The Mothers Child Study Club and the Junior Child Study Club. In 1938, a fourth group was organized and they called themselves the "Pro To Child Study Club".

The Pro To Child Study Club name was a shortening of the club goal…"Progress…Together". The club members were to be mothers of very young children.

It is not always clear what characteristics distinguished the members of one club from another, although it appears that the children of the Junior Child Study Club were younger than those of The Child Study Club.

For example, some members of the Child Study Club such as Mrs. Louis Reidel (Jean and Richard), Mrs. Floyd Hartley (Jack and June), Mrs. Than Chesnut (Barbara and Margaret), Mrs. George Pellett (George), Mrs. Hoyt Glaspie (Betty Jayne and Joyce) and Mrs. Claude Sinclair (Donald) were all mothers of high school students. Whereas, the Junior Child Study Club members such as Mrs. Warren Roberts (Jacqueline), Mrs. Henry Alchin (Marian and Carol), Mrs. Earl Helmboldt (Donald and Joyce) and Mrs. Charles Edinger (Eileen, Richard, William and Juanita) had children in the lower grades.

Most of the time the Child Study Clubs met every other week in a member's home. On occasion, they would meet outside one's home to accommodate the program presentation or for a special event.

One such special event was the Mother-Daughter Banquet. The banquet, sponsored by the first Child Study Club, was held at the Methodist Episcopal Church in April and was supported by the other three clubs. Mrs. G.C. Walcott was in charge of the event and Mrs. C.R. Heesmstra served as the Toastmaster.   As was the case for these banquets it was well attended, had excellent food, an interesting program and was enjoyed by all.

For the most part, the club meetings provided a social setting for a group of women friends to discuss a variety of subjects, including the welfare of the children. Generally, one of the members presented a "paper" on a subject of interest.   For example, the following programs are representative of the presentations for the year of 1937:

Mrs. Floyd Hartley CSC ..."Interesting Our Young People at Home"
Mrs. Claude Sinclair at CSC..."Planning our Finances"
Mrs. Ivah Rolland at CSC..."Family Councils"
Mrs. Maurice Matthews at CSC...A Book Review
Mrs. Sidney Hay at CSC..."Interest in our High School Students"
Mrs. Henry Alchin at JCSC..."Children's Pets"
Mrs. Earl Helmboldt at JCSC..."Presenting Nature to a Child"
Mrs. Delphine Bender JCSC ..."Choosing My Children's Playmates"
Mrs. Edna Brown at Mother's CSC..." School Facilities"

There were many women's clubs active in the community during this period.   Most of the clubs had reports of their meetings and events regularly printed in the two weekly newspapers.

A review of the newspaper articles reveals the Clubs and their leaders most frequently mentioned were: The Golden Rule Club (Mrs. William Henderson, Maria Morea, Helen Munson and Mrs. Maude Reed); Home Economics Club (Mrs. Perry Brunson); "In and Out" Club (Mrs. J.C. White, Mrs. George Hall, Mrs. Arthur Clement, Mrs.Fred Williams, Mrs. Judson and Mrs. Helmboldt); the Penelope Club (Mrs. M.A.Stallworth); Women's Music Club (Mesdames Bell, Skillen, Powlison, Mytinger, Polson, White, Bell, Hiscox and Hamilton), Priscilla Club (Mrs. George Giles and Mrs. Roy Wood), Monday Night Review (Misses Margaret Crane, Janet Conrad, Barbara Barnes, Marguerite Lea, Eleanor Yerdan, and Verda Welch), Quinzedias Club (Miss Vera Jarvis, Miss Lucille McCarthy and Miss Laura Bautan), Coterie Club (Miss Edith Crane), Home Economics Club (Mrs. A.T.F. Butt), Aw Kum On Club (Mrs. Jed White, Mrs. Guy Merrick, Mrs. Harry Reed, Mrs. Perry Brunson, Mrs. Myrtle Swanebeck , Mrs., Cleo Steward and Mrs. Ivah Rolland)

The Masonic organization was strong in Fenton throughout the Thirties.   They owned their own three story building on the northwest corner of Leroy and Caroline Streets.   They used the upper two floors for their organizations and leased the ground floor to the State Savings Bank and to George Tamlyn for his photo store and studio

The Masons chose their leaders for the coming year in December. Those elected were: Worshipful Master Hollis Winn, Senior Warden Allen Moyer and Junior Warden John C Martin.   Other members included: D.R. "Ray" Stiles, R.A. Cummings, Roy Polson, Nelson

Curtis, Albert B. Ives, Murray Chase, Paul Bristol, Wesley Goss, M.G. Sanders and John A. Johnson.

The Order of the Eastern Stars, one of the Masonic organizations, was very active in the community. While men were associated with the O.E.S it was considered primarily an association for women. In their elections for the upcoming year of 1938 they selected Mr. and Mrs. Raymond Hyde, respectively, as their Worthy Patron and Worthy Matron. The Associate Matron was Mrs. Virginia Lonsbury and Mr. Plynna Faye served as Associate Patron

The brothers and sisters of O.E.S. had been considering sponsoring a chapter of the Rainbow Girls, an organization concerned with the welfare of young ladies Ages 13 through 20. After visiting the Holly chapter of the Rainbow Girls, the Fenton group, led by the Past Worthy Matron Mrs. Maurice Matthews, Mrs. John Hoffman, and Mrs. Raymond Hyde, the O.E.S. organized the Fenton chapter.

Miss Helen Hockett was elected as the first leader, the Worthy Advisor and Nellie Davis was the assistant. The girls who joined the Rainbow Girls at the beginning included most of the active young women in the Fenton High School at the time. The founding members were: Dorothy Polson, Margaret White, Violet Bachus, Jayne Glaspie, Dawn Hagerman, Joan Smale, Mary Simmons, June Hartley, Dorothy Austin, Jean Richmond, Laura Lewis, Gloria Reid, Jose Davies, Jeanne Brooks, Kathryn Dode, Joyce Glaspie, Clara Davis, Rosa Westman, Doris Hunt, Rose Buffmeyer, Lois Atherton, Virginia Sluyter, Noreen Carpenter, Virginia Poppy, Carol Lutz and Marjorie Hinkley. Twenty-nine young ladies were initiated!

The Oddfellows (I.O.O.F) and their "Favorite" Rebekahs were one of the most active fraternal groups in the area. As owners of a building with a big meeting hall, they were generous in their willingness to provide space for the meetings and events of other organizations without such facilities.

In January of 1937, the Oddfellows installed their officers for the coming year. The Noble Grand Master was Cleon Moorman. The others in leadership positions were: Ryan Strom, Murray Chase, Lloyd Kelley, George Anglen, Henderson Graham, William Stocken, Ross Henderson, Kenneth Robbins, A. Sears and W.A. Gamble.

Noble Grand Matron Mrs. Marie Steward and Vice GM Emily O'Berry, Secretary Esther Lora and Treasurer Ida Gould led the Favorite Rebekahs. In December Mrs. O'Berry was elected to the

Noble Grand position with Nellie Lockwood and Violet Vandercook assuming new positions.

In today's environment, it is difficult to relate to a very active group of women (and men) who were opposed to the consuming of alcohol. However, in 1937 there was an active chapter of the Woman's Christian Temperance Union, the W.C.T.U. The Prohibition Act had only recently been repealed, and there were some citizens who were working to deny the consumption of alcohol. The wives of many prominent citizens were active in the organization: The wives of the men listed here were active at the time: Maurice Matthews, Ray Welch, Albert Sparks, Ralph Winn, John Howe, Fred Clark, A.T.F. Butt, Julian Bristol, Mark Robinson, Alexander Currie, Walter Brown, Grant Fricke, Ray Marsh and John Holtsforth.

Supporters of the "Townsend Plan" were also present in the community and they formed a chapter of the nationwide Townsend Club. Their President, the Reverend W.H. Hutton, with officers M.A. Conrad, Joseph Beebe and F.M.Granger had frequent meetings throughout the year and continued to support Dr. Francis Townsend's Old Age Revolving Pension Plan to work the country out of the depression.

One of the clubs operating in 1937 and still functioning in the present day is the XX Club. The club members were many of the leading businessmen and other leaders in the community. In 1937, their President was Howard Craft and Daniel L. Hogan DDS was the 1st VP. Tom Swingle was the 2nd VP and K.C. Asmer was the 3rd VP. Secretary George Tamlyn and Treasurer Horace Hitchcock filled out the slate of officers. It is interesting to note that the club held their election meeting at Frank's Tavern on Lake Ponemah, which like the XX Club, has survived the many years to the present day.

In August, the XX Club met at Charles Butcher's cottage on Lake Fenton for their "Annual" Meeting. William W. Blackney talked about "Our Constitution", a male quartet from the American Legion in Flint sang several numbers and to top off the evening, J.C. Peck and George Tamlyn showed some "home movies".

Scene Eight…Church People
…And All the Things They Do!

The Methodist Episcopal Church played a large role in community activities. The general population benefited about as much as the members of the church. The downtown location provided a convenient facility for banquets, meetings and other gatherings, which was not restricted to the church members only. The organizations sponsored by the church had a very active calendar of events. The church had been a significant part of village life for a long time; in fact the Methodist Episcopal Church celebrated its 100th Anniversary in May of 1937

The Men's Fellowship, in its seventh year as a group, hosted several banquets and events during the year and none was more anticipated than the annual Father-Son Banquet. The banquet drew a record crowd of over 250 fathers and sons. Dr. William J. Rynearson served as the MC while Sheldon Latourette led the singing. The guest speaker was Walter Hastings of the State's office of Conservation. He regaled the audience with pictures of Michigan's great outdoors.

And as if not to be outdone by the Men's Fellowship, the ladies of the church "banded" together and held a Mothers-Daughters banquet with great interest and success. Miss Jean Reidel and Miss Janet Conrad teamed up to toast the mothers. Miss Phyllis Lenzner, of Fenton High School seated those attending in step with her piano music.

The Men's Fellowship held an earlier gathering in March of the year which featured FBI Special Agent Jay C. Newman. Mr. Newman had been active in pursuit of "Baby Face" Nelson, one of the periods more notorious criminals. He told of a confrontation with the fugitive in which his deputy was killed. Needless to say, those attending were captivated by his remarks.

The Men's Fellowship was quite aware of the role the women of the church and community played in the making good things happen. They honored their contributions with a "Ladies Night" at which a Professor C. H. Nickels from Michigan State College spoke of "A Poetic Scrapbook"…to the pleasure of all in attendance.

Harvey Swanebeck of Fenton Township was elected as Chairman of the Men's Fellowship. Mr. Swanebeck was a wonderful combination of farmer, politician, real estate developer and Community activist. He was well regarded in the region and was the principal developer of the property along the southwest shore of Lake Fenton.

70   The Village Players

At the time the Ladies of the Methodist Episcopal Church were organized into "Bands". In later years, these groups were referred to as "Circles". The big event for "Band #4" this year was producing a "Style Revue", a fancy name for a Ladies/Children's Fashion Show. The minister's son, William Butt, acted as MC/Announcer and conducted the event as a radio program The attendees set at tables of four, there was the music of a piano duet by Alice Van Atta and Miss Elsie Lehtinaki and a two vocal solos, one by Mrs. William Ruckel.and the other by Mrs. Ellen Lea Wysong. The Rollands Dry Goods, Pelletts Department Store, Becker Federated Department Store and the Faulkner Hat Shop donated the clothing and other accouterments worn by the models (all local people) in the show.

The M.E. "Band leaders" for 1937 were Mrs. David Bradley, Mrs. Alex Currie and Mrs. E.J. Lord for Band #1; Mrs. E.R. Sluyter, and Mrs. John Howe for Band #2; Mrs. Floyd Poppy for #3 and Mrs. Perry Brunson for Band #4.

The Presbyterian and Baptist ladies were not to be outdone by the Methodist women. The Presbyterian women called their groups "Cornerstones". They were active throughout the year with various projects in support of their church and the community in general.

Their President Eleanor Lee led cornerstone #3. She was assisted by Mrs. William Henderson as VP, Secretary Mrs. Arthur Embury, Treasurer Mrs. William Stocken and Retiring President Mrs. William Gould.   Cornerstone #2 officers were: President Mrs. George Pettis, VP Mrs. Walter Conrad, Secretary Mrs. Martin Stiff and Treasurer Mrs. Ray Smith.   Cornerstone #1 had Mrs. L.A. Damon as their president, Mrs. A. Munson as VP and Mrs. C.R. Heemstra as Secretary/Treasurer

The Baptist Ladies Aid and Missionary Society was an active group in their church. Mrs. Garl Albers and Mrs. George Antis provided strong leadership

In August, the people of St. John held a Bar-B-Que party, not only for their members, but also as a community event. They set up some stands for exhibitions and sales of craft items and arranged for dancing in the evening. As part of their program, they had Judge Ira Jayne attend and act as Master of Ceremony for the program. At 8PM the City Band played a concert. Father Tighe was reported to have invited some Detroit Tiger baseball players, namely Billy Rogell and Hank Greenberg to make an appearance. Whether any of them showed is not known, but it probably added to the citizens' interest in attending the event.

Scene Nine...The World of Entertainment?

Speaking of "bands", one is reminded of Fenton's City Band. It all began in the 1800s and was still going strong in 1937. The Village of Fenton had a "City" Band. However, as time passed and the Village became a City, the City Band organization disappeared. But in 1937, the City Band played a concert every week during the summer months and played several "winter" concerts as well.

The City Band organization was very democratic and held an election of officers each year. In 1937, Fred Parker served as President and Charles A. Simmons was the Band's Business Manager. Henry L. Willing was the Secretary and Arthur Claspil was the Treasurer.

The Band Stand was located on the south side of East Ellen Street near the old Water Works. The Band was forced to relocate their bandstand when the Water Works was demolished to make way for the new Municipal Building.

Their concert programs were quite varied, however some of Sousa's rousing Marches were generally among the numbers played. The Band played some classical works as well as some of the more modern tunes. They played at all civic functions and marched in the parades on Memorial Day and the 4th of July. There was no hue and cry about public involvement with religious institutions when the Band played at the St. John church Barbeque or used the Methodist Church for one of its indoor concerts.

In July, Maestro Clarence L. Wilder announced the future Band concerts would have "special features". One special night was scheduled for featuring noted Clarinetist Wilber Grier of Michigan State College. There would be "guest" conductor nights when the conductor of an acclaimed Michigan band would be invited to lead the band.. Then there would be "Old Time" Nights when the band music most had learned and loved in the past would be played. Most programs would include Sousa Marches such as "Stars and Stripes Forever" and "El Capitan".

One of the concerts on the Band's busy schedule was at Genesee County's "Pioneer Picnic" which was an annual event. The Pioneer Picnic was held at McCann's Grove at the north end of Lake Fenton and was attended by many of the pioneer's descendents from Fenton, Holly and the surrounding area.

It is interesting to note that William "Billy" Thompson was the snare drummer in the band in the late 1800s. Mr. Thompson was a jeweler in Fenton earlier in his life but lived in poverty in his later years. He is not remembered as a businessman in town, or even as a musician in the City band. He is remembered as an unusual "character" and the partner of another town "character", Herb Dutton, who played drums in downtown Fenton. More importantly, he is remembered.

When "Billy" died in April of 1937 at the age of 78, he was buried in Oakwood Cemetery. The Reverend A.T.F Butt officiated at his funeral services, which were held at the Craft Funeral Home. Messrs. Ray L Parker, Fred Parker, Basil Chappelle and William Conrad served as pallbearers. Several of the town's citizens showed their respect and attended his funeral

Early in the year, there was a weak attempt to start up a new "modern' dance band in town to play at some of the dances. *The Fenton Courier* ran a front page article about the "new' band, but from all indications it didn't play many "gigs". Miss Phyllis Lenzner, FHS's English and Latin teacher, was an accomplished pianist and the other members were students: Garwood "Fuzz" Marshall-Drums, Jim DeVoght-Trombone, Jean Brooks-Trumpet, Ken Pettis-Violin and Loreen Harding-Clarinet.

Entertainment wasn't all with local talent. 1937 was a great year for movies in Fenton. While the *Rowena* was the only theater in town, the owner, J. C. Peck, brought in "first run" movies, had three different pictures per week with two showings on a weekday and three on Saturday and Sunday. The theater had very good projection and sound equipment and the price was right! At 25 cents for adults and 10 cents for children all times except Sunday evening when adult fares were 30 cents many of the villagers could scrape up the "tab" most of the time. In addition, in the summer months it was nice to go to a movie and as the advertisement in the *Fenton Courier* proclaimed "Enjoy Cool Air Conditioned Comfort".

J.C. Peck served as an officer of the Michigan theater owners' organization and as such made certain his theater was included with the "big boys" in the distribution of first run movies. Some of those on the *Rowena*'s silver screen were:

William Powell and Myrna Loy in "The Great Zeigfeld"
Joe E. Brown in "Polo Joe"
Johnny Weismuller in "Tarzan Escapes"
Jack Benny and Gracie Allen in "College Holiday"
Warner Oland in "Charley Chan at the Opera"

Charles Laughton in "Rembrandt"
Jeanette MacDonald and Nelson Eddy in" Maytime"
Janet Gaynor, and Frederic Marsh in "A Star is Born"
And these were just a few of the movies shown in 1937 at the *Rowena*.
…Scores of actors of the era appeared in a variety of movies…
Names of the "greats" included Errol Flynn, June Harlow, Robert
Taylor, Joan Crawford, Marlene Dietrich, Charles Boyer, Claude Rains,
Robert Young, George Brent, Claudette Colburn, Jane Withers, the
Marx Brothers and Shirley Temple

In November, J. C. Peck purchased the McCraken Building directly across Leroy Street from his *Rowena* Theater and began to remodel the building for use as his second theater. The building housed the Tyrone Gift Shop operated by Mrs. W.H. Alexander. It was one of the widest buildings on Leroy Street and it was intended to use this space for a theater and also provide space for one store on the street front which Mrs. Alexander could occupy and continue her gift shop business.

It had been rumored that an outside group was going to open another theater in Fenton, and it was suspected that J. C. Peck had made the move to head off any second theater being built. However, J.C. had just been thwarted in his attempt to enlarge the *Rowena*. He had petitioned the Village Council to vacate that portion of the alley behind his theater to enable him to use that space to enlarge the theater building. Other merchants who used the alley opposed him and he withdrew his petition and negotiated the purchase of the building across the street from the *Rowena*.

Not all the "spectaculars" occurred on the silver screen. The Knights Templar of the Fenton Commandery No. 14 would occasionally hold military formations and drills for public viewing. The Knights Templar would turn out in splendor with their black double-breasted Civil War style uniforms, with a large white plumed chapeaux and form in ranks and march about the field.

The Knights Templar members were, for the most part, well known businessmen in the community. Their membership included D. G. MacFayden (Commander), John Hoffman (Generalissimo), Maurice Matthews, L.M. O'Dell, Robert G. Stoddard, Clifford J. Phillips, D.R. Stiles, Edgar Webber, Elton Austin, Howard J. Craft, Bryan Bowles of Linden and A.W. Hay.

The Masons, acting as the Fellowcraft Club, were the local sponsors with the Chicago radio station WLS in producing a "Talent Show". The "Talent Show" was based upon the popular "Prairie Farmer" nationally broadcast program. Persons from WLS auditioned local people at the Masonic Hall. WLS were looking for people who could impersonate the radio stars of their show as well as other singers, dancers and those with other talents that would be entertaining.

The "Home Talent Show" was held in the Fenton High School Auditorium for three nights in May. The cast of characters was amazingly lengthy, and in the opinion of those who knew the performers, the skill level of a few of them was very questionable. Nevertheless, the show went on, was well attended and considered a success. Some wag said he would rather have watched young Charley Case wrestle that bear again!

Generally, the community could depend on the Fenton High School play productions to provide some very good entertainment. Consequently, those attending the school productions far outnumbered the parents of the students in the cast.

The FHS Dramatics Club presented one such "good show" in late April. The group presented the comedy, "Meet My Wife" with Ruth Rounds "stealing the show" in the comedic lead. Earl Alberts (the Class valedictorian) played the opposite lead role magnificently.   The supporting cast, directed by Gordon Thomas, was composed of: Don Rowley, Jim Bachus, Jean Reidel, Garwood Marshall, Jeanne Copp and Don Sinclair.

Cole's carnival came to town in April and set up operations on the Grand Trunk lots south of the Train Depot. The event was sponsored by the V.F.W. post that was careful to announce, "…This is a clean cut affair, no gambling, nothing indecent…" Generally, this was the case, however it did not deter some parents from essentially locking up their young daughters and cautioning their young sons to maintain good behavior.

It was August before the Circus came to town. The Lewis Brothers had a three-ring circus and menagerie. The ads read "…great death defying wizards of the air…" They set up in the open fields, called Zoll's Field, west of town on the Silver Lake Road where they had two shows a day, at 2PM and 8PM. Many of the merchants used "courtesy tickets" to the circus as sales incentives, giving away "kids" tickets, which regularly cost 15 cents.

Scene Ten…the "Fade out"

In the last months of the year, the people of Fenton were making their plans for the celebration of Thanksgiving and Christmas. Guy Merrick, the local Buick dealer located on the northwest corner of North Leroy and Roberts (now Silver Lake Road) Streets offered a free Christmas turkey with every used cars sold in the month of December. He was offering a 1937 Buick 4 Door Sedan with radio and heater for $725. If that wouldn't get the free turkey for you, maybe the 1934 Ford DeLuxe 2 Door Sedan, with a new motor and a heater, for $225 would do the trick?

For the past few years, the State of Michigan had been selling ½ year motor vehicle licenses. This was done to allow those vehicle owners to spread the cost of licensing over two payments. The half-year sticker was placed on the front windshield of the vehicle and it was reported that about 40% of the owners used the ½ year program. Claude Cohoon, the editor of the *Fenton Courier*, reported Louis Reidel came into his office in mid-March, just before the March 16th deadline for the 1938 license. He was waving two new license plates in his hand and loudly complaining he had just paid $12 for these "two pieces of metal".

More evidence of things getting better was the completion of a new lumberyard in town. The Sweet and Lee Lumber yard opened near the Grand Trunk railroad crossing at Lincoln Street. Mr. Jack Sweet was an experienced lumberman who joined Mr. Floyd Lee in the enterprise. Mr. Lee had run the White Star service station at the corner of South Leroy Street and Shiawassee Avenue for years. The new manager for the White Star was Russell Carmer.

The town's only bank, the State Savings Bank was actively promoting thrift for the young people in our schools. Early in the year the Bank in cooperation with the Schools initiated a "School Savings System". Those participating students were issued a bankbook, opened an account with a minimum deposit of 25 cents and could make weekly deposits of 10 cents of more.

In the present this program sounds rather "ho-hum", however, in 1937, the general populace had recently, in the early 1930s, had a very bad experience with banks. Many had lost their savings as the banks closed and lacked the solvency to restore the customer's funds. However, the State Bank had earlier demonstrated their financial soundness and as a result, their management believed it was time to promote thrift and at the same time restore confidence in the local bank. The State Bank had earlier in the year observed its Fifth Anniversary of re-establishing banking services in Fenton. Those individuals managing the bank were recognized among the "pillars" of the community: Directors George W. Cook, George Green, F.H. Hitchcock, J.H. Jennings, D.E. Kelleher, George W. Pellett, Charles F. Rolland and E. Clair Reid. While George Cook and George Green were respectively the President and Vice President of the Bank, Clair Reid, the Cashier, was in today's terms, the "CEO". Robert F. Smith was the Assistant Cashier.

As the year was closing, the Junior class as Fenton High School presented the obligatory "Junior Play". Under the direction of Drama teacher Gordon Thomas, the group presented "Headed for Eden". The principals in the cast were: Blanche McLenna, Yvonne Vosburg, Don Peterson, Mary Simmons, Jose Davies and Jean Lee.

In the "outside world" the town's people marveled at the Blue Water Bridge under construction at a cost of $2,500,000. The span connecting Port Huron, Michigan with Sarnia, Ontario, Canada was to be completed in late 1938. However, in Europe and Asia, more ominous events were occurring.

The Civil War in Spain was underway and Hitler's Germany, Mussolini's Italy and Hirohito's Japan were threatening the peace of the world. In the United States, the City of New York was preparing a World's Fair for 1939. New York's colorful Mayor Fiorella LaGuardia suggested they build a "Hall of Horrors" at the Fair and include "…that brown-shirted fanatic who is menacing the peace of the World." Germany's response was to call the "paesano" Mayor a "scoundrel super Jew".

While the people of Fenton were not completely unaware of what was transpiring in the "outside World" they were more concerned about what was happening in their daily life and the lives of their neighbors

On Armistice Day, November 11th, as the children in the Fenton Schools were pausing at 11AM and facing east for a moment of silence, in tribute to those who perished in the great World War, the W.E. Wood Company reported the new Community Center building had reached its structural height. A milestone in the construction, but with much more to be done before the Center became a functioning facility in our community …planned for early in 1938.

There wasn't much commotion among the general public when the Village Council acquiesced to the complaints of a new resident on

Shiawassee Avenue, and ordered the removal of a captured German artillery piece from World War from the park bordering Shiawassee Avenue and Elizabeth Street.

The old gun had been procured by Charles Damon in 1930 from the U.S. Army and positioned in the park, where it was used to celebrate the 4th of July. It replaced a lighter cannon, which had been manufactured locally and originally fired in celebration of the victory at Gettysburg and in later years for the celebration of the 4th of July. The gun was removed to a location near the water works, where two other larger Civil War cannons were also located. The two larger cannon were relocated to the Oakwood Cemetery about 2005.

As the year was coming to an end so was the tenure of the Goodfellow Store after "30 years of faithful service". Their "Going Out Of Business" advertisements offered "Boy's Fleeced Union Suits for 39 cents...Men's Union Suits for 79 cents (Regularly $1.29). They also were selling Men's Overcoats for $14.88, Men's Suits for $14.88 to $18.88, Men's Fine Dress Shirts for 47 cents and Men's Felt Hats for $1.88...regularly $3.50

In December, another "Goodfellow" organization came to life. It was the "Goodfellow Club" which solicited the town businesses, organizations and citizens to donate food, toys clothing and other articles needed to make up Christmas baskets for some needy families in the community. In the end 32 baskets were filled and donated.

Most of the organizations contributed cash for a total of $52.50. The Michigan Bean Company donated a bushel of Michigan beans and George Pettis contributed two bushels of apples.

As the people of Fenton looked back on the happenings of 1937, they were probably amazed at what had transpired. The town had suffered several very tragic events and at the same time experienced some very upbeat happenings that would positively affect their lives and the lives of their children and grandchildren for years to come. They may not have had it in their minds as they excitedly opened presents on Christmas Day, but the biggest and best present for the Village of Fenton was about to be opened in the New Year.... The Fenton Community Center!

Specials For This Fri. and Sat.

TOMATO JUICE 3 Tall Cans	25c
SUGAR 10 Lbs.	53c
TOILET TISSUE 4 Rolls	19c
BUTTER, Linden Lb.	33c
COFFEE, Millar's Real Good, Lb.	17c
BAKER'S COCOA Lb. can	14c
BAKING POWDER Calumet, lb. can	20c
RINSO Pkg.	20c
LIFE BUOY SOAP 3 Bars	19c
SALT Large Box	5c

Gould's Market

Phone - 73   We Deliver

Both the *Fenton Independent* and the *Fenton Courier* published on Thursday of each week. Each of the newspapers carried advertisements for the local grocery stores. Each paper appeared to have certain stores as regular customers. Ed Gould obviously preferred the *Fenton Courier* since his ad appeared every week in that newspaper with rare exceptions.

The advertisement to the left appeared in the May 6, 1937 edition of the *Fenton Courier*.

Act Two...The Year 1938

Scene One...And the Rains Came!

In early February, the region was plagued by thunderstorms and heavy rain. South of town, most of the Tyrone Township bridges in Livingston County were swept away by the raging waters.

In Parshallville, the floodwaters took out their dam, bridge and roadway. Witnesses reported that huge cakes of ice came tearing down the river and only the trees protected the mill itself from damage or destruction.

The newly constructed dam in Fenton was severely threatened by the rising waters that in turn endangered the village's water supply. Men of the village worked all-night and day for two days without relief sandbagging the embankments to prevent erosion. Village President Harry Lemen and other officials stood side by side with the many volunteers protecting the dam and the water works in the park immediately below the dam.

Harry Lemen

Part of the "water works" was a one-story circular building of red brick. The building housed the pumps and the wells that provided the water for the village. The pumps for the water system usually driven by waterpower were being operated by the electric motors. However, as the high waters began to run into the pump station and the pit containing the electric motors, the city engineer called upon the village's fire trucks to pump the water from the pit. Both of the fire trucks, plus an engine from the Wood Construction Company, were used for two days pumping steadily to remove water from the building.

The road to Linden was flooded at the north end of Silver Lake, near the cement plants, and a young entrepreneur was reported to have made a fair amount of money assisting motorists through the flooded area. The young man, wearing hip boot waders, would sit by the road and when the automobile reached the flooded area, he would offer to push them through for fifty cents.   The area remained flooded for three weeks.

The primary reason flooding was so bad in the area of the cement plants was because of the Grand Trunk Railroad embankment between Silver Lake and Lake Ponemah (then called Mud Lake). In order to solve the reoccurring flooding in this area, workers drove a 42-inch diameter metal tube through the Grand Trunk railroad embankment to allow the water to drain away from the area.   This was not an easy task and the company doing the work imported some West Virginia miners to dig the tunnel and install the drain.

Before and after the heavy rains, the various units of the town were busy doing their "things": The Village Council had the opportunity to review the first plans for the new municipal building, which everyone was calling the "new fire hall".

At the same time the village had some workers rapidly transforming Dubord's garage on the "Southside" into a combination fire hall, council chambers, and jail.   Once the fire siren had been mounted on the garage roof, the various operations soon began.

The Village Council met for the first time in Dubord's garage in February and the *Fenton Courier* made an interesting observation concerning the meeting room.   The *Fenton Courier* reported, "The Building Committee had the customary cuspidors and all other equipment arranged in good order in the office of the garage building and the heating plant was performing well".

The plans for the new fire hall were approved and the council urged the contractor, the W.E. Wood Construction Company, to employ local labor as much as possible in the "tear down" of the old fire hall.

It seemed there was all kinds of construction and construction planning going on around town. There was the need for a new fire hall, but before they could build the "new fire hall" it was necessary to tear down the Water Works plant that was on the southeast corner of Ellen and South Leroy Streets.   In years past, the Water Works was the meeting site for the Village Council. In addition to the council meeting room, the rooms in the plant were used to store equipment and as a jail.

The Council had plans to salvage many items from the "old" fire hall for use in the "new" fire hall. As was reported in *The Fenton Independent*, the council instructed that the "…heating equipment, lighting fixtures and other equipment will be carefully taken out to be used in the new building."   How much of the old equipment was actually used is not known, but they probably found most of the old material to be unusable in the new structure. They intended to use the same old clock and bell in the new tower, however the Council ended up purchasing a new $1,300 Seth Thomas illuminated clock while keeping the old bell.

However, the cornerstone for the "new" fire hall did come from the "old" fire hall. A large sandstone block from the old building, was inscribed with the number "1938" and moved to the new building to serve as the building's cornerstone.

Councilman John Hoskins was placed in charge of the Ceremonies for the dedication of the building and the laying of the cornerstone at the base of the tower. The ceremony was set for Sunday, April 24th.

The day of the Cornerstone Dedication ceremonies was a very cold and blustery day. Overcast skies had threatened rain all afternoon and in the middle of the ceremony, the rain began to fall. In spite of the inclement weather a sizeable crowd estimated to be over 1000 turned up at the corner of Ellen and South Leroy Streets for the event. Over 600 individuals had visited *The Fenton Independent* offices in prior weeks to sign a register, which along with many other historical documents was deposited in a copper box and placed inside the cornerstone. (See Appendix Two for the list of the contents of the copper box.)

Councilman John Hoskins had prepared an inspiring program. The Fenton City Band was present and started the festivities by playing several rousing patriotic numbers. Following the invocation by Reverend J. Stanley Mitchell of the Presbyterian Church, John H. Jennings, a respected elder citizen, made several remarks reflecting on the past history of the town. Fire Chief Fred J. Horrell expressed the gratitude of the "fire boys" for the new facilities and Reverend A. Clare Whaley of the Baptist Church closed the ceremony with his Benediction. Whereupon, Village President Harry Lemen stepped forward, with trowel in hand, and ceremoniously laid the cornerstone.

It wouldn't be until June 16th before the Council was to hold their first meeting in the new hall, at which time, with the Fourth of July festivities approaching, they promptly passed an ordinance prohibiting the igniting of fireworks in Fenton

Six months later, the Council decreed that no Christmas trees could be erected along Leroy Street. It seems the State had banned the erection of Christmas trees along all State trucking routes...and Leroy Street was one of those routes. Bah Humbug!

Soon after the passing of the "no fireworks" 4th of July, the people of Fenton learned of the approval of a $72,000 grant to build a new Post Office. The search for a site was conducted and the chosen location was the corner lot on East Caroline and Walnut Streets. This was the location of the home and office of Dr. Burton G. McGarry. About a year later, Dr. McGarry accepted the offer for his property and the construction of a much needed post office building began.

In October, the public found another use for the new fire hall when a jury trial was held on its premises. With Judge E. M Beckwith presiding and a jury composed of Hoyt Glaspie, Ross Henderson, Ford Dormire, John Hoskins, Harry Reed and Roy Goodrich, the trial of William Diehl vs. Gerald Mereness was conducted

It seems that Mr. Diehl had performed some work for Mr. Mereness and claimed he had not been fully compensated for his efforts in the amount of $300. Attorney George McNeal represented Mr. Diehl and Maurice Matthews was the Attorney for Mr. Mereness. The jury decided in favor of the defendant and Mr. Diehl was required to pay $20 in court costs.

On August 11, 1938 the *Fenton Independent published* a special edition devoted to the new Fenton Community Center and pictured the Village leaders during the period. Top Row L-R Shull Woodworth, William Marshall, Floyd Chapin and Robert Beach. Others named but not shown here were: John Hoskins, William Stocken, Gus Lutz and Floyd Poppy.

Scene Two...The Community "House"

The construction of the Fenton Community "House" was making substantial progress and continued to be the "main attraction" in town. The reference to Community "House" was rapidly changing to Community "Center" in the newspaper articles and "town talk".

Most all of the five buildings along South Leroy Street were gone by mid-year. In the process of acquiring the buildings, the Village also picked up a two-story wood frame building behind the Walcott Mill that the Walcotts used for storage. The Village gave this building to the American Legion Post.

After the end of World War I, the State of Michigan gave a large parcel of land on Higgins Lake to Michigan's American Legion. Each of the American Legion posts in Michigan were allowed to request a portion of this large tract for the use of their Post and its members. The Fenton American Legion Post was prompt to act and acquired a large lot on the lake.

After the Village gave them this two-story building, they carefully dismantled the structure, carried it to Higgins Lake where they had enough material to build a large cottage. Post members from the time of its completion

American Legion Cabin at Higgins Lake-1939

in 1939 to the present day have used the cottage.

Even before the buildings along Leroy Street were razed, construction on the Community Center had started. The work of the steam shovel had been completed early and the shell of the building had reached its height in the early months, cement walks were in and landscaping was underway. In May the furniture arrived! Even so there was a still a lot of work to be completed before the scheduled dedication on October 3, 1938.

Under the conditions of the Rackham Foundation providing the funds for the construction of the Community Center, there was to be a local Board of Governors for the Center.

This Board was to be composed of the President of the Village, the Superintendent of Schools and five citizens of the community. The Board was to be self-perpetuating, in that as the citizen members retired from service, the Board would select the successors.

The first Board members were: Harry G. Lemen, the President of the Village of Fenton, Clarence R. Heemstra, the Superintendent of the Fenton Schools; and citizens Charles E. Rolland, Charles Crane, Daniel L. Hogan, Floyd A. Chapin and Don Alchin. Mr. Rolland served as the Board's first President. Horace H. Hitchcock had been originally appointed to the Board but declined and Mr. Chapin was appointed in his stead.

It is interesting to note that while the Community Center was not yet "officially" open, let alone dedicated, it was opened for a very special occasion. Roma Bly, Village Engineer, who had worked so diligently on the Community Center project from its inception died suddenly on September 10, 1938.

For many years, Mr. Bly was "the" Public Works department for the village and he was well respected for his work for the village. For years after his passing, the citizens would be reminded of his work as they walked the town's sidewalks. It seemed like every "square" of cement in every sidewalk in town had an impression bearing his name. To this day, when asked if one remembers Roma Bly, the reply is often the query: "Isn't he the one with his name impressed in the sidewalks?"

Mr. Bly's funeral was held at the Community Center on September 14, 1938 and attended by a large gathering of mourners. The town's businesses closed from 1 to 3 PM for his funeral.

The Reverend A.T.F. Butt of the Methodist Episcopal Church officiated at the service. Roma Bly was the son of Fenton's Union Army veteran, Andrew Bly and the brother of one of the founders of Fenton's Veteran of Foreign Wars post, Andrew Bly, Jr.

The formal dedication of the Fenton Community Center was on October 3, 1938 and it was an elegant affair…and an event anxiously awaited by the townsfolk.

Charles E. Rolland, President of the Center's newly appointed Board of Governors was in charge of the Dedication Ceremonies. As one would expect, Mr. Rolland organized a day of celebration for the coming of a building, an institution, that would materially contribute to the well being of the community for many years, decades, to come.

In the early afternoon, following a prayer of dedication by the Reverend Dr. J. Stanley Mitchell of the Presbyterian Church, music by the Fenton City Band and the singing of Mrs. Helen Kennedy Snyder of Detroit, Village President Harry Lemen stepped forth to officially accept the "gift" of the Rackham Foundation, the Fenton Community Center.

Dr. Alexander Ruthven, President of the University of Michigan delivered the principal address, which was followed by a vocal solo by Mrs. Harriett Mortimore Toomey of Detroit. Mrs. Toomey was a graduate of Fenton High School in the Class of 1922. The Fenton City Band played a couple rousing numbers as the members of the Board of Governors conducted a tour of the new facility.

At about 4PM, the boys and girls were treated to movies in the "ballroom" of the new building, where later that evening there was more entertainment.

The evening entertainment was quite varied. There was a talent show conducted by Mrs. Sheldon Latourette that included community singing, tap dancing, vocal selections and "other pleasing features". Later there was dancing to suit all "tastes".

Square dancing started the evening and "modern" dancing to the music of the Bryan Bowles orchestra followed. Bryan Bowles was from Linden and was well known to the Fentonites. The members of Bryan's band were: Bryan on the piano; Edith Gene Johnson-sax; Fred Aldrich-banjo; Jack Youck-drums; Gerald Bowles-sax and Emma Lou Bowles was the singer. It was quite an aggregation and Linden's contribution to the celebration.

The Board of Governors had begun a search for a Director for the Center, however they could not wait for a Director to be hired and began scheduling events almost immediately. The newly formed Fenton High School Alumni Association and the local Republicans "rented the hall" almost immediately for a banquet and a rally.

There are records of the alumni of Fenton High School coming together for "reunions" as far back as the late 1800s, so it should probably have been expected that one of the first groups to request the use of the new Community Center would be an alumni group.

The Alumni Association sponsored the first banquet in the Community Center following the Homecoming football game in October 1938. Over 150 people attended the event that featured Judge Ira W. Jayne, Class of 1900 as the Toastmaster. Years later, Fenton's

Jayne Road was named for him as were two Jayne Hill communities which were built on his former farm. Al Stickney led the group singing and Mr. Frank Manley was the guest speaker. Frank Manley of the Mott Foundation was a pioneer in the area of community education for which both he and the Mott Foundation earned national recognition.

Soon after the Fenton High School Student Council held the first dance at the Center. Gorton "Bud" Milliken and Al Turco were in charge and it is interesting to learn that the "new Victrola" at the Center provided the music for the dance.

Soon the Board of Governors appointed a Youth Program Committee to coordinate the activities for the younger citizens. The committee was composed of: Mr. And Mrs. Charles E. Rolland, Mrs. Don Phillips, Miss Abbey, Mr. And Mrs. Horace H. Hitchcock, Mr. and Mrs. Hinkley, Mr. William Scott, Mr. Eldon Austin and Mr. Hugo Theisen

The Fenton Independent printed a questionnaire on its front page that solicited the public's input as to the kinds of programs they wanted to see at their new community center.

As the Board of Governors struggled in their search for a Director, they received abundant advise from the academics at the University of Michigan. Most of the applicants were solicited from the colleges in the State and it was not surprising when the Governors announced they had selected Loran Brabon of Hillsdale College. Brabon was formerly from Fenton before going to college at Hillsdale. It is not clear as to what occurred, but Mr. Brabon's did not accept the Directors position and the search for a Director continued.

And the Gods were smiling on the Board when, in December of 1938, they selected Russell D. Haddon to be the Center's first Director. Russ Haddon was a recent graduate of Michigan State Normal College in Ypsilanti, Michigan (now Eastern Michigan University). During an interview in November of 2005, he said that he had prepared for a career in education. However, he smilingly remarked, the offer of a position in his hometown at a salary of $1,400 per year, "was hard to turn down".

Russell Haddon was a 1932 graduate of Fenton High School and was very well known and well liked in the community. During his last year in college, young Russell Haddon was traveling from Ypsilanti every Sunday to serve as a lay reader in St. Jude's Episcopal Church. For almost a year after the departure of Reverend Edward Platts and before the arrival of Reverend William Thomas Smith, Russell conducted the Sunday services at the church.

He would serve as Director of the Fenton Community Center until September of 1948 when service in the U.S. Navy ended his tenure. He established the policies and procedures and guided the activities and services for the Center and contributed significantly to the continuing success of the institution. As the saying goes "...as the twig is bent, so grows the tree..." Russell Haddon is the one who bent the twig!

As the year was drawing to a close, the Community Center was the site of the Christmas Ball sponsored by the Young Ladies Sodality of St. John Church. It was a semi-formal affair and sported the Reade Pierce Orchestra of Ann Arbor. Reade Pierce and his orchestra were well known in the University community and Detroit society.

The funeral procession for Roma Bly leaves the Fenton Community Center following the funeral ceremonies. The white building in the center top of the picture is the Industrial Machine Tool Company's facilities. Note the angle parking along the length of South Leroy Street.

"Mr. Fenton"...Harry G. Lemen

Harry Lemen was the first Mayor of Fenton when it became a city in1964. He was first elected to the Village Council in 1923 and elected Village President in 1931. He served in that capacity for 31 years. When he retired in 1965 he had served 40 years as a Village or City official. He was born in 1895 in Hartland, Michigan and was orphaned at the age of six. After both of his parents died he lived with his uncle w in a three-story log cabin on Lake Fenton. He is best known as the proprietor of Lemen's Market in downtown Fenton. In 1964, over 300 people attended a retirement banquet in his honor. The main speaker for the occasion was Judge Louis D. McGregor of the Michigan Court of Appeals. Judge McGregor said of Mr. Lemen, "Harry Lemen is a man of vision. He is the type of man who gives strength to a community.. I have often heard that the character of a community can be judged by the shadows of a few men who live there, and I'm sure the shadow off Harry Lemen will be around here a long, long time.

Scene Three…School Happenings!

The two-story addition to the north side of the existing High School building was competed at a total cost of about $75, 000. The addition provided ten classrooms for the use of the elementary grades as well as offices for the Superintendent of Schools. The addition allowed the Board to close the North Ward School building and discontinue using the classrooms at the Methodist Episcopal church on Leroy Street

In order to provide some perspective it is interesting to note that at this time Michigan State College was observing its 80th year and building a men's dormitory (Mason Hall) for $500,000.

In July, at the end of their fiscal year, the School Board reported on the financial condition of the schools and *The Fenton Independent* printed the whole report, including the individual salaries of each and every teacher and employee.

Each of the teachers received a raise however so nominal. Mr. Arndt's salary was $1,450.75, an increase of $47.25. Miss Lenzner was at $1,145.70 a gain of $112.20. The Superintendent's salary was increased and Mr. Heemstra was paid a total of $2,053.75 for the year. The average annual salary for an experienced high school teacher in Fenton this year was between $1,100 and $1,300.

However, one must remember that a new car could be purchased for less than $1,000, a new two bedroom home for around $3,000 and anyone making $50 a week considered himself as "doing very well".

While teachers' salaries in this period were quite low compared to those of today, most of the teachers were at ease with the income and were able to maintain an above average standard of living. Furthermore, most of them were very happy to have a job in the middle of a worldwide depression.

Further evidence of the income levels experienced in Michigan during this period is found in how the State of Michigan funded the Old Age Pensioners. In July 1938, the State nearly doubled the yearly funds provided for Old Age Pensions, from $35,883 to $70,638. This raised the recipients' average monthly stipend to $18.56, up $2 from 1937.

As usual the election for the Board of Education was not very well attended. In July 1938, only two incumbents were up for reelection. The two were President of the Board Harry A. Lowe and member J. Weidman. Both were re-elected with 46 ballots cast. This was an improvement over last year when the number voting was only 25.

Board members Lowe and Furlong took time out to accompany Superintendent Heemstra to a meeting in Lansing where over 500 school officers gathered to protest a proposed cut in "State Aid".

One of the school expenses was the cost of books for the elementary grades, 1 through 8. High school students were required to purchase their books and the school sold them to the students at their cost. The school would buy back used books at a "liberal allowance".

On the first day of April, the Student Council honored a long-standing practice and sponsored the All-Hi banquet. Each class competed for honors for the best in table decorations. The officers of the Student Council were: President Donald "Bud" Lemen, Vice President Garwood "Fuzz" Marshall, Secretary Mary Thompson and Treasurer Robert "Junie" Atkins.

One of the school student activities that did not attract much attention was debating. However, Fenton High School had a very active and successful debating program. The team debated most of the high schools in the surrounding area in addition to the private Cranbrook Academy. The team was composed of Marna Houser, Dorothy Wood and Harold Schupbach. Most interesting was the debate topic for the season: "Resolved: That the United States should establish an alliance with Great Britain." With Europe about to erupt in armed conflict; the issue being debated was very appropriate.

School enrollment continued to increase in 1938. The total enrollment for all grades was 974, where it had been 905 in 1937 and 869 in 1936. In view of the increased number of students, Superintendent Heemstra held a "Guidance Meeting" for the parents of those students entering 9th Grade this year.

Mr. Heemstra presided at the meeting and he was assisted by Miss Wagbo (Home Economics), Mr.. Brunell (Manual Arts), Mr. C. D. Arrand (Academics) and Miss Bessie Cramer (Business). Music by the FHS Orchestra under the direction of Mr. Wilder was provided and Miss Thelma Barker's Glee Club also performed.

The school people had other things on their mind besides salaries debate topics and enrollment. In fact it seemed as if every one in the schools was responding to an irresistible urge to put on a "show". Thelma Barker, Vocal Music Teacher took the first step and presented her student Glee Club in the operetta "Hollywood Bound".

Then the teachers at Fenton High School felt the need to hit the "boards". They presented a mystery drama entitled "Green Light" with English/Latin Teacher Phyllis Lenzner, the Principal C.D. Arrand,

History/Civics Teacher Raymond Lee, Miss Miller of Kindergarten renown and Geography/Coach Roger Leestma as featured players. Mrs. Caneror, Misses Betram and Oole also contributed. The proceeds of the play were used to purchase a new "movie machine" for the high school.

Operettas seemed to be one of the preferred forms for a theatrical performance at Fenton High School during this period. The students at the school selected the operetta "The Count and the Coed" for presentation in April of the year. The cast included: Harold Bristol, Beth Hall, May Thompson, Jean Richmond, Eugenia Buckingham, Pauline Stiff, Rose Nakovic, Justin Ruckel, Donald Peterson, Art Barnard and Jim Frew.

The Annual Junior Class Play, "Shirtsleeves" was performed in the auditorium of the new Fenton Community Center. It was the first group to present a stage play in the new facility. The Director of the play was Beth Nixon and the cast was as follows: Dave Dawson, Clara Davis, Jim Frew, Katherine Dode, Ken Lawless, Gorton Milliken, Helen Neely, George Bard, Gordon Sumpter, Jayne Glaspie, Theresa Allen, Dorothy Austin and Loreen Harding.

While performing on stage was exciting for the students, most of them found dancing to the new "swing" music even more pleasing. Consequently, the coming of the "J-Hop" was anxiously awaited.

The "J-Hop" was the most important event on the social calendar and on the "minds" of the students at Fenton High School. It was the premier prom for the school. In fact it was the only prom for the school. Fenton High School had not yet turned to the "Senior Prom" for the big "dress up" dance and "extravaganza"

The Junior Class President Paul Bottecelli and his committees had adopted a Mexican theme for the event and the high school gymnasium was adorned with what the students considered to be festive Mexican decorations. Jack Dowling and his Orchestra were engaged for the dance and when the Grand March music played, Paul escorted Jean Lee to head the procession.

There were TWO graduations in the Fenton Schools in 1938. Not surprisingly, the Fenton High School garnered most of the attention sending 78 hopefuls into the world. Alice Bell Matthews was the Class Valedictorian and Rose Nakovic was the Salutatorian. (See the class list in Appendix One.)

Miss Lucille Miller was a highly respected Kindergarten teacher in the school. She was well liked by students and parents alike and was especially respected for making her classes interesting and exciting. For this year, Miss Miller arranged for the parents to make an academic robe and "mortarboard" for each of her students "graduating" from Kindergarten. A traditional graduation ceremony was conducted and each of the Kindergarteners marched across the "stage' and received a Diploma…it was the Class of 1950.

Jean & Raymond
Durant

Some families, as it was with Harry and Eleanor Durant, were celebrating two graduates this year: daughter Jean in the Class of '38 and young son Raymond in the Class of '50.

Graduates and former students at Fenton High School were very supportive of their "old school" and in May of 1938, a group of alumni met at the high school gymnasium for the purpose of organizing the Fenton High School Alumni Association

In June, 1938, they met again and elected the following officers: President Lynn Welch, Vice President William Dode, Vice President Phillip Hazazer, Secretary Etta Marie Green and Treasurer Walter Hill.

On June 23, 1938, the new Alumni Association held a dance at the High School in honor of the new Graduates, the Class of 1938. Over 100 couples attended the dance held at the high school where they danced to the music of Bill Walls Band, with songs by Harriet Mortimer Toomey and a "guest drummer" in Garwood "Fuzz" Marshall. Former Superintendent J. William Burkett delivered an inspirational talk at the intermission.

Scene Four...Sports and Stuff

As the New Year began, the bowling season was well underway. As in the previous year, the league was divided into two divisions: The Tigers and The Bearcats.

The Tiger teams were sponsored by Hoffman's, Consumers, Industrial #2, Swingle, Michigan Bean, The Fenton Courier, Gould's and the I.O.O F. The Bearcat sponsors were: Butcher's, The Fenton Independent, Merrick's, the V.F. W., Woodworth Brothers, Mickey's, Industrial #1, and the American Legion.

When all was over, the Woodworth Brothers won the league Championship. Butcher's came in second followed by Merrick's in third place.

The V.F.W. team challenged a championship woman's team to a match and surprisingly defeated the Argyle Recreation Girls of Detroit. The *Fenton Courier* found it necessary to expose the fact that the Veterans' team had added a couple of "ringers" to their team for the match. It seems the Veterans had borrowed Howard Reasner and Bill Halls-"star bowlers with Swingle's team". The *Fenton Courier* commented thusly..."The only war either one of them was ever in was the War of Matrimony".

Once the bowlers were finished, the softballers took the field.. Industrial Tool, Matthew's, Gould's, Gamble's, Hagedorn's Dairy and Locke's were sponsors of the teams for the 1938 season.

From the published reports, it was the Industrial Tool Company that kept the game of golf in the Fenton papers. As in the past, it was the Industrial people who sponsored a golf league at the Long Lakes Golf Club. Two teams with a total of twenty-four players participated in the company league. One team represented the "upstairs" workers and the other the "downstairs" workers. In the end, the individual winners were: C. Levendowski, B. Walker, A.Westman, E. Westman, F. Bachus, Jr. and M. Richmond.

The 2nd Annual season ending "Tournament and Banquet" was held in October. With 43 entrants, the winner was Frank Bachus, Jr..

As in past years, the citizens followed the sports program at Fenton High School throughout the year...FHS teams were the *town's* teams!

The FHS basketball team for the 1937-38 season did not disappoint their supporters. While finishing in Second Place in the County Conference, they were the District Champions and lost a close game to

Plymouth High School in the Regional Tournament Finals. Even more importantly, Fenton beat archrival Holly to earn the Tamlyn Trophy again this year.

Don Herman was the team captain and his teammates were: Jack Hartley, Robert "Junie" Atkins, Donald "Bud" Lemen, Garwood "Fuzz" Marshall, Jack Lea, Joe Craft, Donald Sinclair, Albert Turco, Roy Goodrich, and Howard Goodrich.   Don Herman was selected for the First Team All-County Conference and Garwood "Fuzz" Marshall and Robert "Junie" Atkins were honored with selection to the All-County Second Team. Jack Hartley received Honorable Mention.

Coach Lester Miller put all the basketballs away and took to the diamond in early April and found thirty-nine hopefuls awaiting the start of the baseball season. This was the largest turnout in Fenton High School's history with nine lettermen returning. The lettermen consisted of Jack Hartley-1st Base; Bruce McLenna-2nd Base; Don Herman-3rd Base; Joe Craft-Shortstop and David Black-Catcher. The others were John Case-Left Field; Howard Cronk-Center Field; and Don Watters-Right Field and Robert Atkins-Pitcher. Others who played during the season were: Roy Goodrich, Brad Hoffman, Al Hagerman, Pat Barkey, Lee Gordon, Ed Rusinski, Bob Zoll, Al Turco, Gorton Milliken, Sid Smale and Pat O'Connell. Jack Hartley was elected Honorary Captain for the year.

The track team featured two "speedy" athletes in Don Herman and Brad Hoffman. Coach Leestma had a very successful season placing several team members in the County track meet. Others who lettered in Track this season were: Harold Bradley, Howard Cronk, David Dawson, Robert Dode, Dee Marshall, Lorimer Sarosky, Robert Black, Harold Bristol and Ed Rusinski.

During the summer many of the high school baseball players played with the American Legion team coached by Bernard Weber. But most of the towns' folk were more interested in the American Legions Baseball excursion to a Detroit Tiger baseball game

This year the Knights of Columbus joined with the Legion Post to cosponsor the "Baseball Excursion". Consequently, over 500 people made the trip to a Detroit Tiger- Boston Red Sox game. About 200 of those making the train trip to Detroit and back were from Fenton and the rest from Linden, Holly and Flint.

Soon the summer had passed and it was football time again. The Fenton High School football team had a team of "veterans" and started the year with a lot of promise. However, overall it had a disappointing season. They had a winning season, but failed to repeat as County champions and "tied" with archrival Holly. Coach Miller awarded 21 letters to the varsity players: Ronald Covert (Honorary Captain), Don Clark, Ron Longworth, Dee McKinley, Earl Robinson, Larry Sugden, George Bard, Ralph Elliott, Art Barnard, Lem Sarosky, Bob Schleicher, Jim Rash, Bob Harris, Bob Morea, Dave Dawson, Bob Zoll, Sid Smale, Brad Hoffman, Joe Craft, Dee Marshall and Al Turco.

FHS Football 1938. 1at Row L-R Bob Runyan, Lee Gordon, Francis Trimmer, Don Hunt, Wilbur "Bib" Swartz, Gerald Durand, Tom Merrill, Allen Kerton, Sid hay, Jr. Lutz, Carroll Butts. 2nd Row L-R Jim Rash, George Bard, Joe Craft, Dave Dawson, Dee Marshall, Brad Hoffman, Rollie Covert, Sid Smale, Bob Schleicher, Al Turco, Larry Sugden. 3rd Row L-R Dick Smale, Jim Frew, Dave Lathrop, Ron Longworth, Jim "Red" McKinley, Earl Robinson, Bob Harris, Lorimer Sarosky, Bob Morea. 4th Row L-R Dick Smith, Ray Heemstra, Arnold Schutt, Bill Rynearson, Wayne Townsend, Bob Zoll, Art Barnard, Keith Burdick. 5th Row L-R Bob Perry, Ernie Neely, Unkown, Bob Biggs, John McCann, Howard Goodrich, Richard Cronk, Duane Loomis, Leon Shelby. 6th Row L-R Coach Lester Miller, Unkown, Edwin White, Bruce Sinclair, Dean Cox, Ralph Elliott, Jack Kean, Coach Roger Leestma.

The Football Banquet was held in December in the new Fenton Community Center. Honored guests and speakers were; Vincent Valek, a graduate of Holly High School and a member of the University of Michigan football team and Clarence "Biggie" Munn, then line coach at the U of M, and later Head Coach and Athletic Director for the Spartans of Michigan State University.

A.J. Phillips Library located on South Leroy Street. Now the
Fenton Museum.

The Fenton "Water Works". Along Shiawassee River in middle
of town below the dam. Round brick building housed wells
providing water for the village.

Scene Five...Doing Business Downtown

The High School alumni weren't the only ones organizing and getting things done. The local businessmen were very aggressive and were providing incentives to stimulate sales. For example, Winglemire's furniture store was offering "...a real talking Charlie McCarthy free with the purchase of a Grunow or Philco radio..." The doll came with "...full dress, tux, top hat, shoes and gloves".

Rolland's Dry Goods Store was offering "Red Trading Stamps" with each purchase. "Trading Stamps" given with purchases was a relatively new idea in marketing at the time. The customer would collect the stamps in a booklet provided by the merchants, and the stamps could be exchanged for merchandise at a later time. The merchants furnished a catalog of the merchandise and each item was listed with its "price" in stamps.

The use of "trading stamps" continued for many years and during the 1950s and 1960s trading stamps helped revolutionize the way retail goods were marketed.

Stan Swartz operated the Fenton Taxi service and offered "...ride to any place in town for 15c till 6PM...25c after 6PM". Stan also provided "...messenger and delivery service night or day". It was wintertime when Mr. O.A. Gordon first advertised his taxi service but Stan changed his ad in the *Fenton Courier* to read, "Now has heated Cab—15c until 6 PM".

All of the town's automobile dealers joined together for the "National Used Car Week". Their motto was "Drive in your old...Drive out a better". Swingle Chevrolet had a 1930 Chevrolet Coach for $95, "...a real bargain".

It was encouraging to learn that the Industrial Machine Tool Company had received new orders for products and had more men working again. Industrial Tool was one of the major employers in town and "what was good for Industrial was good for Fenton".

This was all good news for the businesses in Fenton, but some "really big" news for the community was the announcement by the Michigan Bell Telephone Company of the introduction the "Dial System" for Fenton. This new system was to be installed at a cost of over $60,000 and would offer its customers "...one, two, four party lines and private lines".

The new equipment was installed at the new company quarters on the second floor of the former Commercial Bank building on the southwest corner of Leroy and Caroline Streets As the new dial phones replaced each of the 72 phones in operation at the time, the installers instructed the owners in the operation of the new dial phone. With the new dial phones, one would need to dial "0" for assistance, to place a long distance call, obtain the time of day or request repair service.

Before the "dial system" , an operator would answer your signal when you lifted the receiver from the "hook" on the telephone.. Then you would give the number of the phone you wished to call and the operator would make the connection to that line and ring the phone being called. For example, if you wished to call Stan Swartz for a taxi ride, you would request "394". You would probably not have to be concerned if you failed to remember the number, because the operator would be able to complete your call if you either asked for the "Taxi" or "Stan" by name.

"Party lines" were "something else"! Even before the dial system was used, party lines existed. Private lines for individual homes or businesses were more expensive, so, consequently, a greater number of the phone users were on party lines. Each user on a party line would recognize their call by the number of rings. If your calls came on two rings for example, the other parties on your line would (should) ignore the call, since it was not for them. However, many felt a strong urge to "listen in" on the conversations of others…and they did!

While the new dial system would not eliminate the "problems" presented by party lines it would make the cost of a private line more acceptable to a greater number of customers. However, it would replace the human operator with an electrical switching device. One would no longer have that "small town" human touch of personal service provided by "your friend" at the switchboard.

Only last year, Michigan Bell's office in Fenton had hired recent FHS graduates Gladys Welch, Mavis Cobb and Wanda Simmons to be "Number Please girls" and work with Senior Operator Phyllis Camm in the Fenton office.

Progress had now brought the townsfolk a more efficient, but less personal, means of communicating. The new dial system was put into operation on December 15th, 1938.

As Faye Beach, the Editor/Publisher of *The Fenton Independent* saw it; the arrival of a modern telephone system in Fenton wasn't the only sign of progress in town.

Mr. Beach wrote a small article for his paper describing his visit to the Fenton Lumber Company where its owner Bill Ruckel demonstrated a remarkable new device he had purchased for mixing paint. As Mr. Beach described it, one would take an unopened can and clamp it in this motorized device, turn on the switch and the device would shake the can very vigorously. Within a few minutes, one would turn the switch off and remove the can of paint. Upon opening the can, one would find a perfectly mixed can of paint. Remarkable!

In May, Mr. Arthur Dubord, who for years had the "Southside" grocery business to himself, found Charles Truchan opening his Sanitary Market only a couple doors north of his store. Truchan's first advertisement in *The Independent* advertisement featured the fact he had "Home Killed Meats"!

In May, Johnny Hoskins also found new competition near his restaurant on North Leroy Street when the Log Cabin Restaurant opened for business a few doors south of his location. Logs that had been split in half and attached to the exterior of the storefront identified the new restaurant. In June, Charles MacGillvray purchased the restaurant.

John Hoskins seemed to counter by announcing a new night chef, Mr. Arthur Senecal and offering "Genuine Italian" Spaghetti for 40c…Fish and Chips 40c…and Chop Suey for 50c". From 1923 to 1924, Mr. Senecal had operated a restaurant in Fenton at the location of the Piccinni Shoe repair store.

The Gordon Bakery moved next to Grant Whitman's Grocery across the street from Hoskins Restaurant and Maude Hunt opened a Hat Shop nearby…all signs of an improving economy.

But the "big news" downtown in the retail business, was that Harry Lemen, after selling his trucking business, which he ran for over 15 years, had purchased the Judevine Grocery and was joined by Burt Burrows as head of the meat department. "Fritz" Judevine, longtime grocer and Village Councilman had died and his business became available. So began Lemen's Grocery on South Leroy Street.

Village President Harry Lemen now had a downtown "office"…a real positive for a politician, but now he had no place to hide! Actually, Harry Lemen really didn't seek or need a place to hide. He was one of the most respected and most liked individuals in town. He served the community for 33 years as a Councilman, President or Mayor

Later a new Dentist arrived in town. Dr. Noble Peckham moved into the offices vacated by Dr. Kochenderfer above Lemen's Grocery Store.

100 The Village Players

Dr. "K" had built a "bungalow" house for use as an office directly across the street from the A.J. Phillips Library next to "Water Works Park".

In October of the year, Mr. Art Gruner and Mr. Merritt of the Genesee Toll Company announced they were going to develop a new housing area to be called "Fairfield" in the northwest section of the village. They planned 100 lots for the new subdivision and planned to build three homes in the near future. Mr. Leon Pavey, who was in charge of the heat-treating facility at Genesee Tool Company, was the first to purchase a house in "Fairfield".

There were many signs of a recovery in the Fenton economy, however in a region where the economy was dominated by the automobile industry, the condition did not significantly improve for several years to come. The Village of Fenton issued their financial report for the fiscal year ending on February 28th and it showed the Village to be in the "black". The Village had started the year with $6,551 and after expending a little more than $42,000, had ended the year with a balance of $9,285.97 and a bonded indebtedness of only $20,500.

The Village leaders had used the funds available very prudently and had made many improvements such as the building of storm and sanitary sewers. In the March elections, which were held in Dubord's Garage building, with 102 citizens casting ballots in an uncontested election, the incumbents were returned to their respective offices: President Harry Lemen, Clerk Robert Beach, Treasurer Horace Hitchcock and Assessor Floyd Chapin. Councilmen Gus Lutz, John Hoskins and Bill Marshall were elected for two-year terms. Trustees Shull Woodworth, Will Stocken and Floyd Poppy were not up for reelection this year.

While the Village "politics" generally found two local parties, the "Citizens"

Horace W. Hitchcock

and the "People's", presenting candidates for the Village offices, the Fenton Township had the Republican and Democrat Parties vying at the ballot box. Fenton's Ray L. Parker was a popular Republican candidate for the County's Registrar of Deeds and was elected as the Township voted overwhelmingly Republican.

In November 1938, the nation went to the polls to elect their Representatives to the U. S. Congress. In 1936, the Democrat A.J. Transue of Flint defeated Republican Congressman William W. Blackney of Clio. Blackney regained his seat in Congress in the 1938 elections with the help of the voters of Fenton and Fenton Township and went on to serve until January of 1953. He did not run for office in the election of 1952.

The State Government passed a new "Primary Election" law. Henceforth, those voting in a primary election would not have to openly declare their party affiliation. From now on, the voter would receive two ballots, one for each party, and would vote only one, turning in the unmarked ballot along with the voted ballot. Those at the polling place would not be able to ascertain the voter's party as both the marked and unmarked ballots would have the same external appearance. So, in 1938, they thought they had solved this problem…never happened Charley!

In August of the year, those that had deposits in the old Fenton State Bank received a final payment on those accounts that were in the bank on June 6, 1931 when the Bank closed. This represented 92.65% of the total deposits. Those who followed such matters reported that most banks in similar circumstances failed to pay such a large return.

A very important election was held in October. The Village Council had called a special election on a $20,000 bond proposal to help finance the building of a sewage disposal plant. The need for such a facility was well understood and unsurprisingly the bond issue was approved by a vote of 113 to 12. In December, a Federal grant for an additional $20,000 was approved. Later, though the grant had been approved, there were no funds allocated to the P.W.A. and the grant was never funded.

The only controversy concerning the sewage plant was about its location. The proposed site, just off Remington Road (now North Road) in the north section of the village, was upsetting to some of the citizens. However, the opposition failed to change the selection of this site.

On several previous occasions, Mr. William H. Keddy, a resident living on Remington Road, had complained and actually filed a suit for $12,000 because of the damage the polluted Shiawassee River was inflicting on his property. The Keddy claim was bounced around for several months before Judge Gadola dismissed the case because Mr. Keddy did not follow the proscribed procedure for handling such claims

The Council then referred the claim to their attorney, Maurice Matthews for him to investigate and report his findings to the Council.. Matthews found the claim to lack "specificity" and recommended the claim to be rejected. Village President Lemen appointed a committee of the whole, with Floyd Poppy as Chairman to investigate the claim and report their findings. The committee determined the claim to be unsubstantiated.

However, the Council offered Mr. Keddy an opportunity to present evidence at a hearing. Mr.. Keddy and his attorney, Mr. Jackson H. Kelley of Pontiac, appeared at a Council meeting and argued their case. During the argument, *The Fenton Independent* reports that Mr. Kelley made a very unusual remark, which essentially brought the hearings to an end. He remarked, "…You would be surprised how much less than $12,000 we would settle for…" After more discussion the Council voted to reject the claim. *The Fenton Independent* account leaves one wondering if the hearing was adjourned because of what the attorney said.

In January, Mr. Keedy's attorney, Jackson Kelley, received some very unfavorable publicity. He was charged with felonious assault after shooting one of several youths who were skating on an ice rink he had prepared in front of his lake home.

During the hearing, President Lemen commented on the sewage situation and the need to address the problem of polluting the Shiawassee River.

A week after the new "Dial" telephone system was "cutover" and went into effect, Mr. and Mrs. Maurice J. Matthews held a. dinner party for the employees of Michigan Bell's Fenton office. It was a "Farwell, Christmas and Cutover" party. Many of the women in the Fenton office were being transferred to other cities: Mary Wakeman-Detroit; Lena McCullley-Pontiac; Phyllis Camm-Lapeer; Wanda Simmons, Gladys Galloway and Glenys Welch-Flint. Only Mrs. Howard Reasner, Mrs. Ed Renwick and Mrs. Mavis Silver would remain in the Fenton office.

Scene Six...A Bit of the World of Entertainment

The Fenton City Band found a new home in the bandstand at "Shiawassee Park". The park, now called "Freedom Park", is a triangular piece of land bordered by Shiawassee Avenue, West Elizabeth and Parke Streets. The Band continued their Wednesday evening concerts every week during the summer months and had several indoor concerts during the colder weather. They participated in the holiday events such as Memorial Day, the July 4th festivities and played at St. John Church's annual Barbeque. Their first appearance at the new Community Center was their concert in late October. Their old "home", the bandstand on Ellen Street, was removed with the beginning of the construction of the new Municipal Building.

C.L. Wilder was the conductor of the band.. Mr. Wilder was also the Instrumental Music teacher at the Fenton schools and Director of the high school band.

The preeminent piano teacher in Fenton during this period was Miss Alice Van Atta. Miss Van Atta was also an accomplished organist and the organist at St. Jude's Episcopal Church for several decades. In the 1800s, Miss Van Atta's grandfather was the proprietor of a furniture store that provided furniture for many of the early residents of the community. She lived on High Street with her sister and brother, all of whom remained unmarried.

At least once a year, Miss Van Atta's students presented a recital, which was not only attended by the student's parents, but also by many of the town's people who enjoyed the event. In July of 1938, the recital featured piano performances by Gloria Reid, Donna Austin, Jean Woodworth, Joan Hitchcock and Robert Gearhart.

Another popular piano teacher, Mrs. Meda Hinkley also presented her students at a recital for the public. The students who performed in her June recital were: Alice Jean Kelly, Lloyd Mitchell, Adelaide Stein, Phyllis Kelly, Bessie Johnson, Ann Hicks, Jerue Lue Lucas, Bruce Mitchell, Kenneth Petts, Betty Ann Grenier, Joyce Ellison, Erma Mitchell, Eileen Edinger, Jane Walcott, Geraldine Pettis, Annie Burgstaller and Leone Hagerman.

Fenton was fortunate to have a theater owner who was continually working to improve his facility. For example, for years J.C. Peck had been hearing his customers complain, "I can't sit down in front, it hurts my eyes". So working with the RCA engineers, modifications were made in the location of the screen and installation of a new lens for the projector. The result the brilliance and clearness of the picture was dramatically improved and those in the third row had the same vision as previously enjoyed by those in the middle seats.

As an added incentive to have his customers sit down front and try the new improvement, Mr. Peck installed new seats in the front portion of the theater. The new seats were of the latest design of free floating springs with "Lazy Boy" style posture backs.

Along with these improvements, J.C. Peck's *Rowena* theatre continued to offer a variety of movies, including many "first run" showings of newly released films.

Few of the movie titles would be remembered today, but the list of "stars" appearing at the *Rowena* would fill the Hollywood "milky way" for generations to come. In just a few months the local folks would see film stars such as: Jane Withers, George Raft, Gary Cooper, Carole Lombard, Fred MacMurray, the Barrymores...Ethel, Lionel and John, William Boyd (better known as "Hopalong Cassidy"), Joan Blondell, Kay Francis, Gene Autry (the "singing cowboy"), Pat O'Brien, George Brent, Buddy Rogers, Betty Grable (who became #1 pinup in WW II), Ned Sparks, Sonja Henie, Don Ameche, Frederick Marsh, Myrna Loy, Rosiland Russell, Franchot Tone, Charles Boyer, Claudette Colburn, Mae West, James Stewart, Robert Young, Bruce Cabot, William Powell, Shirley Temple, Walter Pigeon, William Powell (The Thin Man), Spencer Tracy, Joan Crawford, Robert Taylor, Randolph Scott and Jack Haley. Quite an array!

Along with all the entertainment movies, in June 1938 the theater showed an account of a real life incident that had occurred in China only a short time before. The movie was entitled "Panay Bombing and Sinking". The film related the story of the *Panay* incident in whiich the United States gunboat, the *Panay* was attacked and sunk by Japanese aircraft while she was anchored in the Yangtze River outside of Nanjing on. December 12, 1937. Japan and the United States were not at war at the time. The Japanese claimed they did not see the United States flags painted on the deck of the gunboat, apologized and paid an indemnity. Nevertheless, the attack and reports of the Nanking Massacre caused US opinion to turn sharply against the Japanese.

As in past years, the springtime brought the visits of the Cole Carnival and the Lewis Brothers Three Ring Circus. And also as in the past, the performances attracted a good share of the people in the community.

The prices for admission to the Lewis Brothers Circus remained the same as in past years.... Adults 40c and Children 25c.

Also as in past years, wintertime was for Bowling and spring and summer for Softball. In May the softball season began with over 300 participants. The managers of the sponsored teams met in early May to review the rules and set the schedule. Those attending were: Bernard Weber (Locke's), Thor Neilsen (Hagedorn's), Kleber Merrick (Industrial Machine Tool), John Joslin (Matthews Law), Lee Lanning (Gambles) and Harold Fowler (Gould's).

Bowling gained more participants this year and the league was divided into two divisions: The Tigers, with sponsors Swingle, Courier, Cutups, Industrial #1, Gould's, Hoffman's and Michigan Bean. The Bearcats, with sponsors: Woodworth Bros., Independent, Goodwill, Mickey's, Joe's Shell, Butcher's and Industrial #2...

The "Tigers" found the leading bowlers to be Mssrs Fowler, Groll, Savage, Hockett, Hillis, Reasner, Jess Pasco and the Reverend Mroch of the Trinity Lutheran Church. The *Fenton Courier* and Swingle's Chevrolet were the team leaders in the Tiger Division.

The "Bearcats" individual leaders were Mssrs Rector, Theisen, McBroom, Richmond, Simmons, Taylor and Tom Woodworth. The team leaders were The Woodworth Brothers and the Industrial Machine Tool Company.

The Industrial Machine Tool Company facility on west side of South Leroy Street opposite Ellen Street

The Michigan Bean Company elevator on North Leroy Street just north of railroad intersection.. House in distance on left of photo is residence and office of Dr. William Rynearson.

The Grand Trunk Railroad Passenger Depot

Scene Seven…Activities, Churches, Clubs, Etc.

The people of Fenton didn't need movies, band concerts, circuses and carnivals to provide all of their entertainment. They didn't rely on banquets, bowling, softball and the high school athletics to keep them actively engaged. The activities of their clubs, their church groups and "characters" like "Herb and Billy" provided interesting and rewarding diversions.

The people of Fenton's churches continued to be an active sector in community. The Men's Fellowship kicked off their program for the year with a January meeting featuring the State's Attorney General Harry S. Toy as their speaker.

In February, the Men's Fellowship held their annual Father-Son banquet at the church. The speaker for the event was the Reverend Floyd Sullivan who had lived in Malaya and Burma for over 25 years. Mr. John Hoffman and Dick Reidel gave the toast to the Sons followed by a toast to the Fathers, a tradition at these banquets.

In May, the Child Study Clubs held a Mother-Daughter Banquet with over 250 attending. The affair was held at the Presbyterian Church and Mrs. C.D. Arrand, wife of the High School Principal, acted as the Toastmaster. Mrs. Ray Welch and Mrs. James Piatt made the traditional toasts.

The Men's Fellowship re-elected Harvey Swanebeck as their President as well as returning Ralph Peterson and Dr. William J. Rynearson respectively as their Secretary and Treasurer. John Cox was elected, for the first time, as their Vice President.

Harvey Swanebeck

The Methodist Episcopal Church, now in it's 101st year, re-dedicated their church building. Reverends A.T.F. Butt and Ira Cargo took part in the ceremonies. The Reverend Cargo had served as the Church's pastor at a prior time. The re-dedication was occasioned by the completion of the rebuilding of the facility, which had been destroyed by fire on May 12, 1929.

For the Episcopalians at St. Jude's it was a celebration of having a new pastor. The Reverend William Thomas Smith was the new priest after the position had been vacated for almost one year. Perhaps as part of their exuberance they installed a new musical unit including an amplifier for the church chimes and organ music.

Further, St. Jude's was celebrating their 80th year. From a humble beginning in the home of Mr. and Mrs. Landenberg to the present, the church, its pastor and its members had been active in the community.

The annual Bar-B-Que at St. John was held again this year with much the same agenda as in the recent years. The Fenton City Band was a featured attraction...along with the Bar-B-Que pork...and despite the rain; the event attracted a "big" crowd.

Father Tighe and Banquet Chairman John Dery introduced an inventive solution to the ever-present fly problem for the dining tent. He had a revolving screen door made for the tent entrance and all sides were covered with mesh netting.

In the evening, Bryan Bowles Orchestra from Linden played for dancing. With the rain over, many couples stayed for hours after dining.

The daughters of Dexter Horton made some substantial contributions to Fenton Churches during this year. Mary A. (Horton) Rackham had executed the will of her husband Horace H. Rackham, had already provided the funds for the construction of the Fenton Community Center and a new Municipal Building. Now she provided the funds to build a new meeting hall for the Christian Science community in her hometown. The new hall for the Christian Sciences on East Rockwell Street was dedicated in May of 1938.

As further evidence of the generosity of the Horton ladies, Mary's sister, Myra (Horton) Bussey, a Presbyterian, purchased a new organ for her church on South Leroy Street.

The "old" Fenton clubs continued to meet as in the past. Each issue of the *Fenton Independent* and *The Fenton Courier* was replete with reports on what was happening in the various clubs: Townsend Club, Girl Scouts, Boy Scouts, Epworth League, Entre Nous, the Bayview Club, the Women's Music Club, the four Child Study Clubs, I.O.O. F., the F & A.M., Rainbow Girls, Knights Templar, O.E.S., the Isaac Walton League, the XX Club, the Rebekahs, the church Bands and Cornerstones, "In and Out" Club, Penelope Club, W.C.T.U., D.U.V., W.R.C., Lincoln Club, Fenton Grange and the Veterans organizations, namely the American Legion and their Ladies Auxiliary, the Veterans of Foreign Wars and their Ladies Auxiliaries. The Fenton G.A.R. was still represented by Andrew Bly (92), Charles Bentley (93) and Henry Hartman (90).

The XX Club started the year by electing Daniel Hogan, DDS as their President and Thomas Swingle as 1st VP, K.C. Asman as 2nd VP, Elton Austin as 3rd VP, H.W. Hitchcock as Secretary and G.W. Tamlyn as their Treasurer.

The Women's Music Club conducted an ambitious program with great success. Under the direction of Miss Alice Van Atta, the club held a "Colonial" luncheon at the Presbyterian Church.

After Club President Van Atta's introduction depicting the adoption of the U.S. Constitution, the following program was presented: American tunes-George Pellett and Robert Gearhart; Organ solos by Miss Van Atta; A one act play, "Mrs. Washington's Minuet; "Spring is Coming"-Miss Lehtimaki and eighth grade girls; The Federal March-Miss Phyllis Lenzner on piano; and "Beneath a Willow's Shade"-vocal by Mrs. William Skillen. The program ended with all singing "America".

The Entre Nous ladies elected Mrs. Mark Gordon as their President for the New Year. Other officers elected were: Mrs. C.D. Arrand-VP, Mrs. Martin Stiff-Recording Secretary, Mrs. Walter Conrad-Secretary and Mrs. Robert beach-Treasurer.

The Child Study Clubs continued to be very active during 1938, and a new club, the Pro To Child Study Club was organized and elected the following officers: President Mrs. Marie Stewart, VP Mrs. Grant Wright, Recording Secretary Mrs. Dennis Watson, Corresponding Secretary Mrs. Edna Witherall and Treasurer Mrs. W. A. Gamble.

The Rebekahs held their election and Nellie Lockwood was elected to the top leadership position. The other officers elected were: Charlene Goddard, Violet Vandercook, Grace Wright, Ida Gould and Maude Reed.

The Rainbow Girls were beginning their second year and they elected Nellie Davis as their Worthy Advisor. Dorothy Polson was elected as the Associate Worthy Advisor.

The Order of the Eastern Stars, (O.E.S.) sponsors of the Rainbow Girls, selected Virginia Lonsbury at Worthy Matron and Albert Ives as Worthy Patron. Their respective assistants were Mrs. Claude Sinclair and Mr. Ray Cummings.

The Knights Templar selected their leaders to be: Eminent Commander John B. Hoffman and Generalissimo L. M. O'Dell.

The "In and Out" Club was a card playing club and included Mrs. George Hall, Mrs. Ida Brunson, Mrs. Ada Weber, Mrs. Betty Bender and Mrs. Susie Dort.

110 The Village Players

The veterans' organizations continued to be very active during this period. The American Legion and the Veterans of Foreign Wars each began new programs and continued many the community had come to expect. While the V.F.W.Post was only a few years old and essentially in its infancy, the American Legion Post hit its peak membership of 90 in the year 1938.

The American Legion Post elected Joe Bottecelli as their Commander. Walter Conrad and Mark Gordon were elected to serve as Senior Vice Commander and Junior Vice Commander respectively. The Legion's Ladies Auxiliary elected President Zella White, Senior VP Ella Poppy, Junior VP Lillian Goodrich, Secretary Marie McCoy and Treasurer Myrtle Franks.

The Veterans organizations in Fenton and throughout the nation, had adopted as their principal goal the promotion of "Americanism". With the continent of Europe struggling with Communism, Fascism and the National Socialists of Germany, the Nazi, patriotic Americans were concerned about future of the country. The Communist Party in the United States was openly advocating Communism as a solution for America's economic woes. The German-American Bund was holding rallies in support of Hitler's Germany. So the Veterans organizations became active in their defense of democracy and freedom for the United States and began organizing meeting and conferences in support of "Americanism".

One such rally for "Americanism" was held at the IMA Auditorium in Flint, Michigan.. There was a banquet at which over 1000 attended to hear Homer Chaillaux, the American Legion's National Director for. Americanism. Another 3000 people occupied the balcony seats at the auditorium for the program, of which over 30 were from the Fenton veteran groups.

The American Legion agreed to participate in the "Wolverines Boy's State". The program was sponsored by the American Legion's Department of Michigan. Teenage boys from all over the State of Michigan were to assemble on the campus of Michigan State College for a week in June. At that time the program would organize the boys into a "State Government" modeled after the governmental structure of the State of Michigan. There would be a State Senate and House of Representatives and a Governor. The boys would elect fellow campers for each of the many positions.

Fenton was to send two boys to the Wolverine Boys State encampment. The XX Club and the Industrial Machine Tool Company agreed to pay the expenses for the two boys. The two boys selected were: Richard Reidel and David Dawson.

The Legionnaires were successful in conducting another "Baseball Excursion" to a Detroit Tigers game. This time they had a special train and still only charged $3.00 per person and that included the price of the ticket to the baseball game. Joe Bottecelli was in charge of this excursion, which is one of the programs the public was beginning to expect!

The V.F.W. found a home! After meeting in what available space they could locate, the Post was able to lease the second floor hall in what was known as the Goodfellow building, the second building north of the Masonic building on Leroy Street.

They immediately held a fun and fund raising "Old Time Dance" featuring Kentucky Ben and his Orchestra. The admission charge was 25 cents per person.

About the same time they elected Sam Casazza as Post Commander with his Senior Vice Commander as Andrew Bly, Jr. and his Junior Vice Commander as Eugene Bush. Fred Slover was elected Quartermaster.

In July of the year the V.F.W. post joined two new members, William G. Harris and Deland Shafter DeWitt, both residents of Long Lake. William "Bill" Harris served the Post faithfully for 46 years until his death in 1984. During that time, he had the unique distinction of being the only member to serve as Post Commander on three separate occasions.

The V.F.W. members and others expended considerable effort in the community in the formation of a "Bicycle Safety Club". Since many of the young people in town were bicycle riders; it seemed to be a good idea to teach safety by organizing a club.

The V.F.W. formed a committee with Jesse Straugh as Chairman and Guy Gillem, Sam Casazza and Andrew Bly Jr. as members. They obtained the services of high school student Gilbert Klein as a "recruiting" officer. Gilbert Klein was a likeable young man who was very energetic and had an entrepreneurial spirit. Gilbert was also known as one who repaired bicycles.

It was December before the club was organized and elected their officers. The youngsters elected Murray Bell as their president, Warren Boilore as V ice President, Verne Walters as Secretary and Dean Cox as their Treasurer. Other members were Walter Zabitch, Norman Reed, Wesley Burgess, Harold Annis, Jack Groll, Ralph Pettis, Wallace

Bronson, James Lorang, Theodore Zabitch, Bob Dery, George Stewart, John McCormick and Gilbert Klein

Several of the businesses in town provided financial support for the club and the V.F.W. sold "Booster" auto plates for $1.00 each. With some of these funds they purchased Safety Club Emblems, which the members were encouraged to sew to their jackets.

The Veteran's organizations organized The Patriotic Council whose purpose was to plan and conduct the parades and ceremonies in observance of the major National holidays. The Patriotic Council met in late April to organize and plan for the observance of Memorial Day. The council elected Hollis Winn as their President, Mrs. George Anglen as their VP and Mrs. Kate Hempsted as their Secretary –Treasurer. Mrs. Margaret Metcalf of the Women's Relief Corps was named the Chairman of the program committee for the upcoming Memorial Day festivities. Her committee members were the Presidents of each of Fenton's patriotic organizations.

The efforts of the Patriotic Council was evident to all who observed the "best ever" Memorial Day parade. The *Fenton Courier* reported it was a "large, well formed and orderly parade". The Fenton City Band earned "high praise" for their performance, especially during the ceremony at Library Park. In the ceremony at the Phillips Library, Mr. Milton Hill rendered a trumpet solo that inspired all in attendance. Mr. Hill played "Sleep Soldier Boy, Sleep" in an artistic manner. The Reverend Dr. J. Stanley Mitchell of the Presbyterian Church delivered an inspiring patriotic address in which he cautioned the citizens of the need to protect and defend the values that had made the United States the greatest country in the world.

Scene Eight…Fading out…House Lights Up!

.

While the international news was not very bright and cheery, certainly nothing to laugh about, one event captured the attention of the nation. This occurred when airplane pilot Douglas Corrigan supposedly read his compass upside down and flew to Ireland, across the Atlantic Ocean, non-stop. He had been denied permission to make the flight, and took off from New York for a flight home to California. . Some suggested that he purposely defied authority and flew to Ireland, not withstanding his denial. He stuck with his story and became known as "Wrong Way" Corrigan.

Claude Cohoon picked up on the "Wrong Way" Corrigan theme and wrote the following in his *Fenton Courier* newspaper opinion column.

> *"Not to be outdone by an Irishman who has been grabbing off all the world-wide publicity with his famous wrong direction Flight, the Fenton Fire Department pulled a Corrigan Monday afternoon when they whizzed down Leroy Street in answer to a fire alarm turned in from Bud Carmer's gasoline station on South Leroy. The fireman, with "Corrigan" John Bacon at the controls, opened the throttle wide as they left the station in the wrong direction. Way out north Leroy street they went with the Marshall, Consumer's Power truck and various other cars wildly pursuing them. It was only a short time later when bystanders on Leroy street were surprised to see the fire truck madly dashing back down Leroy street to the other end of town, the siren shrilly clearing the way.*
>
> *Many rumors were started about the wrong direction flight of the firemen. Some maintained that the fire truck couldn't be turned from the fire hall to the south. Others suggested that the truck needed to go up north to get a good start to make the hill, while others said that the firemen went to the Cobblestone to pick up Chief Basil Chappelle".*

The men of the XX Club seemed to have more "fun and games" than other organizations. Perhaps, that is because they lacked many of the more formal aspects of other clubs and organizations.

The editor of the *Fenton Courier* provided the following story. Early in the year XX member Don McGuire had planned to marry, but have a secret, private ceremony. Somehow his secret plans were "leaked" and Howard Craft, the Undertaker, gathered six other friends to covertly accompany him to the church in Flint where McGuire was to wed.

As the bride and her mother entered the church, the mother noticed Howard Craft and his six friends standing in the back of the church. She was heard to remark to her daughter, "They must have a funeral scheduled for after the wedding.... I see the undertaker and his six pallbearers are here already".

When hunting season arrived, they estimated 160,000 Michigan hunters would be in the field. A couple hundred of them were certain to be from the Fenton area.

Claude Cohoon, the publisher of the *Fenton Courier* provided a story about Mel Walden, the proprietor of the Cobblestone Tavern. This is another story representative of his humorous writings.

> "The top hunting story of the season has to do with Mel Walden, proprietor of the Cobblestone Tavern. Last year Mel shot himself a fine cock pheasant. It was such a beautiful bird that he paid $5 to have it stuffed. Last Sunday he saw another fine cock pheasant out in a field behind the tavern and with great care he got his gun and drew a bead on the bird. With one shot he bowled it over before it could move but when he walked up to it to retrieve it, he found that it was the same pheasant he had stuffed last year. How the bird got out in the field will probably always remain a mystery.

While the Fenton Hotel or the Virginia Bar didn't strictly qualify as a "club", they were places where people gathered together for a common purpose.... Talk about things and have a refreshing adult beverage ...and there were some interesting things happening!

Art Dumanois, proprietor of the Fenton Hotel was a very sociable person and consequently his patrons were very sociable and engaged in discussions about a variety of subjects. It was June and on this occasion the discussion turned to the upcoming boxing match between

Germany's hero Max Schmeling and Detroit's "Brown Bomber", Joe Louis. The "discussion" rapidly divided the people at the bar into two camps. Finally, there was a challenge. Those that favored Schmeling as the winner...which happened to be Frank Spear, Earl Ackerman and Bob Snyder...would have to push those favoring Joe Louis...Frank Pratt, Carl Kerbyson and Phil Crane...in a wheelbarrow from the Hotel to the Fire House in the event Joe Louis won the fight. Needless to say, the Schmeling crowd developed some sore hands and muscles after Joe Louis knocked out Hitler's favorite boxer in the first round of their bout

Martin Stiff, who had been an attorney in Fenton for several years, closed his Fenton office when he accepted a position with General Motors. His office, which was located next to the *Fenton Courier* office, was vacant for a time, until attorney Robert D. Long came to town and occupied the space.

This prompted Claude Cohoon, always the humorist, to opine in his newspaper column the following:

> *"We had Stiff and now have a Long. The Courier will be the next-door neighbor to a lawyer next week. Robert D. Long, a young man from Pontiac, has rented the former offices of Martin L. Stiff. Naturally, the town extends a welcome hand of greeting to the new professional man. What would happen if Mr. Long and his predecessor ever decided to go into business together?*

Fenton didn't go the whole year without any crime being committed on and by its inhabitants. The Fenton Lumber Company was burglarized when some unknowns broke a window, entered the building and smashed the company safe. They made off with $511.32. A couple other break-ins occurred where the burglars used the same M.O. (Method of Operations for those not up on the Police lingo!).

The County Sheriffs made three arrests in the township that drew some heavy fines for those that violated the law. Cecil Warmington of the Cobblestone Gas Station, Mrs. Bessie Black of Black's Landing, Lake Ponemah and Mr. Swarzbaugh of the Long Lake Trading Post were each fined $150 for having slot machines on their premises.

Earlier, in the summer, a speedboat carrying several young ladies and driven by a Miss Ruth Piper, struck a boat on Lake Fenton.   Mr. George Clark, an elderly gentleman, and a friend were fishing at the time when they were hit broadside by the speeding boat. Mr. Clark was thrown into the water and when his friend pulled him from the water, it was learned he had suffered some very severe lacerations and was bleeding profusely. He was rushed to the hospital, but died of his injuries and loss of blood. Miss Piper, whom the Fenton papers described as a "Flint socialite" was charged with negligent homicide.

At her trial, she pleaded guilty to the charge and was sentenced to pay a $1,000 fine OR spend 30 days in jail.

With the construction of the Fenton Community Center of prime interest in the town, it was more than an item for the society column when any member of the extended Horton family came to town

In July, Mrs. Charles Crane entertained at her cottage at Long Lake (remember, the natives had trouble referring to the lake as Lake Fenton). Her guests were Mrs. Charles L. Bussey (Myra Horton), Mrs. Horace Rackham (Mary Horton), Mrs. Bryson D. Horton and Mrs. Dexter Horton.

Mr. Bryson D. Horton, Fenton High School graduate, Class of 1921, was a son of the Dexter Horton, one of Fenton's most prominent citizens. By the late 1930s, Bryson Horton had already won fame and fortune and had a distinguished career in the electrical industry.

Bryson Horton had developed a cartridge-type fuse and founded a company that produced the device, an enclosed safety switch. The enclosed safety switch was embossed with a capital "D" for Detroit in a square embossed on the product. The safety switch became so popular that the company adopted "Square D" as its official name.

Bryson Horton built his estate, "The Hickorys" in nearby Holly Township. The Horton estate is now the property of the Great Lakes National Cemetery. As an aside, it is interesting to note *The Fenton Independent* reports in July 1938, Mr. and Mrs. Bryson Horton entertained Charles and Grace Rolland of Fenton at their estate. The occasion was the 29th Wedding Anniversary of the Rollands.

The minutes of the meetings of the Village Council often reflect the attitude and the feelings of the people living in Fenton at that time. On the occasion of the 75th birthday of Henry Ford, the Council members adopted a resolution that may have been characteristic of that time…another time, a different time.

The following resolution was the unanimously approved by the Fenton Village Councilmen…

> " *WHEREAS, Mr. Henry Ford, an industrialist, philanthropist, humanitarian, twenty-five years ago proclaimed and established a minimum wage of Five Dollars a day as an induction rate for his workers, thereby raising the standard of living for the laboring man, and …WHEREAS This horseless Buggy King was the principal factor in making Michigan what it is today, the automobile capital of the world, therefore be it RESOLVED, That the Village of Fenton dedicate the thirtieth day of July as a day on which this great genius of the universe will be feted, honored and respected, giving an opportunity to representatives of the auto industry and others from all corners of the world to salute and celebrate this eventful occasion… "*

It seems very unlikely in today's climate that any of the present day "giants of industry" would receive such accolades from any group of elected or un-elected officials.

As the year was coming to a close, the people of Fenton received some very sad news. On December 13th, Fenton lost one of its most celebrated "characters" Herb Dutton, who drummed on the Fenton streets for years, died at the age of 79 at the County Infirmary. Herb had gone to the County Jail to spend the night in their transient sleeper room. Those in charge found him unconscious in his bed the following morning. He was transported to the County Infirmary, failed to regain consciousness and died. Funeral services were held at the Howard Craft Funeral Home.

Again for the "movie buffs" among the readers, here is some information on what was happening in the "flickers" during the year 1938,

Academy Awards
Best Picture: "You Can't Take t With You"
Best Actor: Spencer Tracy in "Boy's Town"
Best Actress: Bette Davis in "Jezebel"

118 The Village Players
Other films released in 1938 include:

The Adventures of Robin Hood-Errol Flynn & Olivia de Havilland:
Alexander's Ragtime Band-Tyrone Powers, Don Ameche, Alice Faye
Angels with Dirty Faces-James Cagney & Pat O'Brien
Blockheads-Stan Laurel & Oliver Hardy
Bluebeard's Eighth Wife-Gary Cooper
Boy's Town-Spencer Tracy & Mickey Rooney
Bringing Up Baby-Cary Grant & Katherine Hepburn
A Christmas Carol-Reginald Owen
The Citadel-Robert Donat & Rosiland Russell
Dawn Patrol-Errol Flynn
The Divorce of Lady X-Laurence Olivier
The Drum-Sabu
Four Daughters-Claude Raines
Holiday-Katherine Hepburn & Cary Grant
Jezebel-Bette Davis
The Lady Vanishes-Michael Redgraves
Pygmalion-Leslie Howard
Rebecca of Sunnybrook Farm-Shirley Temple
Room Service-The Marx Brothers
Test Pilot-Clark Gable & Myrna Loy

Interlude One...The World at War

During the year we are about to review, a succession of momentous events was moving the countries of the world toward the greatest, most far ranging war in the history of the world.

The actual conflict of arms started on September 1, 1939 with Germany's invasion of Poland. This followed a series of aggressive moves by the Germans that resulted in their acquisition of Austria and Czechoslovakia, and other lands of the former Northeast Prussia.

In September of 1938, British Prime Minister Chamberlain, representing both Britain and France, met with the German leader, Adolph Hitler and signed The *Munich Agreement* that essentially gave Czechoslovakia to Germany

Upon returning to Britain, Chamberlain acclaimed the agreement as having secured "Peace in our time".

With the invasion of Poland less than one year later, both Great Britain and France declared war on Germany and World War II began.

PM Neville Chamberlain and Adolph Hitler after signing the Munich Agreement

As you read "Act Four...1940", we suggest you be aware of what was happening in background on the larger stage...the world. The people of Fenton, and for the whole nation as well, were still not willing to accept the war in Europe as *their* war. The country's leaders, primarily the President Franklin Roosevelt, had gained the people's support for strengthening our defenses and providing material assistance to Great Britain, while publicly proclaiming we would not engage in the war. One of Roosevelt's election campaign themes in 1940 was that " he kept us out of war".

Following is a "Timeline" of some of the major events of the war in Europe, Japanese operations in Asia and the related actions of our government. (Timeline obtained from <u>thehistoryplace.com</u>)

Jan 30, 1939 – Hitler threatens Jews during Reichstag speech
March 15/16 – Nazis take Czechoslovakia.
May 22, 1939 – Nazis sign 'Pact of Steel' with Italy.
Aug 23, 1939 Nazis and Soviets sign Pact
Aug 25, 1939 – Britain and Poland sign a Mutual Assistance Treaty.
Aug 31, 1939 – British fleet mobilizes;
               Civilian evacuations begin from London.
Sept 1, 1939 – Nazis invade Poland.
Sept 3, 1939 – Britain, France, Australia and New Zealand
               declare war on Germany.
Sept 4, 1939 – British Royal Air Force attacks the German Navy.
Sept 5, 1939 – United States proclaims neutrality;
               German troops cross the Vistula River in Poland.
Sept 10, 1939 – Canada declares war on Germany;
                Battle of the Atlantic begins.
Sept 17, 1939 – Soviets invade Poland.
Sept 27, 1939 Warsaw surrenders to Nazis
Sept 29, 1939 – Nazis and Soviets divide up Poland.
Nov 8, 1939 – Assassination attempt on Hitler fails.
Nov 30, 1939 – Soviets attack Finland.
Dec 14, 1939 – Soviet Union expelled from the League of Nations.
Jan 8, 1940 – Rationing begins in Britain.
March 12, 1940 – Finland signs a peace treaty with Soviets.
March 16, 1940 – Germans bomb naval base near Scotland.
April 9, 1940 – Nazis invade Denmark and Norway.
May 10, 1940 – Nazis invade France, Belgium, Luxembourg
               and the Netherlands; Winston Churchill becomes
               British Prime Minister.
May 15, 1940 – Holland surrenders to the Nazis.
May 26, 1940 – Evacuation of Allied troops from Dunkirk begins.
May 28, 1940 – Belgium surrenders to the Nazis.
June 3, 1940 – Germans bomb Paris
June 10, 1940 – Norway surrenders to the Nazis; Italy
                declares war on Britain and France.
June 14, 1940 – Germans enter Paris
June 18, 1940 – Soviets begin occupation of the Baltic States.
June 22, 1940 – France signs an armistice with the Nazis.
June 23, 1940- Hitler tours Paris
July 25, 1940-FDR orders Partial Trade Embargo to Japan
July 1, 1940 – German U-boats attack merchant ships in the Atlantic.

July 5, 1940 – French Vichy government breaks off relations with Britain.
July 10, 1940 – Battle of Britain begins.
July 23, 1940 – Soviets take Lithuania, Latvia and Estonia.
Aug 13, 1940 – German bombing offensive
   against airfields and factories in England.
Aug 15, 1940 – Air battles and daylight raids over Britain.
Aug 17, 1940 – Hitler declares a blockade of the British Isles.
Aug 23/24 – First German air raids on Central London.
Aug 25/26 – First British air raid on Berlin.
Sept 4, 1940- US warns Japan to stay out of Indochina
Sept 22, 1940- Japanese troops cross over into Indochina
Sept 26, 1940- FDR imposes embargo on scrap iron to Japan

A French man weeps as the Nazis march into Paris, June 14,
1940 - beginning a four-year occupation of the 'City of
Lights.' (Photo credit: U.S. National Archives

Leroy Street looking south from the intersection of Leroy and Roberts (now Silver Lake Rd.) Note Virginia Tavern on left corner and Lutz "Tire" Store on right corner. Angle parking was ended in 1940.

Worker in process of building tower for new Municipal Building....
"Fire Hall"...at southeast corner of South Leroy and Ellen Streets.

Act Three…The Year 1939

Scene One…"While the Storm Clouds Gather"

"While the storm clouds gather far across the sea," sang Kate Smith, popular songstress on her weekly radio program. Kate Smith introduced

Irving Berlin's "God Bless America" in November of 1938 and her recording of the song is the most recognized version even in the present day. Moreover, the lyrical prayer expressed the patriotic spirit of the country then as it does today.

The people of Fenton, not unlike most of the nation's people, many with a keen memory of the World War…"the war to end all wars"…were not inclined to become involved in "Europe's troubles".

Kate Smith

Representative William W. Blackney's letter to the *Fenton Independent* probably reflected a common attitude:

> *" We must not forget that fighting Europe's battles is not the best way to preserve our civilization, and we must no longer delude ourselves with the vain hope of making the world safe for democracy, but realize that we are facing the grim necessity of keeping democracy in the United States"*

In an edition of the *Weekly Reader* used as school instructional material, the publisher included a question for the students to consider and discuss in their classes. The question was "In the event the United States entered the conflict in Europe, which side should they join? The Axis Powers, Germany and Italy? or The Allied Nations of Great Britain and France? There was no clear-cut support for either side among the students or the general populace.

Supporters of Germany, mostly Americans of German heritage were organizing the German-American Bund and holding rallies in some of the nations largest cities. The newsreels shown in the movie theaters showed the big rally of over 22,000 people in New York's Madison Square Garden where their leader, Fritz Kuhn, led the participants in using the stiff armed hand salute of the Germany Nazi party. It was rumored several men from Fenton attended the Bund rally in Detroit.

However, the Bund and its program were not well received by the American people. A public opinion survey in 1939 showed that Fritz Kuhn was seen as the leading anti-Semite in the country.

In January, *Time* magazine selected Adolph Hitler as their "Man of the Year", probably because he had successfully annexed the German-speaking portions of the nation of Czechoslovakia.

In spite of what was happening in Europe, life in the village and the State went on much as it had for the last few years. The signs of recovery from the deep economic depression were everywhere, even though times were still "tough" for many people.

Most of the village activities were similar to those activities in the most recent past. However, Village politics was the exception. For the first time in a couple of years, both local parties presented a slate of candidates for the Village's elective offices.

The People's Party, which had been "inactive" in the past year, caucused and nominated Dr. M. B. Smith as their candidate for Village President. The big surprise came when the Citizen's Party caucused and presented their candidates. The Citizen's Party nominated Shull Woodworth as their candidate for Village President. After six terms as Village President, Harry Lemen had been "passed over" and his party had nominated another person.

During his tenure as Village President, Harry Lemen had essentially operated as a "one man" Personnel Department. Generally, he would interview job applicants and make the employment decisions. His actions were generally approved after the fact by Council action.

Since he was now the proprietor of a downtown grocery store, some of his detractors had started a rumor that Harry expected Village employees to do their grocery shopping at his store. While there is no evidence the rumor was the reason his Citizen's party "passed" on his re-nomination, it is a strong possibility. Especially, considering the way Harry Lemen handled the rebuke and the events that followed.

Harry Lemen decided to run as a "sticker" candidate in the upcoming election. Along with his public announcement of his candidacy, the *Fenton Independent* published his open letter. A portion of his letter follows:

> *"I also wish to correct any rumors whereby I have used my office as Village President to gain financial benefit for myself; I wish to emphasize therefore that that never occurred and never will."*

In the March election, a record number of voters turned up at the polls and overwhelmingly returned Harry Lemen to office. The total number of citizens voting was 905, which far exceeded the 102 votes cast in the 1938 Village election.   Harry Lemen received 683 votes while Shull Woodworth had 106 and Dr. M.B. Smith only 77 votes.

Others elected were: Walter Conrad-Clerk, D.R. Stiles-Treasurer and Floyd Chapin-Assessor. Trustees elected were: Charles A. Stein, Nelson Curtis and Floyd Poppy.   The incumbents who did not stand for re-election this year were: Gus Lutz, William Marshall and John Hoskins.

Soon thereafter, the Council confirmed the appointments of Howard Craft as Fire Chief, Lewis Rector as Assistant Fire Chief and Fred W. Williams as Fire Marshall.

Earlier in the year, the Village Council directed a reorganization of the Village's police department and eliminated some of the practices used in the past to supplement the officer's incomes. In Fenton and many of the smaller towns in Michigan, the "Nightwatch" would solicit contributions from the town's businesses to supplement the salary paid by the village. Other services were rendered the citizens for which a fee was charged. For example, if you were going to be on vacation for a time, you could engage the "Nightwatch" to check your property while you were away. For this service, you would pay the Nightwatch a small fee.   It was recognized as an antiquated method of compensating the community police for a long time, however the situation was never directly addressed. The Fenton Village Council decided to eliminate this practice before it became a problem.

The "Nightwatch" name was abandoned in favor of "Deputy Marshall". Compensation for the services of the Deputy Marshall and all others performing police functions would be authorized by the Village Council and paid from public funds.

The Council set the salary of the First Deputy Marshall, Leon Durkee, at $45 per week for full time. The Deputy would be required to "furnish and maintain his automobile." Further the council stated "all officers fees earned by him in connection with village business to belong to the village". The council also directed that "All collections from merchants to be discontinued". For the first time, the Village was to supply uniforms for the Deputies and pay the automobile liability insurance premiums. The *Fenton Courier* complimented the Council members on their actions and opined "…Leon Durkee will surely feel more proud and dignified to be on a regular salary and not forced to collect quarters and half dollars up and down the street to maintain himself and his family."

126 The Village Players

Another important "police" policy change happened at the same Council meeting. At the urging of the Justice of the Peace Julia Sweeney, the Council established a system to handle traffic violations

Traffic tickets would be issued to violators as usual. If it were a first time violation, there would be a procedure to avoid trial or expensive court procedures. Typical of the violations which could be paid in this manner were: Parking violations, $1.50; failure to stop at a stop street, $2; driving through a red light, $3; disobeying an officer or fireman at a fire, $3; more than three in driver's seat, $3; following fire truck, $3; speeding, $5 plus 50 cents for each mile in excess of the speed limit; improper muffler or cut-out, $1.50; driving over a fire hose, $5; making a U turn on Leroy Street in the business district, $1.50.

Village President Harry Lemen and the council members had been concerned about the sewage problem facing the city for some time, and the skies darkened on the prospects of solving the problem in the near future when the Village's request for PWA funds was "killed" for lack of PWA program funds.

However, the Council did take a positive step toward solving the pollution problem. Late in the year the Council obtained a lease for some property owned by David and Hazel Belle Black of Tyrone Township, just south of the Genesee County limits. For the sum of $450 the Village obtained the rights to use the property "as a public dump".

It is interesting to note that about sixty years later, the issue of the use of this property as a "dump" came into question, when the then owner sued to have the City of Fenton clean up the property to facilitate his sale of the property. At first the City denied ever using the site as a city dump. The owner visited Fenton's Historical Museum and found positive evidence of the City's use of the site as a "dump", which convinced the City authorities as to the merit of his claim. It seems the City had "forgotten" about the action of the Village way back in 1939.

Early in the year, the Reverend W. Thomas Smith of St. Jude's Episcopal Church appeared before the Council and urged them to create an ice skating rink. The Council responded positively and soon thereafter the Fire Department flooded a portion of the athletic field behind the Fenton High School building. But, as in the past, the variations in weather, along with snow and rain, presented some insurmountable maintenance problems and the outdoor rink was less than a complete success.

As during most summer months in the past, the Council directed the "oiling" of most of the village's dirt streets. Parking in the downtown business area was becoming a bigger problem, especially on Saturday. The building of the Community Center had severely reduced the number of downtown parking spaces, particularly during the construction period. But now, the many activities being conducted in the Community Center and an apparent increase in commercial activity, parking spaces were at a premium, especially on Saturday morning, afternoon and evening!

They didn't solve the parking problem, but they did ban making right turns on a red light!

One of the many "modern" dances held in the ballroom of the Fenton Community Center in the late Thirties.

Large crowd attending "Craft Show"
at the new Fenton Community Center in Fall of 1938

The New Fenton Community Center

Scene Two…the Center of Activity!

There was no doubt about it! The Fenton Community Center was up and running. The Board of Governors had selected a Director for the Center and planning for the use of the facility was well underway. Even though the public "Open House" was not scheduled until late in September, the public was coming and going in the building while the doors were open. The citizens were anxious to see the inside of the building they had witnessed rising from the former "City dump". They were not disappointed in what they found…a modern well-furnished building…much needed by this growing and active community. Even though many of the citizens continued to insist the building was built backwards, they were rapidly adjusting to the progressive architecture evidenced by their new Community Center.

The Village's agreement with the Rackham Foundation required the approval of the appointment of the Director of the Community Center by the Board of Governors for the Rackham Graduate School at the University of Michigan. The local board had selected Russell Haddon and his appointment was submitted for their approval.

As Russ Haddon relates the story, the Dean of the Graduate School

thought Mr. Haddon was deficient in Social Work courses.. Consequently, he withheld final approval of Mr. Haddon's appointment as the Director until Mr. Haddon completed a number of courses prescribed by the Dean.

Consequently with a "temporary" appointment in hand, Russ Haddon spent most of the following year traveling on nights and weekends to Ann Arbor or Detroit taking the required courses. Finally, after having completed the prescribed courses to the Dean's satisfaction, he was appointed as

Russell Haddon

the Director of the Community Center in February 1939.

Even before the Rackham Board at the University of Michigan formally approved Russell Haddon, the Board of Governors of the Community Center aggressively pursued an activities program for the Center.

130 The Village Players

A group of citizens, about 50 in number, met in late January to plan an activities program. The group designated a number of activities to organize and support. The following activities and the leaders were named:

Table Tennis-. Delphin Bender
Sewing- Mrs. Lillian Norgen
Bookkeeping-Miss Gladys Abbey
Public Speaking- Russell Haddon
Discussion Forum- Mr. C.D. Arrand
Home Economics- Miss Martha Wagbo
Dramatics Club- Mrs. Eugene (Helen) Cooley
Glee Club/Chorus- Miss Frances Hicks
Orchestra- Miss. Frances Hicks
Contract Bridge- Mrs. James Pratt/ Mrs. R. Silver
Men's' Horseshoes- Richmond Browne
Old Time Dancing-John Martin
Village Players- Mrs. John Johnson
Book Club- Miss Mildred Cady
Women's Athletics- (HS P.E. Instructor)
Rug Weaving- Mrs. Helen Kerber
Knitting- Mrs. A.D. Duesberry
Men's Athletics- Lester Miller
Interpretive Reading- Russell Haddon
Agriculture- James Campbell, County Ag Agent
Lecture Series- Prof. Hall, Herman & McDowell

In addition to the "fun and Games" nature of most of the planned activities there was a more serious program put in place. The new Director for the Fenton Community Center established an Employment Service. The service worked in liaison with the State's employment service, and maintained a list of both employers and persons seeking employment. As economic conditions improved, the persons seeking employment were primarily seeking work as domestics, waiters/waitresses and child or health care assistants.

For the first time, the community had a modern auditorium with a well-equipped stage. Consequently, those interested in stage productions were one of the most aggressive groups and in a matter of days things were happening. By mid-year they had recruited 55 members even though they had limited their membership to "out of school" persons.

The Dramatics club at the Fenton Community Center (FCC) held an organization meeting. At this meeting Mrs. A.T.F. Butt, the wife of the pastor of the Methodist Episcopal Church, was chosen as their President. The other officers elected at that time were: VP- Mrs. L.A. Wilson, Secretary- Mr. Graham Bell, Treasurer- Mr. Ronald Butler and Director- Mrs. Eugene Cooley.   Months later, In September, Miss Gladys Decker was elected unanimously to replace Mrs. A.T.F. Butt as President when her husband, the Reverend Butt was transferred to Algonac.

The Dramatics Club Committees and their leaders were as follows: Reading: Mrs. Cooley, Chairman; Misses Martha Wagbo and Miss Gladys Decker: Production: Rev. W.T. Smith, Chairman and Mrs. Gladys Abbey; Finance: Mr. Russell Haddon; and Stage Setting: Mr. J. Johnson and Mr. Ryan Strom.

It is interesting to note that at their second meeting the Dramatics Club voted that. "...from now on we will be known as the 'The Village Players' ".

In May, the Village Players offered two nights of drama at the FCC. On each of the two evenings the "Players" presented three one-act plays.   On the first evening the plays were "Sunset by Slantsky", "Another World" and "Light". On the following night, the three plays were "Cassandra", "So's Your Aunt Anna" and "The Knight in Spain"

Miss Florence Mantha directed "Sunset by Slantsky" with a   cast including Barbara Barnes, Nellie Davis, James DeVogt, William Dode and Rev. W.T. Smith.

Ramona Burrows directed "Another World" and her all female cast was headed by Marlene Wessendorf.   Ruth Wakeman, Thelma Barker, Director Ramona Burrows, Ann Hungerford were the supporting actors.

"Light" featured S.F. Beach as an unscrupulous mine owner who turned off the "lights'. Gloria Reid, William Butt and Dawn Hagerman were in the supporting cast.

For the first play of the second night of shows, Mrs. C.D. Arrand directed "Cassandra" where Mrs. L.A. Wilson played the lead role of a famous crystal ball gazer. Don Sinclair, Joan Smale and the dance team of Neva Neely and Jack Klinger played roles in this unusual play.

The second play of the evening. "So's Your Aunt Anna" was directed by Miss Gladys Abbey with a cast composed of Helen Neely, Margaret

Durkee, Ethelyn Burrows, Lucile Cheesbrough, Eleanor Yerdon and Mildred Smith.

The last play, "A Knight in Spain" found Ronald Butler and Jean Hagerman playing the leading roles. Ryan Strom, Mildred Alchin, Graham Bell and Betty Cook were in the supporting cast.

The Village Players weren't the only group anxious to use the new theater facilities provided by the FCC. Before the "Players" got started the people at the Methodist Episcopal Church, often the scene of many of the town's functions, sponsored the "Community Home Talent Program" at the FCC.

Those involved: Carol Jean Walden, Mrs. Earl Bell, Mrs. Eugene Cooley, Richmond Browne, Mrs. Paul Bristol, Miss Alice Van Atta, a Men's Chorus of Ten Voices, Lee Kelley, Miss Francis Hicks, a play presented by FHS students with Miss Nixon directing, Tap Dancing and Acrobatics by Marjorie Bachus, Barbara Jean French, Murray Bell and Lois Searight with Mr. Leon Jolly

The faculty and students at Fenton High School were also eager to use the new facility. In March they presented the play "Stage Door " at the FCC to a large audience of students and townspeople. Junior Theresa Allen played the lead role made famous by Ginger Rogers in the movie version of the Broadway play and Bob Harris was the male lead. Gordon Thomas directed the play.

Not all the playing occurred on the Center's stage. A large, well-attended semi-formal "Cabaret Party" was held in late April. Many round tables were placed throughout the auditorium floor with a dance floor space left in the center. There was a floorshow and dancing to the music of Jack Dowling and his Orchestra. It was an excellent simulation of a New York Cabaret...except the covenant with the Rackham people did not allow the serving of alcoholic beverages. Regardless "booze or no booze" the party was a big success!

The Community Chorus under the direction of Miss Frances Hicks performed in June at the Center with cello solos by Mrs. Kenneth Klingbeil. Richmond Browne and Miss Hicks were also featured as soloists on the piano and violin respectively.

The Village Players returned to the FCC stage later in the year, but only after many other events had transpired, including the "Open House" on September 21st.

A couple hundred citizens, many of them seeing the facility for the first time, attended the Open House. Ronald Butler was in charge of the Open House and with the FCC staff prepared a full day of activities.

Members of the FCC Board of Governors proudly escorted groups of citizens on a tour of the facility. Many of the activities, such as the book club, Community Chorus, Sewing, Knitting and Contract Bridge had their participants on hand to talk with others with similar interests.

In the evening, the Village Players presented a one-act play in the auditorium. The play was titled "Long Distance" and its cast included Willard Hatfield, Ronald Butler, Harvey Walters, Ryan Strom, Margaret Durfee, and Joanne Smale. The play's Director was Miss Gladys Abbey. Roger Leestma was the Stage Director.

The play was followed by two dance sessions: Lewis Gage and his orchestra played "Old Time" music with John Martin as the "Caller". The "old timers" were promised an "old time dance" with schottisches, square dances, circle two steps and waltzes. Following the "old timers", modern dancing to the music of Dick Smale and his band held forth for the rest of the evening.

The "permanent" residents of the Fenton community were very much aware of how the population changed during the summer months. Lake Fenton and the many other lakes in the Fenton area were very popular with summer vacationers from Flint, Detroit and other locales outside our region. The Director of the FCC and his activities chairmen wanted to include the summer visitors and planned a number of activities to attract and entertain the "resorters".

They held well-advertised "Resorter's Night Dances" in July and August with Thor Neilson, Ron Butler, Jim Frew and Norm Neiniger in charge of arrangements. Jack Dowling and his orchestra provided the dance music.

In late October, the very active Village Players began the casting for a "long' play, "Old Lady Thirty-One" for presentation in the early part of the next year.

There was another "change of pace" in the stage presentations when Miss Frances Hicks began rehearsals for a light opera, "The Bartered Bride" and another group decided to put on an old-fashioned Minstrel Show.

The Minstrel Show, under the direction of Gerald Rawson, was to be presented in March of 1940. It was to have an all Male cast just like the "genuine old time minstrel shows". Ryan Strom and Gerald Rawson would share the responsibility for the script and casting. Instrumental music would be the responsibility of John Hoskins, while Grant Wright and Miss. Frances Hicks would handle the vocal music. Leon Jolly would be in charge of the dancing. It was planned to have a chorus of 30 Fenton men.

At the annual meeting of the Board of Governors for the Fenton Community Center, Floyd Chapin replaced Charles Rolland as President of the Board. The other officers elected for the coming year were Harry Lemen as Vice President, Don Alchin as Secretary and Dr. Daniel Hogan as Treasurer.

More or less as a Christmas present, late in December, the Rackham Foundation announced they had purchased property on West Caroline Street, east of the Shiawassee River and was donating the property to the Fenton Community Center. Eventually, two tennis courts would be built on a good portion of this property.

One was also reminded of the fact Fenton was part of a large farming community when the FCC became the scene of a "Farm Festival". In early November, The Fenton Grange was the sponsor of the event, with George Petts as the General Chairman. The exhibits were wide ranging and covered most of the farm products and activities. The exhibits and those responsible for the showings are listed below:

Potatoes	W. A. Sheldon
Fruits	George Petts
The Grange	Harvey Swanebeck
Poultry	Chet Hillis
Floral	Mrs. Cheney
Gardens	Mrs. C. Dibble
Grain	Mr. C. Morgan
Future Farmers	Mrs. F. Kirshman
Home Economics	Mrs. C.A. Simons
Special Exhibits	Mr. Elwood Elsworth
Commercial Exhibits	Raymond Hunt CofC

Scene Three…Who's doing what in the Clubs?

How anyone found time to engage in other activities outside of those programs sponsored by the Fenton Community Center is difficult to comprehend. However, the many clubs, church groups and patriotic organizations continued to meet and conduct their many faceted agenda

Two of the most active Womens clubs in town were the Bayview and the Entre Nous. As in the past, both clubs met on a biweekly basis and generally one of its members would present a paper to stimulate thought and discussion. A review of the members also indicates the members were, for the most part, the wives of the town's "movers and shakers".

Early in the year, the Bayview Club selected Mrs. Anson Wolcott as their President and Entre Nous selected Mrs. C. D. Arrand as President and Mrs. Martin Stiff as their Vice President.

The Child Study Clubs continued to be very active and a fifth Child Study club, the Senior Child Study Club, was organized as part of the FCC program. The others were the Child Study Club, Junior Child Study Club, Mothers Child Study Club and the Pro-To Child Study Club.

The Fenton Women's Music Club elected Mrs. Don Smale as their new President in November and tapped Mrs. Lowell Swanson as VP and Mrs. Clair Reid for Recording Secretary and Treasurer.

The members who were recognized for their active roles in some of the town's clubs during the year included those listed below:

Bayview Club	Mrs. C.E. Rolland, Mrs. E.R. Sluyter, Mrs. Anson. E. Wolcott, Mrs. Wm. Alexander, Mrs. Thomas McKinley, Mrs. Charles Morehouse, Mrs. Raymond Hyde, Mrs. D.A. O'Dell, Mrs. E. C. Reid
Entre Nous	Mrs. Frank B. Mytinger, Mrs. C. Heemstra, Mrs. Than Chestnut, Mrs. S.F. Beach, Mrs. F.J. Horrell, Mrs. Roger Leestma, Mrs. Mark Gordon, Mrs. Harry Lowe, Mrs. C.D. Arrand, Mrs. Kleber Merrick, Mrs. Martin Stiff, Mrs. Flora McKeon,
Child Study Club	Mrs. Than Chestnut, Mrs. Sydney Hay

Junior Child Study	Mrs. John Millington, Mrs. Henry Alchin, Mrs. Ivah Elrich, Mrs. Ralph Richmond, Mrs. Earl Helmboldt, Mrs. Wm. Johnson, Mrs. M.B. Shaw, Mrs. Phillip Garvey, Mrs. Gordon Robbins, Mrs. Clarence Edinger, Mrs. John Chapman, Mrs. Richmond Browne, Mrs. Delphine Bender, Mrs. George Paine
Monday Night Review	Misses Joyce Minnock and Eleanor Yeardon
Womens Music Club	Mrs. Thor Neilson, Mrs. Earl Bell, Mrs. F.B. Mytinger, Mrs. Leo Hall, Mrs. W.H. Skillen, Mrs. Roger Leestma, Mrs. Mark Gordon, Mrs. Harry Lowe, Mrs. Sorensen, Mrs. Paul Bristol, Mrs. D.C. Smale, Mrs. Clair Reid, Miss Mabel VanAtta, Miss Alice VanAtta, Mrs. A.B. Stanton, Miss Frances Hicks

There were many other clubs, mostly organized to play bridge, "pedro" or other card games Some of the clubs that received mention in the weekly newspapers and members were: Aw-Kum-On Club (Ivah Rolland, Myrtle Swanebeck, Gladys Ford, Violet Bachus, Hazel Merrill, Grace Wright, Zella White, Minnie Moore, Nina Ford, Marie Steward); Oke-Doke Bridge Club (Mrs. Harold Freeman, Mrs. Earl Goddard, Mrs. Harry Reed, Mrs. George Atherton, Mrs. Peter Morea, Mrs. Gordon Bly); Penelope Club (Mrs. Stallsmith);

The patriotic organizations continued to lead all others in the number of members and the range of their community activities. The American Legion James Dewitt Post and the Veterans of Foreign Wars Curtis-Wolverton Post, along with their respective Ladies Auxiliaries, were most prominent. The Daughters of Union Veterans, Womens Relief Corps and the Lincoln Club were smaller, but still very viable.

The Colonel Fenton Post of the Grand Army of the Republic had been essentially non-operational for several years. Now with the death of Andrew Bly, at the age of 92, only Charles Bentley remained as Fenton's lone survivor of the Civil War. There were only two others who remained in Genesee County. They were James Taylor, age 92, and Craydon E. Foote, age 89, both residents of Flint.

The more active women in the D.U.V and its Lincoln Club were: Mrs. Louis Seaton, Ruby Anglen, Helen Munson, Alberta French, Florence Robbins, Violet Vandercook, Ruth VanAlstine, Flora Munson and Mrs. George DeWitt.   The D.U.V. chose as their President Jessie Andrews.   Also Senior VP Dorothy Griswold and Junior VP Clara French were elected to office.

The W.R.C elected President Martha Berdan, Senior VP Edith Collins and Junior VP Clara French.   Others active in the W.R.C. were Mrs. Wm. Dode and Mrs. Alta Hall

The V.F.W. Curtis-Wolverton Post celebrated their Fifth Anniversary and elected Spanish War Veteran Sam Casazza as their commander. Others elected were Isaac Stiff as Senior Vice Commander, Andrew Bly Jr. as Junior Vice Commander, Fred Slover as the Quartermaster, Harry Dobbs as Chaplain, Walter Stiff as Judge Advocate and William G. Harris as the Adjutant.

Soon after his election, V.F.W. Commander Casazza had a mission statement published in the *Fenton Independent* that read as follows:

> *"Our organization is dedicated to the care and welfare of the disabled and unemployed veterans. We are seeking justice for the dependents of deceased veterans. We are promoting the "Keep America Out of War" campaign which deserves the support of every loyal American"*

One of the new projects undertaken by the V.F.W. Post was to raise the funds necessary to purchase uniforms for the Fenton High School Band.   It was an ambitious project that James Tribbey was assigned to conduct, but with a combination of fund raising events and the solicitation of citizens and businesses, the members were confident they would reach their goal in the coming year.

The V.F.W. Auxiliary President Lelah Stiff was supported by a number of very active members: Irene Boilore, Zelma Slover, Naomi Bennett, Edna Bly, Delia Palmer, Agnes Bottecelli, Hattie Rohm, Arthie Westfall, Emma Hall, Margaret Petts and Mrs. Martin Piccinni.   Myrtle Harris and Fannie Schleicher joined the Auxiliary this year.

American Legion James DeWitt Post elected Commander Mark Gordon.   Early in the year, the James Dewitt Post renewed their "Americanism" program with a meeting at the FCC with Mr. Walter S. Reynolds of Detroit as the speaker.   Other programs that received their continued support were the American Legion Baseball program and participation in the Wolverine Boys State.   Harold Schupbach and Joe Craft were sponsored at the Boys State and spent a week on the Campus of Michigan State College in June with that program.

As a fundraiser, the Legionnaires brought the donkeys back to town. Only this time, they were "Texas" burros and instead of playing basketball, they were playing softball! The "game" was held at the High School baseball field in mid-July and all those involved had a good time and made a little money for the Legion Post.

Men and Women of the American Legion visiting Cabin at Higgins Lake: L-R (in rear) Harry Reed, Charles VanAlstine, Unidentified Man, Roy Goodrich, L-R (in front) Lillian Goodrich, Ruth VanAlstine, Maybelle.Reed.

The American Legion Ladies held their annual election of officer in early October and selected Lillian Goodrich as their incoming President. The 1st VP was Zoe Jenison, 2nd VP Mabel Reed, Secretary Ruth VanAlstine, Treasurer Ida Gould, Chaplain Hattie Rohm, Historian Margaret Petts and Sergeant at Arms Gladys Dobbs. Others active were: Zella White, Mary Matthews, Minnie Winn, Grace Williams, Myrtle Franks, Linnie Sparks, Norma Reed, Emma Curtis, Marion Crego and Artie Williams.

The American Legion and V.F.W. posts often worked together on special projects and as members of the Fenton Patriotic Council. On one occasion, the Post members arranged to present an American flag to the Community Center. The time of the presentation ceremony arrived. The members of the posts and other patriotic organizations were there and ready to make the presentation. However, there was no member of the Board of Governors in sight. Finally after several phone calls, Harry Lemen arrived on the run. He explained there was some confusion on the Board and everyone thought the other person was going to represent the Board at the ceremony. Mr. Lemen's apologies were graciously accepted and the flag was presented and received in an elegant and proper manner.

The Armistice Day parade was exceptionally well done on this November 11th. The American Legion and V.F.W. veterans, with their ladies, turned out in force for the parade with their respective color guards. The Fenton City Band led the way for two Drum and Bugle Corps from the Flint V.F.W. posts. The celebration of the day that ended the "Great War" was topped off in the evening with a dance at the Legion Hall in the old Macabee Building on the corner of Walnut and Caroline Streets.

The V.F.W. continued to support the "Bicycle Club" in the community. The town marshals, Leon Durkee and Basil Chappelle conducted instruction about the traffic laws and how they applied to bicycle riders. The program attracted more than fifty boys and girls who met on a weekly basis at the V.F.W. hall downtown. Murray Bell was elected President by the bikers.

The Masonic Temple was the scene of constant activity during the year. The Masons, Knights Templar, Order of the Eastern Star and the Rainbow Girls always had something going! The O.E.S. held elections and chose Mrs. Ruth Sinclair as their Worthy Matron and Ray Cummings as their Worthy Patron. The Associate Matron was Mrs. Elsie Welch and the Treasurer was Mrs. Myrtle Swanebeck. The Rainbow Girls, in their third year, began the year with Miss Violet Bachus as their Worthy Advisor and Miss Mary Simmons as the Associate Worthy Advisor. In November, the annual election resulted in naming Miss Carol Lutz as the Worthy Advisor and Miss Kathryn Dode as the associate.

The Oddfellows named their leaders for the year as Noble Grand Frank Whitney, Vice Grand Clinton Kelley, Secretary Glen Mathews, Treasurer George Anglen and Trustee Fred hall. Their "Favorite" Rebekahs held their election and named Mrs. Bert Lockwood as their Nobel Grand and Mrs. Earl Goddard as the Vice Grand.

Pellett's Department Store begins remodeling in 1940

Pellett's display window ..."window shopping?"

Looking southeast to Matthews Law Office
(smaller brick building) and Kroger's to right.

Scene Four...Churches and their activities

For many years, the town had been blessed by an exceptional group of Church pastors. With the arrival of the Reverend Dr. J. Stanley Mitchell of the Presbyterian Church, the village clergy acquired an eloquent speaker. His oratory at the Memorial Day ceremonies at the A.J. Phillips Library on that day established his reputation as a speaker. Consequently, he was frequently invited to deliver the invocation or speak at many civic functions.

The new rector at St. Jude's Episcopal Church, the Reverend William Thomas Smith, was another excellent speaker, who soon became engaged in many community activities. He appeared before the Village Council to urge the development of a skating rink in the community, not only for the recreational benefits, but to avoid the acknowledged dangers of skating on the millpond. With the opening of the Community Center, Reverend Smith became involved in their activities program, especially with the Dramatics club where he later directed or acted in several plays.

The Roman Catholic community...as well as all the townspeople knew the Reverend Dennis P. Tighe. Father Tighe was known for his love of cigars, golf and his passionate desire to establish a church school at St. John. As a fundraiser for the church, Father Tighe organized an annual church Bar-B-Que which was held during a late summer afternoon and evening. As the years past, the attendance grew and the programs became more interesting. The City Band always played a concert for the event and that, along with good food, helped to draw a large crowd.

Father Tighe was an acquaintance of several players on the Detroit Tigers baseball team, and he always invited several of them to attend the outing. Whether Billy Rogell, Mickey Cochrane or Hank Greenberg every showed up is not recorded, however the fact that there was the possibility that they might attend was well publicized in the weeks prior to the affair.

Another leader among leaders in the town's clergy was the Reverend A.T. F. Butt of the Methodist Episcopal Church. Here again, the Reverend Butt was a very good speaker and he participated in many community events where he provided the inspirational prayer or the prayer of thanksgiving. His church being centrally located and having the largest facility for a meeting or banquet, was often the scene of functions sponsored by organizations without an affiliation with the M.E. Church.

For several years, the church provided classroom space for the Fenton Schools elementary students. The Methodist church officials transferred the Reverend Butt to Alpena in late September and the Reverend Wesley J. Dudgeon came from West Branch to serve as his replacement.

Paul C. Mroch pastored the Trinity Lutheran Church. The Reverend Mroch became very active in community affairs, especially the sports programs. He was one of the town's best bowlers and played an excellent game of softball.

It is interesting to note that the Reverend Clare A. Whaley, pastor of the First Baptist Church was "ordained" as a Baptist preacher in April of this year. Reverend Whaley was once an ordained minister of the Methodist church, but left that denomination and joined the Baptists

One of the most active Church-sponsored groups was the Men's Fellowship of the Methodist Episcopal Church. Their annual Father-Son Banquet was held in early February at the M.E. Church. Over 200 attended the 1939 banquet that was the largest in the history of the event. Ronald Butler and Fred Kirschner made the traditional "toasts", to the fathers, and to the sons, respectively. Reverend Butt offered the Invocation and Reverend Mitchell served as the Toastmaster.

A Variety program was presented featuring vocal solos by Douglas Fairbanks Kelley, music y Bert Barnes, short talks by James Cole and Jack Kelley and performances by Dick Carter, the "handcuff king" who has traveled extensively throughout this country with his act.

In April, the Fellowship elected their officers: President Charles Wortman, Vice President Bert Clark, Secretary Ralph Patterson and Treasurer Dr. W. J. Rynearson.

The Guild of St. Jude's Episcopal Church held their annual Mother-Daughter Banquet at the Fenton Community Center and attracted about 220 participants. Mrs. Clarence Heemstra offered the "greetings' to those attending and Mrs. Claude Sinclair served as the "Toastmistress". Mrs. J Stanley Mitchell and Misses Barbara Chesnut and Jean Gordon made the traditional toasts. The Village Players presented the one act play "Another World" as part of the program. Mrs. Joe Chene was recognized as the youngest mother present and Mrs. Robert Neely was acknowledged as the mother with the largest number of daughters in attendance.

The "new " season of Men's Fellowship activity began with a banquet in September. This time the speaker was Malcom Bingay, the Editor of the Detroit Free Press. The turnout was exceptional and the Fellowship scored another triumph.

The next banquet produced by the Men's Fellowship was the annual "Ladies Night" in early October. This banquet was held in the Fenton Community Center since the attendance exceeded three hundred persons. Those attending listened to songs by Harriett Mortimer Toomey of Detroit. Leon Maxwell of Flint led community singing. Then a trio composed of Aldrich Locke, Lewis Gage and Richmond Browne serenaded them. Detroit's Director of Recreation, Clarence Brewer was the guest speaker.

It is interesting to note that at these large banquets, at least those held at the Methodist Episcopal Church, there was a "Supper Squad" designated to work with the church ladies who prepared the food. Those assigned to the "Supper Squad" had their names published in the weekly papers and the lists often included men who were not members of the church, but affiliated with or supportive of the Men's Fellowship. On one occasion, the whole membership of the XX Club made up the "Supper Squad".

The juxtaposition of the following advertisement from the *Fenton Courier* immediately following the discussion of the banquets in the town might make one chuckle, but one must remember Fenton was the center of a large farming community and when the farm animal failed to respond to "Doc" Trimmer's treatment, it might be time for the farmer to contact the Valley Chemical Company!

FARMERS ATTENTION!
We Remove Dead Horses and Cattle
We Pay Top Market Price

$5.00 for Horses $4.00 for Cows

Service men will shoot old or disabled animals
Prompt Service   Telephone Collect

Valley Chemical Company
Telephone 3-9154   Flint, Michigan

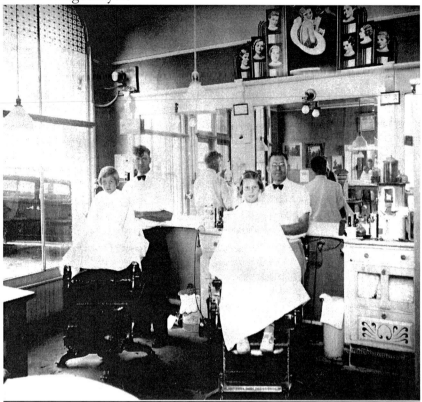

Glen Carpenter's Barber Shop in first block of East Caroline Street in the same building as the D & C Store. The Barber on left is Basil Chappelle who also assisted Leon Durkee, Village Policeman during night hours. Glen Carpenter is the barber to the right. The young lady in the chair is Irene Heemstra, daughter of C.R. Heemstra, the Superintendent of Fenton Schools. The young lady in Chappelle's chair is Betty Holm. Irene Heemstra Camp was a member of FHS Class of 1945. Betty Holm Lamb was a graduate of FHS Class of 1943

Scene Five...What's Happening Downtown?

While the opening of the Fenton Community Center was BIG, the grand opening of Kelly's Ice Cream Bar was a close second! Marge and Lee Kelly held their "Grand Opening" in September, soon after the opening of school. With Sundaes and Sodas at 5 cents and Malted Milks at 10 cents, the business was brisk. While the special prices didn't last the "brisk" business did. Kelly's rapidly became the place to be for all the teen-age students at Fenton High School.

Lee and Marge Kelly had leased the place from Joe Bottecelli when Joe became the proprietor of the Virginia Bar. The Bottecelli family moved to a home on Adelaide Street a couple doors north of the High School building and the Kellys moved into the upstairs apartment vacated by the Bottecelli family. Both Lee and Marge had worked for Mickey's

Marge & Lee Kelley

Dairy, the most popular dairy bar in the region. Lee had learned to make ice cream at Mickeys and he continued to make his own ice cream for his new business.

With a juke box playing almost continuously, Kellys became a warm, friendly place to congregate and enjoy an after school "coke", play the pinball machine, listen to music and visit with your friends. For the high schoolers of the late thirties and early forties, Kellys became a part of your life and is fondly remembered

Robert G. Harris, in front of Kelly's Ice Cream parlor in the 100 Block of North Leroy Street. These buildings were demolished as part of a 1970s urban renewal project

While visiting with Marge Kelly, she remembered those days with equal fondness. Marge said that after World War II, the climate changed. The young people were different, they had many other interests and activities. Further, the market for ice cream had changed completely. After the war, vendors of ice cream were almost everywhere. If they wanted ice cream they could go to the nearest grocery or gas station. They didn't need to travel downtown to buy their ice cream at Mickeys or Kellys.

Another person of interest in the community was Nathaniel Chesnut, better know as "Than". For years Than and his family operated a dairy farm, "The Chesnut Acres" south of town. It wasn't just an ordinary diary farm, but one that produced very special milk that was in demand in the Flint hospitals. For fifteen years, seven days a week, regardless of road or weather conditions, either Than or his wife made a trip to Flint to deliver this special product. After selling the farm, The Chesnut family moved to the Village of Fenton. The family, especially Than, was active in many community activities, an Than was the one to relieve Russ Haddon as the Director of the Community Center when Russ entered the U.S. Navy during World War II.

Than Chesnut was a "fanatic" supporter of University of Michigan football. At each home game, he would carry several bushels of apples from the local orchards to distribute to the players and the U of M Band members. One each trip, he would invite a couple young men to accompany him and help him carry and distribute the apples. This meant that those selected would have "free " admission and a close-up view of the game. To say the least, Than had no shortage of volunteers!

Than Chesnut

The search for a site for a new "Federal Building", the new post office, was announced the previous year and the property at the southeast corner of Walnut and East Caroline Streets had been selected. However, it was not until October before the purchase of the property of Dr. and Mrs. Burton McGarry was completed. Dennis E. Kelleher, longtime Fenton Postmaster, was eager to vacate the storefront post office location at 113 South Leroy Street. It was anticipated that construction of the new post office would be completed in about one year.

In their annual meeting, the State Savings Bank of Fenton elected their Directors and appointed their officers. The Directors were as follows; George W. Cook, George Green, H.W. Hitchcock, J. H. Jennings, D.E. Kelleher, George W. Pellett, Charles E. Rollands, Louis A. Riedel and E.C. Reid. The officers were: President George Green, Vice President and Cashier E. C. Reid, Assistant Cashiers R.F. Smith and Otis E. Furman. The town's people were pleased with how the bank had come through the "bank troubles' of the early thirties and much of the credit for this good management was assigned to E. Clair Reid and Otis E. Furman. Both of these men, experienced in banking, had been brought to Fenton to provide leadership during those difficult years.

During the late summer of the year, Pellett's Department Store underwent a remodeling of their store on South Leroy Street. The Store occupied one of the widest buildings in the business district and the installation of a modern Libby-Owens-

E. Clair Reid

Ford "Vitrolite" front was a sharp contrast to the generally drab century old storefronts of the majority of Leroy Street businesses. A complete eight-page section of the *Fenton Independent* was devoted to the new remodeled store, its merchandise and its employees.

Not all the business activity occurred on Leroy Street or in the retail business. Mr. Roy Polson was operating a cement block manufacturing business on Shiawassee Avenue and using a new machine that produced one block a minute. S. F. Beach of the *Fenton Independent* visited Mr. Polson's shop and reported "Perfect blocks were formed, laid out to dry and ready for sale at a surprising speed."

As if there weren't enough clubs and organizations in the Fenton Community, a group of young men came together in April to plan the organization a chapter of the Junior Chamber of Commerce in Fenton. At a meeting in April, the group, which was chaired by Ronald Butler, approved a Constitution and elected a Board of Directors. The following were elected as Directors: Ronald Butler, Ray Hunt, Neil Woodward, William Ruckel, Edward Mitts, Harvey Walters and Ray Cummings. The Director then met and elected the following officers: President Ray Hunt, VP Ronald Butler, Secretary Ray Cummings and Treasurer Harvey Walters.

In mid-June, the Community Chest program was activated for this year. As in the past, they reasoned that the businesses and the people were being "hit" by solicitors of one cause or another and the Community Chest would allow contributions to one fund which would then provide financial support to the most deserving local charities. The committee, composed of William Burkett, Arthur Becker, Louis Reidel, Hoyt Glaspie and J.C. Peck, set this year's goal at $1,000. "If you continue to give indiscriminately to every solicitor you will encourage what the chest was organized to correct".

Looking northeast on first block of North Leroy Street. Rowena Theater after remodeling is in near right of photo. Moving to the left from theater is Byerly's Grocery Store, Log Cabin Restaurant. Hoskins's Restaurant it to the right with "Lunch" sign. Note three "new" cars of same make parked on street.

Scene Six…What's' Happening in the School Yard?

Not enough is said for and about the school "assemblies" in the present day. Perhaps that is because school enrollments have grown to such numbers that it is not workable to bring the whole student body together for a lecture, demonstration or informational program. However, in the thirties at Fenton High School, several assemblies were held during the school year. The three held in 1939 involving outside talent were of particular interest at the time and in some respects are recalled with a measure of amazement today.

In late January a well know newspaper writer from Grand Rapids named Ben East spoke to the assembled students in the auditorium of the new Fenton Community Center. Ben East spoke of the wonderment of Michigan's wilderness…the lakes and the streams and the abundances of nature. Even at the age of 40 years, he had written extensively about the outdoors and the need to protect the environment. In years to come, he would have a national, even an international reputation for his vigorous defense of the nation's treasures and his willingness to take on powerful forces to protect them.

The next assembly was held in the High School's auditorium (gym) and the presenter was positioned on the stage, about four feet above the gym floor. Mr. John S. Sloan program dealt with "liquid air". He had on the stage with him several canisters containing "liquid air". As he described "liquid air" it was air that had been liquefied by compression and cooled to a very low temperature. His demonstrations were very fascinating. He took a banana, froze it solid in the "liquid air" and proceeded to use it as a hammer to drive a nail through a wooden board. When he fried an egg on a block of ice, he stole the show. Awesome!

The assembly in early November provided a look into the future, however few if any in the audience had a clue as to how it was to affect their lives and the lives of generations to come. The guest presenter was a "television expert". Again the assembly was held in the High School Auditorium and the "expert" was on the stage with his equipment for demonstrating what he referred to as an "electric eye".

At one time in his presentation he invited a couple of our students to the stage. Jim Frew and Harold Schupbach went to the stage and were seated in chairs, one near the "expert" and the other near a "box" on the other side of the stage. The expert directed his "box" (a camera) at

150 The Village Players

Harold and asked Jim Frew to report what he could see in his "box" (which contained a TV screen). Within moments, Jim exclaimed he could see Harold on the screen. Awesome!

Not all the assemblies utilized speakers and presenters from the "real world". Many were strictly "In house" productions, such as student play.

The new Community Center was not available for the presentation of "The Trysting Place" so the gym stage at the high school was the location for the school play. Gordon Thomas directed Joyce Stein and Jim Frew in this romantic comedy. Dawn Hagerman, Rosa Westman, Bob Harris and Dick Riedel supported them.

The Fenton High School dramatics continued with the production of the Stephan Foster's operetta "An Old Kentucky Garden" directed by Thelma Barker. The show was performed at the Fenton Community Center. The female performers were: Mary Jean Rowley, Marjorie Hinkley, Marjorie Williams, Eileen Freeman and Helen Hager. The male counterparts were: Justin Ruckel, Dick Riedel, Don Peterson, Art Barnard, Arnold Westman and Ken Pettis.

The governing body for the Fenton Schools startled the community when it announced the total school enrollment near the end of the 1938-1939 school year had peaked at exactly 1000 students. The prospects of a continued growth were evident and the budget implications did not go unnoticed

At the time, several smaller elementary school districts, such as the Silver Lake School District, surrounded the Fenton School District. Most of these smaller districts were also experiencing growth with a limited budget. In June, the Silver Lake board requested consolidation with the Fenton district, however the Fenton board rejected the proposition as being "impossible to consider at this time".

Consolidation of school districts was not a popular issue at that time and would remain that way for many years to come. Finally, with improved transportation, the recognition of the benefits from the economy of scale and a mandate from the State resulted in the consolidation of many school districts.

In June of each year, the Board of Education published its annual financial statement. This year the statement was severely truncated compared to those published in recent years. The details of the $70,542.16 expenditure budget were for the most part presented in sufficient detail, however the detailed information on the salary of each individual administrator and/or teacher was eliminated. It was probably a good thing. Even though the salaries paid are of public record, no one likes for every "Tom, Dick and Harry" to know exactly how much you are paid!

Also in June, the Fenton High School received notification from the North Central Association, the regional school accrediting organization, of the reaccredidation of Fenton High School; FHS had been accredited continuously since 1926.

The 1938-39 Fenton High School Basketball season was one that started fast...faded...and came back strong in the Tournament. The team was composed of experienced players for the most part and they won their first four games of the season quite handily. They lost twice to arch rival, Holly High School and lost temporary possession of the Tamlyn Trophy for the year. After ending up in 4th place in the County league, they won the District Tournament by defeating Milford and Grand Blanc . However, the County League champions, Davison High School was their first opponent in the regional tournament and, as in the league play, they were defeated.

Joe Craft, Al Turco, Bud Milliken, Dave Dawson Sid Smale were the regular starters. Bob Zoll, Don Clark, Ken Lawless and Ed Rusinski made up the supporting cast.

The springtime sports at Fenton High school featured two of the fastest runners to participate in Track in the recent history of the competition. Senior Brad Hoffman and Junior Roy Perry ran away with the competition. Roy Perry elected the team's Captain, won the 100 and 220-yard dashes at the county meet, as well as running on the first place relay team. He also won first or placed in the regional and State track meets.

Both Perry and Hoffman also played baseball this season. When not running track, they joined with Gorton Milliken, Lee Gordon, Joe Craft, Al Turco, Bob Harris, Verne Walters and Duane Loomis to represent Fenton on the diamond. Brad Hoffman, a three-time letterman, was elected Honorary Captain.

Coach Lester Miller had only ten returning lettermen from last year's football team as he began practice in the fall. In the first week of practice, one of the untested players, Bill Rynearson, son of Dr. W.J. Rynearson, had his leg broken above the knee. He was standing along the sidelines during a scrimmage, when a "mass of players" rolled over him. His football season was over.

About the same time, returning letterman Bo Schleicher severed several tendons in his right wrist as he leaped on a moving car, caught his arm in an open window and shattered the window glass. Surprisingly, Bob Schleicher returned to play the last half of the season's games.

With a large squad of largely inexperienced players, the coach lost a whole week of practice when the school closed down for a week over concern of the spread of infantile paralysis among the student body. However, early on he had recognized he had many talented athletes on his squad and he was able to develop one of his best teams as coach at Fenton High School. His earlier optimistic opinion was more than justified as the 1939 team, starting slowly came on strong to win a share of the County League Championship.

The backfield had Joe Craft and Bob Zoll at quarterback with the fleet footed Roy Perry and Harry Daniels at halfback and Leon Shelby and Carol Butts at full back. The line was anchored by Dave Dawson at center, Bob Harris, Jim Frew and Bob Schleicher at guards, Lary Sugden, Howard Elliott, John McCann, and George Bard at the tackles and Al Turco, Howard Goodrich, Bob Biggs and Dee McKinley at the ends. Albert Turco and Bob Harris were selected to the All-County First team at the end of the season

Interscholastic competition at Fenton High School was not limited to athletics. The school fielded a very competitive debating team that won more than share of debates with county schools and others outside the area, many with larger enrollments such as Cranbrook Academy.

The student debaters were Richard Alexander, Joan Cox, Marna Houser, Harold Schupbach and Dorothy Woods. The Resolution being debated this year was: Resolved: The United States should form an alliance with Great Britain. It was a very timely topic in view of Hitler's Germany threatening the peace of Europe.

For years the High School band, sans uniforms, was relatively small and while individual members possessed considerable musical ability, the band and orchestra was continually struggling.

The band instructor, Mr. C.L. Wilder left the school in the summer and the fall semester started with Mr. Thomsen in charge of the music program. Mr. Thomsen began an aggressive recruiting campaign and by the end of November, the band and orchestra membership had increased considerably. As published in the *Fenton Courier* in November, here is a list of the band members at that time:

Trumpets	Jean Brooks, Bob Zoll, Bernie Greene, Marvin Youker, Jerry Houser, Dale Hagerman, Wayne Young, Joan Morgan, Joyce Bump, Ray Heemstra
Clarinet	Donna Austin, Dick Hiscox, Martha McCann, Jane Walcott, Albert Carlson, Clayton Moorman, Irene Heemstra, Louis Trimmer, Alice Moorman
Flute	Gloria Reid
Saxophone	Dawn Hagerman, Murray Stanley, Robert Harris, Ione Rounds,
Trombone	Gerald Durand, Richard Smale, Carl Alber, Robert Weigant
Baritone	Richard Schaefer
Alto Horn	Duane Houser, Earl Carmer, Carl Pettis,
Bass	Joe Craft
Bass Drum	Jack Klinger
Snare Drum	Ralph Crawford, Tom Merrill, Dee Marshall, Billy Brown, David Stiff
Violin	Don Bump, Edwin White, Joyce Neely, Herbert Lathrop, Margaret Kovitz, Austin Foley (also Bass Violin), Beth Ann Morehouse.

Near the end of the school year, the annual Junior-Senior Banquet was held at the Presbyterian Church. The theme of the banquet was adopted from a popular movie musical of the day, "Big Broadcast of 1939". Senior Kathryn Dode, a winner of several oratory contests, welcomed the Juniors and turned the meeting over to the Toastmaster, Senior James Frew. Jim Frew introduced the speakers for the evening. Senior Ed Rusinski spoke for his class and Principal Charles D. Arrand spoke for the faculty. For entertainment Elizabeth Thornton sang two numbers. Loreen accompanied her on the piano. Senior Richard Alexander presented Mr. Arrand, the Senior class advisor, with a watch in appreciation of his help and guidance. The banquet was adjourned and the hundred or more in attendance adjourned to the high school gym for dancing.

It was graduation time and the 55 members of the Class of 1951 were anxious to get the show on the road! For the second consecutive year, Mrs. Lucille Miller had her young charges outfitted in cap and gown and held a genuine graduation ceremony in the high school gymnasium. The highlight of the ceremonies was the graduates singing their class song, "Play with all your Might". The *Fenton Independent* reported, "During the past week the little folks have been going about town with their caps and gowns and taking on all the airs of the seniors that are completing their school work this year."

A few days later, the Class of 1939 graduated sixty-three students at their Commencement exercises held at the Fenton Community Center. Superintendent Clarence R. Heemstra presented the diplomas at the event. The Reverend A.T.F. Butt pronounced the invocation and the benediction.

The speakers at the Commencement were all members of the graduating class; Maxine Powlison as the Valedictorian, Blanche McLenna as the Salutatorian, and Donald Bell, Joan Cox, Edward Rusinski and Paul Bottecelli on topics related to the class theme. A list of the graduates is to be found in Appendix One.

On the proceeding Sunday evening, the class attended the Baccalaureate services at the Fenton Baptist Church, where the Reverend Clare Whaley presented the sermon.

It is also interesting to note that at the graduation exercises at the University of Michigan this year, two distinguished graduates of Fenton High School were awarded honorary degrees by the university. Bryson D. Horton of Detroit and Dr. Ward MacNeal of New York were so honored.

The Alumni of Fenton High School continued to be very active in 1939 and sponsored a reunion banquet at the Fenton Community Center in late October. At the banquet they elected officers for the upcoming year. Those chosen were: President Raymond Hunt, VP Nathaniel "Than" Chestnut, Secretary Catherine Cook and Treasurer William Dode. For the Board of Governors the group named: Mr. C.R. Heemstra, Mr. C.D. Arrand, Miss Jean Riedel, Mr. Robert Atkins and Mr. Norman "Slew" Neininger. (Mr. Neininger was nicknamed "Slew" as a young boy, a name he never was able to shake, even if he had wished to do so. "Slew" was for "slew foot", it seems he had very large feet...or at least his classmates thought they were exceptionally large!)

Scene Seven…Fun and Games

The bowlers never had it so good! In early February, the NEW Fenton Recreation opened as a new bowling establishment in the old Dubord's garage. In recent times this building had served as the temporary fire hall, village council meeting rooms, jail and an election-polling place. The building was purchased by W. L. Hunt and had been completely remodeled and sported six new bowling alleys.

The Grand Opening of the new six lane alleys was highlighted by a match between the Old Frankenmuth team of Detroit and a team composed of Fenton Firefighters. Even while being spotted 80 pins the "Fire boys" (Howard Craft, Tm Woodworth, Shull Woodworth, Louis Reidel and Bob Beach) were not able to win the match.

In the absence of Village President Harry Lemen, Councilman William G. Stocken threw the first ball on the new alleys and the *Fenton Courier* reported "the packed audience was given a big surprise when all the pins toppled over in spite of the ball rolling down the gutter." Manager Jim Smith could only shrug his shoulders in wonderment!

The league bowling, which was well underway before the opening of the new alleys, continued at the Fenton Bowling Alleys of Clarence "Bud" Edinger. As one reviews the list of bowlers in the league, it is almost a roll call for all the businessmen in town. There was Howard Craft (the undertaker), Carl Tisch (Manager of the D & C Store), Floyd Hartley (owner of gas station), Robert Beach (Fenton Independent), Nelson Curtis (Butcher at Alchins), Guy Merrick (Buick Dealer) and Louis Reidel (manager of Michigan Bean Co.). Others active in the league this year were: Bob Dode, Walter Dorr, Chet Willing, Pete Cutler, Jack Harrison, William Taylor, Harold Fowler, Frank Bachus and J. Hockett.

As soon as the snow cleared, the Softball leagues began organizing for the new season. Most of the sponsors from past seasons were fielding a team again this season: Mickey's Dairy, Gould's Grocery, the Industrial Machine Tool Co., Fenton Hardware, Locke's Gas Station and Law Officer of Maurice Matthews. The league held a banquet at Swanebeck's cottage as a "kick-off" for the season.

The Industrial Machine Tool Company continued to support golf tournaments at the Long Lake Country Club as they had in recent years. Some of the leading golfers were: J. Bachus, L. Louden, L. Davis, T. Nelson, E. Westman and H. Schulte and M. Richmond

In the recent past, both Mickey McBroom and his wife Dorothy had established themselves as champion Skeet Shooters. In 1938, Dorothy McBroom had won the State Championship, but fell two hits short of repeating this year. However, Mickey came through to uphold the family honor by winning the small gauge competition by shooting 95 out of 100 during the competition.

Something new was added to the sports activities during this year when Mr. Roger Leestma, FHS coach, organized a number of young men for competition in the Flint Golden Gloves Boxing Tournament. James Foley, Lyle Pratt, Dee Marshall, Charles Case, Phillip Crane, D. Walker, Bob Black, Leo Schleicher, Clyde Dennison and David Dawson trained for the competition.

In the competition, Lyle Pratt won two fights before losing a decision, Charley Case, Clyde Dennison, and Bob Black were T.O.'d in their first bouts. James Foley and Leo Schleicher advanced to the final, but none of the Fenton boxers won out in the end.

While "jitterbugging" was not considered a "sport", it certainly was athletic and recreational. Consequently, when the "King of Swing" Benny Goodman and his orchestra played at the I.M.A. auditorium in Flint in early May, many of the Fenton young people (and some older ones too!) headed north for the event. The band played for the "jitterbugs" from 4 to 6 PM, so most everyone watched the exhibition on the floor from balcony seats. The concert and dance began at 8:30 PM and the number in attendance increased significantly. When one of the "big bands" would visit the I.M.A. it seemed about half of those in attendance crowded close to the stage to watch the musicians and singers.

Another interesting musical event happened in Fenton, just before Benny Goodman hit town. Mrs. Harriett Mortimore Toomey, a 1922 graduate of Fenton High School, and an accomplished vocalist, brought a group of singers from her church in Detroit, to conduct a concert of sacred music at the Methodist Episcopal Church. Mrs. Toomey was frequently invited to sing at important events in her hometown

The Community Chest funded a summer playground program that served about 100 youngsters. Coach Lester Miller and Music Teacher Thelma Barker were in charge of the program held at both the high school facility and the Community Center. It was open all day, every weekday to all children. Teenagers June Hartley and Jean Woodworth were employed as Student assistants to work with the "little ones".

As in the past years the Fenton City Band played an important role in providing entertainment to the people of Fenton   Early in January the band elected Fred Parker as their President and Charles Simmons as their Manager.

The band played its weekly summer concerts at its bandstand on Shiawassee Avenue. Mr. C.L. Wilder, the instrumental music teacher at Fenton High School, conducted the band during this time. Mr. Wilder left his position at the high school and also left the City Band after the completion of the summer concerts.

The Fenton City Band presented its first winter concert at the Fenton Community Center in early November where it featured the accomplished Harpist Joseph Vito

The *Rowena* remained a major source of entertainment for both young an old.. At 10cents for children and 25cents for adults (30cents on Sunday evenings), the price was right! J. C. Peck continued to operate a clean, respectable theatre. Recent Fenton High School graduate Harold O'Grady, the nice looking young man with the ruddy cheeks, was now a permanent member of the staff and he carried out JC's policy on expected conduct and behavior to the "T".

The year 1939 was an exceptional year for movies; some of the industry's classic films were released during the year. Most of them appeared on the *Rowena* screen. One of the most popular films, even to this day, was "The Wizard Of Oz" with Judy Garland, Frank Morgan, Ray Bolger, Jack Haley and Bert Lahr. Films like "Beau Geste" with Gary Cooper, Ray Milland and Robert Preston, brought action audiences to the edge of their seats and "Babes in Arms" teamed Mickey Rooney and Judy Garland in one of the great "Let's put on as show" movies. The excellent "Confessions of a Nazi Spy" took the gun out of Edward G. Robinson's hand and gave him a pen instead. Errol Flynn romped through "Dodge City" in Michael Curtiz's wonderful western, and Henry Fonda outran the Indians under the loving eye of Claudette Colbert in John Ford's towering revolution/western "Drums Along The Mohawk". All these were shown at the *Rowena* this year.

Tyrone Power and Henry Fonda carved out the myth of Jesse James for movie fans. John Ford gave John Wayne his first defining screen role as The Ringo Kid in "Stagecoach" and Robert Donat created the timeless portrait of a dedicated schoolmaster in "Goodbye Mr. Chips". Cary Grant, Douglas Fairbanks, Jr. and Victor McLaglen battle against an Indian cult at the height of Britain's Imperial rule of India. George Stevens directed the rousing "Gunga Din" with perfect timing and amazing enthusiasm Henry Fonda gave the most convincing screen interpretation of Abraham Lincoln in John Ford's "Young Mr. Lincoln"

There were many others, even the ones referred to as "B" movies that were well worth the price of admission   Bob Hope and Bing Crosby began one of their "road' films and   There were three films in the Blondie series, Bulldog Drummond was included in the title of two flicks, Andy Hardy and The Thin Man series made their annual appearance, Kildare was there and Charlie Chan solved three mysteries.

Fenton Street Scene-100 Block North Leroy.   Store with people entering is Kelley's Ice Cream parlor. To the left of Kelley's is entrance to a barbershop that had replaced the former tenant, Puccini's Shore Repair Shop. To the right, the white building, is McGuire's Hardware Store and further to right is Coles Gift Shop.

Scene Eight...When Bad Things Happen

In mid-May Donald "Bud" Lemen, son of Village President Harry Lemen and his wife Ila, suffered an attack of appendicitis. When the appendix ruptured, he was rushed to Hurley Hospital in Flint where he died on May 22nd. The reaction of the people of Fenton to the death of young "Bud" Lemen is difficult to conceive of in today's environment. The shock of learning of his death occasioned a sense of personal loss with most of the townspeople.

The *Fenton Courier"* expressed the general opinion that "Bud" was of "sterling character...clean, upright...everyone liked Bud."

Donald Lemen was a handsome young man, gentlemanly, and well liked by both young people and adults. He was well known as a leader in high school, having served as President of the Student Council and Vice President of his Senior Class. He was a varsity athlete in football and basketball "Bud " Lemen graduated from Fenton High School in June of 1938 and he deferred going to college to work in his father's grocery. His plans were to enroll at Hillsdale College in the fall of 1939 along with his long time friend and classmate, Garwood Marshall.

On the afternoon of his funeral, all the stores in downtown Fenton closed their doors. His funeral was held at the Methodist Episcopal Church and the Reverend A.T.F. Butt conducted the service. The church would only seat 400 people, but the number who attended far exceeded that number. There were hundreds of students, classmates, friends and family in around the Church. Following the service, he was buried at Oakwood Cemetery. The *Fenton Independent* published the names of those who served as Pallbearers and Flower Girls at the funeral. They were as follows:

Pallbearers	Bernard Weber, Ronald Butler, Kenneth Bristol, Wayne Wessendorf, Edison Stiles, Harold O'Grady, Bud Birch of Lapeer, Gerald Niles of Holly, DeForest Marshall, Donald Herman, Kenneth Burrows, Burton McGarry, Neil Woodward, William Dode, Bruce Cox and Harry Bender.
Flower Girls	Mary Thompson, Mae Thompson, Nellie Davis, Yvonne Stein, Marie Dery, Dorothy Polson, Margaret White, Margaret Adams.

Close friends, Garwood Marshall and Robert Atkins attended with the Lemen family, father Harry, mother Ila and sister Margaret. It was a small town tragedy that affected many who knew him and many who wished they had known him.

Just a couple months later, the townsfolk learned of the passing of Andrew "Sandy" Bly at the age of 92. Andrew Bly was one of the three surviving Union veterans of the Civil War. Mr. Bly had enlisted in the 8th Michigan Infantry at the age of 16. As a member of the 8th Michigan, where on September 17, 1862 he fought in the Battle of Antietam, one of the most horrific and bloody battles of the Civil War. There were over 23,000 men killed or wounded on that day, more than nine times the number of casualties on "D" Day, June 6, 1944.

He survived Antietam, but later became ill and very weak. He was discharged from the Union Army and sent home to Michigan. Later, having regained his health and strength, he enlisted in the 10th Michigan Cavalry and campaigned with the Regiment until the war ended. Returning to Fenton, he became a mason and general building contractor. He is credited with building the first cement walls in the Village of Fenton. He was active as a member of the Colonel Fenton Post of the Grand Old Army and was the only G.A.R. veteran to walk the parade route during their convention in Detroit in 1938.

He was the father of Roma Bly, devoted servant of the Village of Fenton and of Andrew J Bly Jr., a combat veteran of the first World War and one of the founders of the Curtis-Wolverton Post of the Veterans of Foreign Wars in Fenton.

During the hot days of summer, the mothers of the nation were particularly concerned about their children contracting the dreaded disease of *poliomyelitis* or more commonly referred to then as "infantile paralysis". Those afflicted with this disease faced the possibility of death or a life with a crippled body.

The movie newsreels frequently showed polio victims who were required to live in an Iron Lung in order to breathe.

With the first report of a case within the area, the parents would almost panic at the possibility of their children being one of the diseases next victims. Children were often prohibited from going swimming or playing games which might overly exert them and make them more susceptible to becoming a victim of polio. There were all kinds of actions taken out of fear and the general public's lack of understanding of the causes for this devastating viral disease.

In July of 1939, there was an outbreak of polio cases in Wayne and Genesee counties that caused considerable concern in Fenton and the surrounding area.

Later, in September, young Clyde Baker, age 15, a Junior at Fenton High School contracted polio, and after an illness of 9 days, he passed away. Clyde was the son of Mr. and Mrs. Charles Baker who lived about 3 miles south of town. They had taken their son to the Pontiac Contagious Hospital when he was diagnosed with having contracted the dread diseases. He died in the hospital only three days short of this 16th birthday.

His death increased the concern of the people of Fenton about the spread of the disease in the community. School had been in session for a couple weeks when Superintendent Clarence Heemstra announced the schools and all school activities would be closed for one week. All classes and football practice was suspended for the week. Furthermore, all the students were urged not to congregate in fear that the disease may be spread to other individuals.

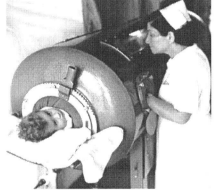

Polio victim in Iron Lung

Those who lived through the thirties lived with the fear of polio. It was not until 1952 when Dr. Jonas Salk developed a successful vaccine to fight polio that his fear subsided.   Later in 1957, Dr. Albert Sabin's Oral Vaccine was recognized   as   the   preferred vaccine and is now used almost exclusively in the United States.

Today polio is virtually unknown in the United States and rare in other parts of the world. Each year in the United States the effects of the Sabin vaccine prevent about 25,000 people from getting polio; prevent 2,000 people from dying, and prevent about 2,500 people from being completely disabled   This all came too late for Clyde Baker but thousands of other youngsters like Clyde have been saved from death or living with a crippling handicap.

Come Christmas time, all the worries and troubles were set aside and it was a time for joy and happiness…. especially for the children…of all ages!

For years the very best Santa Clause in town…and perhaps the whole State of Michigan was Aldrich Locke. He was a relatively was short and stocky man, jovial by nature and he loved playing Santa for the young children in the town.

In the last days before Christmas, he would visit each of the nursing homes in the area. The residents enjoyed his visits, but not as much as Aldrich enjoyed them. The picture below is "Santa" sometime in the early Forties. The children's identities are unknown except for the girl is directly behind the young boy on the far right of the picture. She is Sara Hunt Sherff, the daughter of Ray Hunt, local insurance man and community activist. Ray Hunt was the first President of Fenton's Junior Chamber of Commerce.

Scene Nine…Uptown, Downtown-All Around the Town!

Following the sicknesses, injuries and death of our friends and loved ones, and after a period of grief and sorrow, a person begins to feel alive again and his daily routine begins to return to normal. It's the nature of the human beast? Right?

So it was for the people of the Village of Fenton in the summer of 1939. It was time for the "boys of summer" to take the field and the collective attention of the town was on more pleasurable things. The Detroit Tigers were "our" team. Every game day, as you walked down almost any street or especially past the fire hall, you could hear either Harry Heilman or Ty Tyson giving the play-by-play account of what was happening at Navin Field Harry Heilman, a Hall of Fame Tiger outfielder of the past was the broadcasting Tiger games on WXYZ. On WWJ, Ty Tyson was also broadcasting the same game! There was a real division among the radio baseball fans as to which one did the best job.

So, in October, when Art Dumanois arranged for Harry Heilman to make an appearance at the Fenton Hotel, half the town wanted to meet this former slugging Tiger outfielder. Harry Heilman held a "Town Meeting" and spent several hours answering all the stupid questions his fans could conjure or conceive.

Margaret Crane, FHS Class of 1933, turned her attention to aviation. Margaret, the daughter of Mr. and Mrs. E.E. Crane of Lake Fenton, not only learned how to fly at nearby Flint Bishop airport, but also had became a part owner in a small private plane. In late December, Miss Margaret Crane flew her plane solo to Miami, Florida to attend a "meet" where over 200 planes from all around the nation gathered. Miss Margaret Crane would remain active in aviation her entire life, dying in year 2005

Her parents were owners and developers of considerable acreage on the western shore of Lake Fenton. Today's automobile driver can turn east off of Torrey Road on to "Margaret" Drive and travel a mile or so along the lakeshore before turning on to "Ruth" Drive and finally exiting on Torrey Road. Ruth Crane was Margaret's younger sister.

On Saturday, June 17th, the *Fenton Courier* ran a story about a runaway "doodlebug" in downtown Fenton. As reported a "doodlebug" belonging to Jim Pratt had been driven in to town by Rolland Harris who backed the "bug" into the curb on Roberts Street along side Joe Bottecelli's Virginia Tavern. Rolland, who needed crutches to walk, upon returning the "doodlebug", placed his crutches inside the homemade contraption. Then when he started the machine "it jumped out from under him and streaked across Leroy Street, missed Merrick's air tower by an eyelash and took a course up the railroad tracks toward Linden." The "doodlebug" was finally stopped when it hit the fence of a coal yard near the tracks.

The report defined a "doodlebug" as a reconstructed old car with a shortened wheelbase generally used for light tractor work

"How the tractor get across Leroy Street on a busy Saturday afternoon with hitting a car is a wonder". Witnesses said the traffic was heavy that day but at that particular moment when the "doodlebug" shot across the street there were no cars coming from either direction

Another interesting news article appeared in the *Fenton Independent* in late December. It told of Freddie Rolland, oldest son of Ivah Rolland, who was a civilian employee of the U.S.Army. Fred Rolland had just left San Francisco aboard the U.S.S. Sirius headed for Midway Island in the western Pacific Ocean. Fred Rolland, a Fenton High School graduate in 1935, was a part of a group of civilian and military engineers who were going to Midway to blast a deep-water channel in the reef to provide better access to the U.S. Naval base on the island.

. The last days of September and the first weeks of October were exceptionally "hot" days. The temperature soared and the citizens, almost all of them without air conditioning, were wondering if fall and winter would ever arrive. On one such day, Frank Seger came to visit with "Faye" Beach in his office at the *Fenton Independent*. Frank brought with him an ear of corn picked out of the field on which the kernels had "popped". Mr. Beach kept the ear on display for some time in case anyone asked, "How hot was it?"

In late April at the annual meeting of the Fenton Fire Department, longtime fireman Fred J. Horrell resigned as President of the organization and was replaced by Harry Moore, a member since 1915. However it wasn't until mid-October before the members of the Fire Department, the Village Council, the Water Commission members and their wives honored Mr. Horrell upon his retirement. The banquet for the 45-year veteran fireman was held, appropriately, at the fire hall. The Firemen presented Mr. Horrell with a watch and pendant depicting his service. Over 50 citizens attended the event.

In the "outside" world, on September 1st Germany had invaded Poland and the war in Europe was on! The Polish army was defeated within weeks of the invasion. The Germans broke through Polish defenses along the border and advanced on Warsaw in a massive encirclement attack. After heavy shelling and bombing, Warsaw surrendered to the Germans on September 28, 1939. Britain and France, standing by their guarantee of Poland's border, had declared war on Germany on September 3, 1939. The Soviet Union invaded eastern Poland on September 17, 1939. The demarcation line for the partition of German- and Soviet-occupied Poland was along the Bug River.

Congressman William Blackney and most of the citizens were opposed to the United States becoming involved in "Europe's wars" and still held on to the idea of remaining neutral in the conflict.

However, some things had already begun to change, some young men were enlisting in the armed services. It was not unusual to find an article in the newspaper reporting one of the most recent volunteers, for example Harold "Ted" Bradley, a Fenton High School graduate of 1938, had finished his Army basic training and was now stationed in Hawaii.

But the people had not yet accepted the notion that the United States would soon be involved in war. People were more concerned about the condition of the ailing baseball great Lou Gehrig, after watching his farewell address in the newsreel at the *Rowena* describing himself as "the luckiest man on the face of the earth" or the opening of the New York's World Fair.

Every town has its "scrooge". Some of the townsfolk considered Mr. George Wellington Harvey as being of that ilk. However, when you consider the task Mr. Harvey was charged to perform, one might want to give him a bit of "slack". George Harvey worked at being a real estate person and undoubtedly it was his field of endeavor that led him to the job of being a "rent collector" during the depression years. Not a very enviable occupation even in the best of times. George Harvey worked for a man in Flint who owned several rental houses along East Street in the northeast section of the town. Every couple of weeks George made a trip to Flint to deliver the proceeds of his collection efforts to the absentee landlord. The fact that George Harvey didn't possess an automobile didn't seem to faze him as he made his recurrent trek. Winter or summer, sunshine, rain or snow, nothing deterred George Harvey from making the trip. George would stand along North Leroy Street not far from his home in the northeast section of town, and raise his thumb to the approaching motorist. Hitchhiking was quite common, especially for the younger men, during this period. Most people had no fear of picking up a stranger along the road. George Harvey, however, would not accept a ride with just anyone that came along. In the wintertime, while standing in the cold, he would raise his thumb and when the automobile stopped to pick him up, he would first check to see if the automobile had a heater. If there was no heater, he would decline the offer of a ride and resume his thumb raised posture, even in the cold and blustery weather.

These four men were very influential in the early days of the program to build the Fenton Community Center. They are L-R Maurice Matthews, Village Attorney; Charles Crane, Member of FCC Board of Governors; C.R. Heemstra, Superintendent of Schools and Member of the FCC Board of Governors; and Roma Bly, Village Engineer and Member of a Special Committee chosen by the Village Council to work with the Rackham Foundation. Others equally deserving of recognition, but not pictured above are: Charles E. Rolland, Chairman of Special Committee and Member of FCC Board of Governors; George Green, Member f Special Committee and Chairman of State Savings Bank; Dr. D.L. Hogan, Member of FCC Board of Governors; and Don Alchin, Member of FCC Board of Governors. (*Authors Note: The pictures above and several others in the book were copied from the Fenton Independent newspapers resulting in a very poor quality. However, it was deemed important to present an image of these men and women regardless of the quality of the photo.*)

Interlude Two...At Center Stage...
...The Community Center

Nothing more significant occurred in the village during the decade of the 30's than the development of the Fenton Community Center. One can only imagine the pleasant surprise experienced by the Village leaders Fund offered to provide funds to build a "community house" in the Village of Fenton. The five Trustees of the Rackham estate were intent on carrying out a provision of Horace H. Rackham's will to establish a community center in a small community.

Mary A. Horton Rackham

Horace Rackham was known to be very fond of the Village of Fenton and his wife, the former Mary Horton, was born and raised in Fenton. Of the five Trustees of the Fund, three were members of the Horton family. These were Mrs. Mary Rackham, Mrs. Myra Bussey and Mr. Bryson D. Horton. Another Trustee, Mr. Frederick G. Rolland, had lived in Fenton for years.

Several years later, the Fund Trustees described Fenton as "a decorous, tree-shaded, typically American village in the heart of an agricultural district...without a central gathering place" ... with "no community facilities for the promotion of leadership, educational advancement, social enjoyment, or civic improvement."

It wasn't the first time the Horton family had made a substantial gift to the Fenton community. In 1919 the Hortons developed the Dexter Horton Park on a portion of the family farm along the Shiawassee River in the center of the town and gave it to the village. Now, the Trustees proposed the new "community house" be built on the land adjacent to the "park", which over the years had lost the appearance of a park and had evolved into the town dump!

In January 1937, the Rackham Trustees provided a $200,000 fund to buy and clear the land and construct the community building. It would be necessary to buy the buildings now occupied by Frank and Anson Wolcott's milling company, The Wander Inn, Shull and Tom Woodworth's plumbing business, and John L Rohm's barber shop. The "Old Fire Hall" would have to be razed also to provide the required land area. The "Old Fire Hall" housed the fire fighting equipment and was used for meetings of the Village Council as well as some of the town organizations such as the local political party caucuses

These buildings were located on the west side of South Leroy Street, immediately north of the Industrial Tool plant, which sat on the immediate north bank of the Shiawassee River.

Anson and Frank Wolcott relocated their milling business to Argentine where an old mill with waterpower coming from Lobdell Lake was available. The Wolcott Mill operated continuously in that location until 1998 when Frank Wolcott Jr. sold the mill and retired.

Tom and Shull Woodworth moved their plumbing shop into a building next door to Dubord's Southside Grocery on South Leroy Street. Later Tom set up his shop in a building directly behind his residence on Adelaide Street and his bother Shull, who was less of a plumber and did more sheet metal and furnace work, operated out of his house on South East Street.

The two ladies who ran the Wander Inn, Mrs. Martha Lamareaux and Mrs. Grace Faint, moved to Higgins Lake, bought another tavern and continued their business. Some of the locals were sorry to see the Wander Inn close up since they would no longer be able to smilingly remark…"Wander in, Stagger out". John L. Rohm moved in with another barber, Glen Carpenter, on the south side of East Caroline Street just off of Leroy Street.

The Trustees of the Rackham Fund recognized the razing of the Fireman's Hall would necessitate the building of a new Fire Hall. The new "fire hall" would also provide space for the Village Council and other village employees. For this, an additional $28,000 was allocated for the construction of this new "municipal building".

In 1938, the new Municipal building, which was more often referred to as the new "Fire Hall", was constructed on the southeast corner of South Leroy Street and Ellen Street. The old water plant, which occupied the spot, was demolished to make way for the new "municipal building". The operative water works building, a circular red brick building, was located directly behind the old plant, next to the river

As the construction of the "Community House" progressed, *The Fenton Independent*, the most widely read weekly newspaper, provided a "play by play" account of the happenings. With their Leroy Street offices directly across the street from the construction site, the paper's Publisher S.F. "Faye" Beach was able to provide a detailed report on when the "steam shovel" arrived and began digging up the old "town dump". Mr. Beach reported it was not a pretty sight as two truckloads an hour were removing a terrible mess of rubbish and trash that had accumulated over the years.

The Village Council had proclaimed an end to the dumping of trash and rubbish at the future site of the "Community House". The village had opened a "dump' near the intersection of Jayne Road and the south end of East Street. The Village dump was actually in Tyrone Township, Livingston County and was not as conveniently located as the more central downtown site. However, since there wasn't a waste collection and disposal program at the time, the good citizens of Fenton found it necessary to drive to the village limits south of town to dispose of their trash.

The excavating began in June of 1937 and before the former owners of the buildings to be razed had removed all of their machinery, equipment and other material. There was concern that the back entrances of Walcott's Mill and the Woodworth Brothers shop would be blocked with spoil and debris before they could complete their moves. However, they were able to hasten their relocation and complete the moves with time to spare. The building housing Rohm's barbershop was spared for the time being since it was to be used as an office by the W.E. Wood Construction Company of Detroit as their offices during the construction project.

The Rackham fund furnished additional funds for the purchase of properties on West Caroline Street to provide space for an alley behind the buildings on South Leroy Street north of the construction site and another location for building tennis courts along the river.

In accepting the gifts, the Village Council agreed that the operation of the facility was to be a "not for profit" endeavor and while the Village was the "beneficiary" of the gifts, the Village did not "own" the property. The Village had agreed that the maintenance and upkeep of the Center was "not to be a burden to the taxpayer".

The extent of the involvement of the "locals" in the design of the community building was relatively minuscule. The fact that the world-renowned architect, Eliel Saarinen was engaged to design the building is indicative of the control exercised by the Rackham people. It's doubtful, if the village leaders would have had a world known architect, such as Saarinen, on its long list of candidates. His son Eero assisted Saarinen and Mrs.F.W.Whittlesey of Phoenix, Arizona, the daughter of Mr. Horton, designed the landscaping.

Eliel Saarinen had an international reputation for his work and had associated himself with the University of Michigan and Cranbrook

Foundation. His son Eero was already establishing a reputation in his own right, but his "glory days" were ahead of him. Eero Saarinen in later years distinguished himself by designing the "Gateway to the West"...the Arch in St. Louis, Missouri and the terminal building at Dulles Airport outside of our nation's capital

The design of the building was "progressive", as was the Messrs. Saarinen's style. There certainly was no other structure in the area in the same class. Upon its completion, the Fenton "man of the street" often remarked the building had been built "backwards". Most of the citizens had difficulty accepting that the "back" side of a building would have most all of the windows. However, it didn't take the public long to recognize the new building was exactly what our community needed.

The agreement provided for a Board of Governors to manage the facility. Consequently, the Board of Governors for the Community Center were charged with the responsibility to operate the Center with the funds available from the income of an endowment fund provided by the Rackham Foundation and the rental fees and other incidental income generated from those using the building The Governors were also responsible for the appointment of a Director of the Center. An unusual condition was placed in the agreement, whereby the Board of Governors of the Rackham School for Graduate Studies at the University of Michigan would need to approve the appointment of the Director. The inclusion of this caveat is probably best explained by the fact that up until the decision to fund the Fenton Community Center, all of the programs funded by the Rackham Foundation had been conducted by the University, with one of their most recent gifts being the funding of a building for the School of Graduate Studies.

Horace H. Rackham

The construction of the Fenton Community Center was essentially completed in May of 1938 with the arrival of the furniture for the building and a "grand" dedication ceremony was conducted October 3rd of that year. University of Michigan President Alexander G. Ruthven addressed an overflow audience of over 500 people in the Center's auditorium-ballroom.

The Board of Governors first meting was in the Community Center on August 9, 1938. They were required to handle many "housekeeping" issues in the first months of operation; however their principal interest was to find a Director. From the very start there were a number of applications for the position and a significant number of "recommendations" from college administrators and faculty. At an early meeting a professor from the University of Michigan volunteered to assist the Board in finding a suitable person to be the Director. Within weeks, the Board was interviewing many of the applicants and at the same time planning for the Dedication Ceremony which they set for the "afternoon and evening of October 3, 1938".

As a "human interest" sidelight, one should know about the story of Ivah Rolland. For years, Mrs. Ivah Rolland enjoyed telling this story.

It seems it was Ivah's birthday and her mother-in-law, Mrs. Frederick G. Rolland, the former Margaret Eddy, was holding a party for Ivah at her residence.

One of the guests was Mary Horton Rackham. Margaret Rolland and Mary Rackham had been schoolmates in their younger years and were lifelong friends.

Ivah recalled that some time during the gathering, Mary Rackham said she was considering making a substantial gift to the Village of Fenton. She asked Ivah what she thought the village needed most of all. Ivah said her response to Mrs. Rackham was that the town needed a community house, a place where the town's people could gather.

Some time later, the Horace H. Rackham and Mary A. Rackham Foundation made a gift to the Village of Fenton to build a "Community House". Ivah Rolland enjoyed telling her friends the Community Center was "her Birthday gift"!

What a fine gift…one that keeps on giving!

O'Dell's Drug Store on North Leroy Street. Mr. Anible behind soda fountain counter. Center left, D.A. O'Dell holding child. Center right, leaning on counter, L.M. O'Dell. Clerk behind counter on right, Miss June Chappelle Bigelow. Customers' identities unknown.

"The Fire Boys" enjoying their monthly steak dinner. L-R Shull Woodworth, Fred Williams, John Bacon, Tom Woodworth, Louis Rector, Howard Craft, Bob Beach, Harry Moore, Claude Cohoon and Lee Kelley. Calendar on wall for 1940.

Act Four...The Year 1940

Scene One...The Times...They Are A'Changin'

My Old Home Town

My old home town's so different now
To what it used to be
And, I can't make it seem somehow
The same old place to me

The old landmarks are now all gone
New one's are in their places
And I don't see no more downtown
Those old familiar faces

The mill is gone the old town hall
To me it is a pity
To see them go, for I loved them all
Now my home town's a city

So progress marches on you see
To make the whole world better
But the home town of my youth will be
In my memories forever

P.J.R.

The Fenton Independent printed the poem on the front page of its February 15th edition. P.J.R.'s sentiment fairly represented the feeling of most of the town's "old timers", which constituted the majority of the townsfolk. Things "they are a'changin" without question. The new Community Center was up and running at full speed, and the panorama along South Leroy no longer included the old Fire Hall, Walcott's Mill, the Woolworth Brothers Plumbing shop, John Rohm's Barber Shop, the Wander Inn or Fenton's Odorless Cleaners. A couple houses on West Caroline east of the Shiawassee River Bridge were being removed to provide space for a couple tennis courts and some shuffleboard. The grounds behind the Community Center were no longer used as the "city dump" and a bridge across the river at that point was being considered.

The corner of South Leroy and East Ellen Streets was the site of the new municipal building, which housed the fire department, council meeting rooms, the jail, as well as a tower with the new illuminated town clock, old bell and all. The old waterworks building was gone as was the City Band's bandstand on Ellen Street and Kenny Robbins had a new modern Standard Oil station directly across from the Municipal Building.

The noontime siren at the "Fire Hall" sounded at 12 noon on the dot, and to the newcomers, it was often confused with the fire alarm...after all it was the same siren. What would happen if a fire occurred exactly at 12 o'clock was never considered.... and, presumably the confluence of events never occurred.

The southeast corner of Leroy and Caroline Streets sported a new modern "five and dime" variety store, the D & C Store having expanded into "two store fronts" and updated its exterior, with large display windows and appropriate signage. Pellets Department store had modernized its front and evidenced a trend away from the old and dated look of the downtown stores. The old two-lane bowling alley, which had served the town's winter athletes well for years, was about to surrender to the New Fenton Recreation on the south side of town. Likewise, the days for the Post Office being located in the store front next to the bowling alleys, was about to come to an end, as construction had begun on a new Federal Building at the southeast corner of Caroline and Walnut Streets.

The Michigan Bell's "dial" telephone system was working famously, and most of the townsfolk, who had telephones, were able to memorize the four digit telephone numbers of the businesses and friends most frequently called.

Perhaps you are wondering about the identity of the author of the poem who signed the initials "P.J.R.". A search of the City Directories lists only one person with those initials, Paul J. Rector who lived on 507 East Rockwell Street. A number of persons interviewed who knew Mr. Paul Rector, find the notion he was the composer to be very plausible. He was known to be one who was willing to express his opinion and viewpoint on most any subject. Fortunately, his son William L. Rector was able to confirm the fact that his father was the "P.J.R." who authored the poem. Paul J. Rector was a graduate of Fenton High School in the Class of 1926. He was the son of Lou Rector, who, at times, seemed to be the "one-man" public works department for the Village during the thirties. .

Scene Two..."Frankly, my dear, I don't give a damn"

According to film historian Stu Kobak, *Gone With The Wind* "is often considered to be the most beloved, enduring and popular film of all time". Before the film was made, Margaret Mitchell's book had sold more than 1.5 million copies. The film won the Oscar for best picture in 1939, and the people of Fenton were anxiously waiting for the movie to be shown at the *Rowena*. J. C. Peck was very good at getting the first run movies into his theatre, long before the theatres in Holly or Linden. However, in this case the Holly Theatre was the first to show this gigantic movie.

Even then it was not until early May before the Holly Theatre announced the special showings. All the seats were reserved for the evening showings. Because of the length of the movie, there were only two sessions a day, matinees at 3 PM and the evening show at 7:30 PM. The admission was 75 cents for unreserved seating at the matinees and $1.00 plus 10 cents tax, for a total of $1.10 for the reserved seating at the late shows.

The people of Fenton vied with the Holly folks for a seat at the movie and the whole three-day engagement was sold out. It wasn't until March of 1941, before the epic drama was shown at the *Rowena*. Those who waited could attend one of the two daily showing, 1:30 PM and 7:15 PM, where all seats were 55 cents for adults and 25 cents for children.

As in the recent years, over 400 movies were released in 1940, but after the banner year of 1939, the truly movie "gems" were few and far between. The two "blockbusters" for the year were probably Disney's "Fantasia" and "Pinocchio", both of which were products of the artists' pen. But there was a real winner with "Grapes Of Wrath" starring Henry Fonda. The tale of the "dust bowl" farmers' migration to California was a tale of recent history that has since become a classic.

There were several Charlie Chan movies with Sidney Toler in the tile role. Dr. Christian was the lead character in several others with Jean Hersholt as the venerable Physician. Young Doctor Kildare, played by Lew Ayres appeared on the screen in several dramas. Roy Rogers, Ken Maynard, William "Hopalong Cassidy" Boyd, Gene Autry, John Mack Brown, Bob Steele, Tim McCoy and Don "Red" Berry were the leads in a plethora of "cowboy" movies. Even established stars like John

Wayne, Errol Flynn, Wallace Berry, and Gary Cooper did their part in portraying the men of the "wild west".

The Three Stooges, Laurel and Hardy, Bob Burns, Joe Penner, Joe E. Brown, Martha Raye, Judy Canova and The Marx Brothers provided the "laughs"…and did a very good job at it!

As you review the "stars" during this period, it seems Hollywood must have been bursting at the seams with "beautiful people". The "beautiful" men included: Frederic Marsh, Errol Flynn, Cesar Romero, Chester Morris, Gary Cooper, Ray Milland, Robert Montgomery, Preston Foster, Victor Mature, John Garfield, Henry Fonda, Lloyd Nolan, Richard Dix, Dick Powell, Clark Gable, Gene Raymond, Richard Arlen, John Wayne, Edmund Lowe, Dennis Morgan, Lew Ayres, Spencer Tracy, Cary Grant, James Cagney, Robert Young, Buster Crabbe, Joel McCrea, Don Ameche, Wayne Morris, Dennis O'Keefe, Bruce Cabot, John Barrymore, Douglas Fairbanks, Jr., Warren Hull, James Dunn, George Raft, George Sanders, William Powell, William Gargan, John Payne, Jon Hall, Brian Aherne, Ronald Coleman, George Brent, Tyrone Power, Lee Tracy, Ronald Reagan, Tony Martin, James Stewart, William Holden, Walter Pidgeon, David Niven, Ralph Bellamy, Fred MacMurray, Laurence Olivier, Bing Crosby, Fred Astaire, Pat O'Brien, Jackie Cooper, Louis Hayward, Mickey Rooney, Franchot Tone, Paul Lucas, Paul Muni, Brain Donlevy, Bob Hope and Adolphe Menjou.

While some of those listed above may not be as "pretty" as others, they were not among those not noted for their looks: Wallace Berry, Edward G. Robinson, Jean Hersholt, Boris Karloff, Albert Dekker, James Gleason, Peter Lorre, Frank Morgan, Frankie Darro, Walter Brennen, Roscoe Karns, Ken Murray, Sidney Toler, Charlie Ruggles, Leon Errol, Charles Bickford, Charles Laughton, Victor McLaglen and Thomas Mitchell,

On the distaff side, some of the movie "beauties of the day" were: Lana Turner, Dorothy Lamour, Carole Lombard, Vivien Leigh, Fay Wray, Lucille Ball, Priscilla Lane, Ann Southern, Rochelle Hudson, Barbara Read, Maureen O'Hara, Loretta Young, Betty Grable, Norma Shearer, Virginia Bruce, Jane Russell, Rosiland Russell, Joan Blondell, Ann Sheridan, Ginger Rogers, Miriam Hopkins, Bette Davis, Alice Faye, Gloria Jean, Ann Francis, Judy Garland, Joan Bennett, Lupe Velez, Margaret Sullivan, Irene Dunn, Mae West, Olivia deHavilland, Madeleine Carroll, Carole Landis, Jeanette MacDonald, Margaret Lockwood, Anna Neagle, Lyn Bari, Greer Garson, Barbara Stanwyck,

Marlene Dietrich, Linda Darnell, Joan Crawford, Myrna Loy, and Jean Arthur. Shirley Temple and Jane Withers were starting to show their "age" and their roles were changing. Martha Raye, Marjorie Rambeau and Judy Canova were cast in comedic roles.

Of the over 400 movies released in the year about 150 were shown on the silver screen of the *Rowena*. Some of the more significant showings were:

Movie Title	Star
Virginia City	Errol Flynn
The Westerner	Gary Cooper
Wyoming	Wallace Berry
A Dispatch From Reuters	Edward G. Robinson
Edison, The Man	Spencer Tracy
The Fighting 69th	James Cagney
Foreign Correspondent	Joel McCrea
The Grapes of Wrath	Henry Fonda
The Great McGinty	Brian Donlevy
Irene	Anna Neagle
Johnny Apollo	Tyrone Power
Knute Rockne, All American	Pat O'Brien, Ron Reagan
Lillian Russell	Alice Faye
The Mark of Zorro	Tyrone Power
My Favorite Wife	Irene Dunn
Northwest Passage	Spencer Tracy
One Million B.C.	Victor Mature
Our Town	William Holden
Pinocchio	
Pride and Prejudice	Greer Garson
Rebecca	Laurence Olivier
The Return of Frank James	Henry Fonda
Road to Singapore	Bing Crosby, Bob Hope
Swiss Family Robinson	Thomas Mitchell
They Drive By Night	George Raft

In September of the year, J.C. Peck initiated a major remodeling of the *Rowena*. The whole front of the theater, from sidewalk to the top of the building was covered with cream and tan colored porcelain enamel panels with stainless steel trim. The front was trimmed in red and maroon.

The remodeling included the construction of a new canopy, which reached from the Western Auto store to Byerly's Food market. The canopy was a truncated "A" shape with changeable letter boards on each side and with the theater name on the front. The panels were translucent with back fluorescent lighting. The canopy had a running border of colored lights. The "new age" of theaters design had arrived in Fenton!

The remodeling eliminated the Fenton Barber and Beauty Shop operated by Harvey Walters and Arlene Pilmore and the space was used for increased seating and a lounge area. Mr. Johnson's Jewelry store survived the change, as did the offices of Horace Hitchcock and George McNeal on the second floor of the Building.

The July 4, 1940 issue of the *Fenton Courier* carried this advertisement sponsored by the Fenton Chamber of Commerce. A map of the area that accompanied this commercial is on page 242.

Scene Three…The Community Center is "the" Center!

With better than a year of experience behind them, Russell Haddon and his small staff, along with a good number of capable and willing volunteers, had the operation of the Community Center in "full gear". From morning to night, day after day, the people of Fenton and the surrounding environs were making good use of the facility and the programs offered at the Center.

The "theater people" in the community finally had a facility to use and enjoy their passion. The Dramatics Club, which had renamed themselves, the "Village Players", were attracting more attention and people interested in performing, learning theater skills and willing to do the work required to produce quality stage plays

Early in the year, the Village Players elected an executive committee and organized themselves into four groups, each with a group leader. Each group was a complete play-producing unit. The four leaders were: Ryan Strom, Thelma Barker, Gladys Abbey and Madeline Wessendorf.

The Village Players Executive Committee was composed of Walter Conrad, Helen Cooley, Gay Decker, Russell Haddon, Thelma Barker and Ramona Burrows. The Executive Committee was to hold a monthly business meeting and coordinate the four units. Each of the four groups was to meet, as they deemed necessary.

Each of the four groups announced their selection of one-act plays as follows: Ryan Strom's group selected "Quiet Please" directed by Miss Florence Manthey; Thelma Barker's group chose "Little Prison" directed by Willard Hatfield: and Gladys Abbey's unit went for "The White Phantom" to be directed by Miss Gladys Abbey. Marlene Wessendorf's group decided to spend their time studying directing and make-up. In April, the three one-act plays were presented at the Community Center. Before the end of the year, the four groups presented a total of six one–act plays.

The Village Players met in October and they decided to abandon their name in lieu of "The Dramatics Club"…back to their original name. However, they met again in November and renamed the group, the "Mimes Club".

The Dramatics Club, now no longer using the name "Village Players" presented a three-act play in mid-October titled "The Brink of Silence". The cast consisted of: Walter Conrad, Ryan Strom, Murray Stanley,

Wilbur Strom, Ramona Burrows, Katherine Dode, Russell Haddon, Mrs. Leon Pavey, Mrs. Herman Wessendorf and Betty Cook.

The Community Chorus under the direction of Miss Frances Hicks presented the Light Opera "The Battered Bride" to a full house audience of over 320 in early February. Miss Hicks recruited a group of musicians as accompanists: Violins: John Mazago, the Master of the Flint Symphony and Miss Mary Cosgrove. Bass Violinist Miss Marjorbelle Bordeau, also of the Flint Symphony. Richmond Browne of Fenton was the pianist.

A group of folk dancers, in native Czech costume, appeared throughout the opera, as well as the Fenton Chorus group composed of: Thor Neilsen, Mr. and Mrs. Wayne Townsend, Mrs. Rose McCann, Russell Haddon, Miss Gladys Abbey, Mrs. Gertrude Bard, Miss Jane Garvey, Miss Lois Tysse, Miss Lucille Miller, Miss Eileen Freeman, Ralph Petts, Henry Alchin, Edward Mitts, Mrs. Peter Morea, Mrs. August Arndt, Miss Rosalind Gorney, Mrs. Leo Weigant, Dana MaWhinney and Miss Loreen Harding.

In March another group of men came together to produce an old-time Minstrel Show. The Minstrel Show construct had probably waned in recent years, and the local fellows thought it was time to revive it.

In today's political and cultural environment it is difficult to comprehend how this could occur, even be considered. However, during this time and for decades previously, white actors appearing in "black face" was not unusual.

After all, Al Jolson was one of the leading male singers and movie actors, and he traditionally appeared in "black face". His song hits "Mammy", "Sewanee" and "Sonny Boy" were all presented in the Negro idiom.

Two white actors, Charles Correll and Freeman Gosden, were the principal characters in a popular radio comedy show in which they played two stereotype Negroes. Further, professional minstrel shows had toured the country and the minstrels were popular and accepted by the general public

The Minstrel Show was presented at the Community Center on two consecutive nights to standing room only crowds. The Chairman of the "Minstrel Men" was Gerald Rawson. The organizing group elected Grant Wright as their Secretary, Ray Randolph as the Music Director and Property Managers Ray Shepard and Ed Turner.

The *Fenton Courier* reported, "…the show was a surprise to many. Besides good laughs and some good orchestra music, the general staging of the performance deserves mention".

The End Men of the show were: Gerald Rawson, Ryan Strom, Walter Conrad, Charles Joslyn and John Hoskins. The show opened with a number by the chorus and was followed by "Steppin' Around" in which the entire ensemble participated.

Some of the performances noteworthy of special mention were: the dancing of Leon "Snowball" Jolly; Tenor Lee Kelly's outstanding rendition of "A Beautiful Girl Is Like A Melody; Bass Thor Nielsen's "Old Black Joe" and Ray Seger's Harmonica solos.

The men in the chorus were: Lee Kelly, Thor Neilsen, Harold Bristol, Ed Bretzke, Ray Seger, Bud Crane, Russell Haddon, Edward Turner and Joe Bradley.

The band consisted of; Merle Parker, Don Alchin, Al Wheeler, Irving Gould, Bob Harris, Ralph Crawford, Dick Smale and John Hoskins.

The show ran for over two hours and after the final performance, plans to take the show "on the road" were being considered. A short time later, an abbreviated company produced the show in Swartz Creek.

Later, the group reorganized as "The Fenton Variety Club" and elected their officers: President Gerald Rawson, V.P. Ryan Strom, Secretary Grant Wright, Properties: Ed Turner and Ray Seger and Librarian Roy Randolph.

The actors used the stage at the Community Center for a considerable amount of the available time, however they didn't have a monopoly. The Center had scheduled a very ambitious "Lecture Series"

Mr. Winfield Line and his wife, Dr. Grace Song Line, delivered the "kick-off" lecture. Mr. Line and his Korean-born wife spoke on the situation in Japanese controlled Korea. The Lines were very popular on the lecture circuit delivering over 100 lectures in Michigan in the last year. Their illustrated presentation, using colored motion pictures, was very informative and expertly delivered.

Later, Dr. Robert H. McDowell, of the University of Michigan, spoke on a current world problem when he discussed the situation in the "Near East". In the present day, the "Near East" is usually referred to as the "Middle East".

A couple months later the favorite "outdoors" enthusiast, Journalist Ben East returned to Fenton to inform the audience about the wonders of Michigan's wilderness

The main room of the Community Center was a very busy space during the year. Interspersed between the plays and the lectures there were several concerts, dance recitals and vocal presentations.

While all these festivities were happening in the town, the people of Finland were defending themselves from an invasion by the forces of the Soviet Union. Consequently, there were several fund raising and relief efforts underway to provide help to the Finns. One such effort was the appearance of a Finnish Male Chorus at the center. This was accompanied by a fund drive led by George Green, the President of the State Savings Bank. The citizens were quite generous in their support of the Finnish Relief Fund effort.

In early June, the Fenton Community Center was the site of two excellent shows. Frances Hicks presented her students in their "Spring" concert on two consecutive evenings. On the first evening the "young" students were featured. The second evening was assigned to the "older" students. As usual, Miss Hicks and her students delivered an excellent performance.

The "Youngsters" group was composed of: Buddy Roberts, Virginia Ware, Dorothy Tobin, Walter Tobin, Freddie Becker, Martha Jean Swanson, Frances Foreman, Harold Kiess, Joyce Eedy, Martha Marshall, Don Foreman, Mary Nell Walker, Gladys Barton and Milton Rosenbaum.

The "older" group consisted of: Beverly Boyer, Barbara Cosand, Esther Parker, Lauren Kretchmar, Patsy Hagerman, Shirley Shepard, Virginia Parker, Madge Mikesell, Beth Ann Morehouse, Lois Dowen, Ronald Wilson, Edna Hook, Dorothy Wood, Barbara Clark, Neil Walker, Donna Morea, Ann Hultin and Betty Jean DeVore.

Soon after, Leon Jolly offered his students in a dance recital. The year's work of Leon Jolly and his students was presented at the Community Center. The program offered a Harmonica Band, acrobatic dancing, a vocal selection, a comedy skit by the Variety Club, an exhibition tap dance and a number by seven eight-year old little girls.

The pupils of Leon Jolly appearing in the recital were: Elizabeth Ann Dunn, Anne Boilore, Gail Hagerman, Billy Freeman, Jerry Hatfield, Janice Blanchard, Lois Searight, Bruce Trimmer, Jack Pellett, Nancy Bly, Doris Bowman, Barbara Ireland, June Boilore, Rosemary Howe, Marion Eastman, Jane Gamble, Alice Moorman, Marie Moorman, Marion Cooper, Murray Bell, Barbara Crocker, Jacqueline Roberts, Laura Hockey, Joan Clark, Joyce Helmboldt, Phyllis McCormick, Jeannine Turner and Leah Merrick. The pianist was Leone Hagerman.

The Fenton City Band experienced another very successful year. The Band played weekly concerts throughout the summer months, participated in the holiday parades and other civic functions such as Christmas program at the Community Center and the a St. John Barbeque outing in the fall.

The Band began the year with their annual meeting at the Community Center. Before electing their officers for the year, the members participated in a Fish and Chips supper prepared by Willard Hatfield, the meat manager at the A & P and erstwhile performer with the Village Players…and also an excellent cook.

The Band elected Fred Parker as their President, Henry Willing as their Secretary, Art Glaspill as Treasurer and Charles Simons as their Manager. The Executive Committee members elected to serve were: Glen Carpenter, Don Alchin and Clifford Roberts.

The Fenton City Band continued to play weekly summer concerts but no performance received more acclaim than the "winter" concert they presented in cooperation with Miss Frances' Community Chorus in October. Director Stanton and Miss Hicks found the *Fenton Courier* exuberant in their praise for the performance of both organizations.

Miss Hicks continued her good work by arranging to have her Fenton Chorus join the Hartland Chorus in their annual presentation of the "Messiah". The "Messiah" was presented to full houses in Hartland and at the Community Center. The Fenton production was on December 22nd as part of the Christmas celebrations at the Center.

Mrs. W.T. MaWhinney, Miss Marie Warren of Flint, Lester McCoy and Vernon Syring sang the solo parts. A twenty-five-piece orchestra from Hartland and Flint provided the accompanying music

Village President Harry Lemen was the "sparkplug" that ignited the Christmas Party at the Center. A huge tree was well decorated and lighted and placed in front of the Center. On the evening of December 23rd a large group of townsfolk, gathered there to sing Christmas Carols and participate in the Christmas program.

A Brass Quartet composed of Bob Brundel, solo cornet; Alfred Bathhurst, Trombone; Clarence Schoup, First Cornet; and Gerald Durand, Trombone joined with the Fenton Chorus to fill the air with Christmas music. The Reverend W. Thomas Smith of St. Jude's read the Christmas story from St. Luke. Following the outdoor celebration, the public was invited to tour the Holy Manger scene arranged in the Center's Auditorium.

During the year many "dances" were held at the Center. Starting with the "Gay Nineties" costume ball in early January sponsored by the Village Players, with Mrs. L.A. Wilson in charge, to the "Christmas Dance" in late December, the Center was the venue for all kinds of dance parties.

The Community Center was also the scene of some very interesting "shows" other than dances, recitals, plays and parties. The Grange and the Garden Club joined together in the late spring to hold a "Garden Show". And then again, in June, held a "Flower Show". These events, the "first of their kind" were well attended and enjoyed by those in attendance.

In early October, the Community Center was the scene of "…two days of interesting exhibits, programs of music, pictures, speakers, prizes and dancing…" The Second Annual Farm Festival was underway.

The two days of festivities included a concert by the Fenton High School Band, an address by Elmer Beamer, the State Commissioner of Agriculture, Motion pictures, hobby exhibits, "guessing contests", bake sales and the showings of fruits, vegetables, grain, flowers, eggs, canned goods and others farm and home products.

There were commercial exhibitors, including several local merchants, present to show the latest in farm equipment

The evenings were the "fun" time for those attending. The Harvest Old Time dance on Saturday night capped the two-day event.

As a result of an "Interest Survey' conducted in the first year, the Community Center had organized many classes and clubs, with very diverse interests and activities. One of the most prominent, and mentioned most frequently was the Dramatics Club aka Village Players, Mimes Club or whatever.

One of the clubs, the "Hikers Club", for example, met regularly, rain, shine, snow or hail, and hiked! Long winter hikes usually ended up in the home of George Grove or one of the other members where they recuperated with a hot buttered rum or hot chocolate. Russell Haddon recalls being on the hike to the Tyrone Gardens, which was their 16th hike of the year, and put them over the 100-mile mark.

Other clubs required less physical exertion. William "Bill" Marshall, Councilman and Barber, was an avid fisherman and hunter. Consequently, it was not unusual to find Bill Marshall conducting a class on "Fly Tying" at the Community Center.

One of the classes was specifically designed for the young ladies of the community. This was the "Beauty" class. Its motto was "Your Carriage,

Madam".   The class provided instruction to the young women
"showing how the feet, knees, head and chest should be used in
standing, sitting and bending."

While most of the events, especially in the winter months, were
conducted in the Center's building, the summer programs turned to the
outside areas. The Community Fund and some money from the WPA
funded the Summer Playground program. Coach Lester Miller and
Music Teacher Thelma Barker from the Fenton High School were
employed to conduct the summer program. Swimming classes were
held at Silver Lake. It is interesting to learn the transportation of the
swimmers to Silver Lake relied on volunteer drivers from the
community.

The tennis courts, to the rear of the Center Building, just east of the
Shiawassee River Bridge on Caroline Street, were completed and opened
for play in July of the year.   There were two tennis courts, a
shuffleboard court and a horseshoe-pitching pit in the area.

The "Grand" opening of these facilities was done with some
"fanfare". Village President Lemen and some town dignitaries were on
hand for the opening and the "start up " program was well organized.
There were some exhibition tennis matches with Buster Bender and
Clifford Snyder, Shuffleboard instruction by Claude Williams and some
tips on Horseshoes by Richmond Barnes.

As winter approached, the Village decided to create a skating rink on
the tennis court surface. This rink was to be used for the "little folks"
and the "big bruisers" were urged to skate somewhere else, the pond
was suggested since the ice was good and thick there this year.

Even though the Board of Governors began developing programs and
activities before a Director was "on board", the programming of
activities took a major step forward when the new Director, Russell
Haddon, organized the "Community Council" in early May.

A number of citizens were invited to meet an form the Community
Council and at their first meeting they selected Clarence Heemstra, the
Superintendent of the Fenton Schools, as their Temporary Chairman
and Barbara Barnes as their Secretary. The mission of the Council was
described at the meeting as a "policy making body" and to coordinate
the many activities and the 20 organizations expressing a desire to use
the Center's facilities.

At the following meeting in late June, the group elected the members
of the Executive Committee and the Officers for the Community
Council. The officers were: President C. R. Heemstra, V.P. Russell

Haddon and Secretary Barbara Barnes. The Executive Committee members were: Charles Simonas, Alice Merrick, Reverend W. Thomas Smith, Zella White, Lucille Miller, Elton Austin and Joe Bottecelli.

In July, Russell Haddon presented his report to the Center's Board of Governors. He reported that during the last year, the Center hosted an average of 3.4 meetings per day, with a total of 1266 meetings, 74 dances, 78 private parties and 47 dinners.

Even with all this positive news, one should note there were still people in Fenton who were unemployed or underemployed and in a real sense "hurting". While economic conditions were improving, one of the new Directors "pet" projects was the operation of an employment office in the Center. The Center's employment operations were coordinated with those of the State and County governments. The Center kept a list of those seeking employment and responded to those employers seeking help. There were 275 individuals registered with the Center's employment office in June of 1940 and the principal prospects for employment were for girls and women in housework and nursing. For men, the opportunities were principally in farm labor. Most of those who sought employment were for domestic service, waitress and home care positions.

Mr. Haddon credited the success of the Center to the many volunteers who had devoted their time and efforts to "make it work" by leading the 32 classes and clubs. The myriad of adult education programs, recreation, social and youth activities had involved 529 adults and 191 youth leaders, all volunteers. In addition there had been 128 "out-of-towners" volunteering and benefiting the programs.

As an example he pointed with pride to four groups and their leaders who had great success in the past year. He mentioned Gerald Rawson and the Variety Club (The Minstrel fellows), Mrs. John Johnson and Gay Decker of the Village Players, Miss Frances Hicks of the Community Chorus and Ray Seger and his Harmonica Club.

As the year drew to an end, the Board of Governors received the resignation of Floyd Chapin. Mr. Chapin had a long record of many years of public service, having served as President of the Village and as a member of the Village Council. He was presently serving as the Village Assessor. The Board replaced Mr. Chapin with Mr. Elton Austin, then the Manager of the local A & P store. Elton Austin had served the community in a variety of roles, and his character was beyond reproach.

And finally, Russell Haddon was appointed as the permanent Director of the Center, after finally satisfying the additional college courses requirement imposed by the Dean of the Graduate School at the University of Michigan.

At about the same time, the Board elected Harry Lemen to serve as Chairman. Mr. Lemen was serving on the Board as specified in the agreement with the Rackham people whereby the President of the Village would automatically be a member of the Community Center's Board of Governors

The Community Center reported their financial solvency, a large and growing number of activities and participants., and a capable Director and Board of Governors in charge. After its first full year of operation, everyone was looking forward to an even more interesting and successful year in 1941.

Fenton Chorus under direction of Miss Frances Hicks. Two men standing behind pianist on left are Russell Haddon and Thor Neilsen. Man stand in front of drape opening with sweater and tie is Ronald Butler. Young man in back row between two women is Neil Walker. All others are not identified. Location is in main hall of Community Center. Period: Late Thirties.

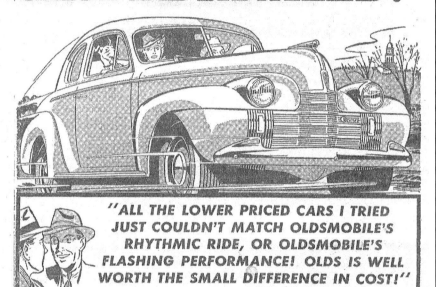

Scene Four…What's Happening in Government?

It has been said that no function of government is more important than providing security for its citizens. This is the principal responsibility of the Federal government and it is equally true for the small communities, just like it was for the Village of Fenton in 1940.

Leon Durkee had served the Village and the community for the past decade, first as the "Nightwatch" and later as the "first" Deputy Marshall. The Village Council had abandoned the common practice of many small communities, whereby the "Nightwatch" collected fees from local merchants and other property owners as part of his compensation for serving. This practice reduced the expenditures of the governmental unit, but it did not contribute to the professionalism of its "police" officers.

In 1939 they had appointed the City Engineer as the Village Marshall and named Leon Durkee as the Deputy Marshall. His part-time assistant, Basil Chappelle, was also made a Deputy Marshall.

As the year began, both Leon Durkee and Basil Chappelle asked the Village Council for "more money". After a week of deliberation, the Council appointed Leon Durkee as First Deputy Marshall at a salary of $2,500 a year with 2 weeks of paid vacation. He would, however, be required to maintain his own car and "try doors of businesses each night". Later, the Council approved the purchase of two new pairs of pants and a cap for his Police uniform.

Basil Chappelle, a full-time barber, was named 2nd Deputy Marshall with a compensation of $6 for each night he worked.

At the same meeting, the Council approved paying Ray Seger $9 per week for operating the City Dump. It was at this time they also approved Mr. Seger's request for a small shanty to protect him during inclement weather. He said that in the past when it rained he would climb under a wheelbarrow, however as he has aged, this is becoming more difficult for him. The Council approved the building of a 10 x 12 foot shed costing $29,95 for material and $20 for labor.

A couple months later Councilman Nelson Curtis caused a bit of brouhaha when he brought up the subject of "stealing" scrap metal from the dump. Some of members seemed to be upset with the course of the discussion and resolved the issue by instructing Mr. Seger to place "NO Stealing" signs at the dump. They further clarified the issue by confirming that the caretaker of the dump, Mr. Seger, had every right to salvage scrap metal from the dump and sell it for his benefit.

One of the first problems facing the new Village Marshall John Bacon and the First and Second Deputies was the State's ban on all angle parking on State road routes. Since US 23 traversed Leroy Street through the town, the entire angle parking in the Leroy Street business district would be required to change to parallel parking!

The scarcity of parking spaces in the "downtown" area was already becoming a problem since the building of the Community Center reduced the available parking in that area..

By June, they had re-marked the lines of the parking space in the downtown area and the citizens had to learn how to parallel park! The change from angle to parallel parking reduced the number of downtown parking spaces by some 40 spaces.

At this time, the Curtis-Wolverton Post of the Veterans of Foreign Wars who held a lease to use a vacant lot owned by the Grand Trunk Railroad south of the Railroad Depot came forward with a proposal. Aware of the problem facing the community, VFW Post offered the land to the Village for use as a parking lot. The Village happily accepted the offer and proceeded to prepare a graveled parking area for 136 cars parking on an angle.

The lot was lighted and on Saturday nights there was an attendant to assist those using the lot. John Bacon, in his other capacity as Village Engineer, announced that parking there was "perfectly safe" and "convenient". The entrance to the lot was on Pine Street and the exit on East Street. The sign over the entrance credited the V.F. W. for their contribution in providing the new parking lot.

Quite often the candidates for the Village offices ran unopposed, even though there were two local political parties, the Citizens and the People's Parties. Usually the candidates nominated by the Citizens group were elected, so frequently, the People's Party wouldn't even bother to caucus and nominate their candidates. The Editor of the *Fenton Courier* was very upset with this situation and often editorialized about the need to have a choice in the elections. In 1940, he was happy to announce that both parties had caucused and nominated a full slate for the annual Village elections.

The Citizen's Caucus met first and unsurprisingly nominated Harry Lemen as their candidate for Village President.. They also proposed the return of Walter Conrad as Village Clerk, D.R. Stiles for Treasurer and Floyd Chapin as Assessor. Their candidates for the three spots on the

Village Council were: Gus Lutz, John Hoskins and William J. Burkett. Lutz and Hoskins were incumbents and when William Marshall declined to run, William Burkett, a former Superintendent of Fenton Schools, was nominated to take his place..

A few weeks later, the Peoples Party caucused and nominated Harry Lowe for Village President. Harry Lowe was serving as President of the Fenton School Board. They nominated Morris Sanders for Village Clerk and D.R. Stiles for Village Treasurer. Their nominations for the three seats on the Village Council were: John Weidman, Bert Lockwood and R.P. Smith.

Since both parties nominated D.R. "Ray" Stiles, he had to decline one of the parties. He chose to stay with the Peoples Party since he had originally won election as a candidate of that party. The Citizens Party subsequently placed Ray Hunt on the ballot in the vacated spot.

The April election did not produce any "upsets". The Citizen's ticket prevailed except for the Treasurer's spot. Consequently, Harry Lemen was returned to office along with William Conrad and D.R. Stiles. Gus Lutz, John Hoskins and William Burkett joined the sitting trustees: Nelson Curtis, Charles Stein and Floyd Poppy.

William "Bill" Marshall may have other "fish to fry" when he stepped aside in the Village election. In the following General election he was the Republican candidate for County Sheriff.

Earlier in the year, the Village Attorney, Maurice Matthews, wrote Harry Lemen and the council, suggesting that the Council instruct the Treasurer to pay and retire the outstanding bond indebtedness. If that would be done, the Village " ...will be out of debt". He further wrote, "that...will be a memorable record, for no Village of Fenton Council has closed its term out of debt for over fifty years". However, the "pay as you go" policy followed by Lemen and the council was about to face a real financial hill to climb, as the need to build a sewage disposal system was imminent.

A very important election was held in October 1938, when the voters approved the sale of $20,000 in bonds to help finance the building of a sewage disposal plant. However, the PWA grant, while approved, was not funded because of the lack of funds at that agency. Consequently, in early February, President Lemen went to the public again with a proposal to approve an additional $23,000 to go with the previously approved $13,000 for a total of $36,000. This was the amount needed to meet the estimated costs of building a new sewage disposal system. Although the turnout was relatively small, the voters overwhelmingly approved the sale of the bonds and the construction of the sewage disposal plant.

President Lemen and the Council immediately began the process of contracting for the building of a sewage disposal plant and system. The site was purchased and surveyed by the County Surveyor. The builder was selected and contracts approved. Construction began as the year was ending.

Another public service problem was addressed directly. Certain parts of the village on the higher ground, on occasion, suffered from low water pressure. It was proposed to build a storage tank on the high ground south of town to remedy this pressure problem. The Water Commission composed of Fred Horrell, Ray Hunt and James Bryce reported the project would proceed on a "pay as you go" basis.

In August an old issue was revisited. Mr. William H. Keddy sued the Village President and each Council member for failure to solve the pollution problem, which was affecting his property downstream on the Shiawassee River. The issue was referred to the Village Attorney, Maurice Matthews.

In January the bids on the construction of the new Post Office were solicited. One month later when the bids were opened the contract for building the "Federal Building" was awarded to Sorenson-Gross Construction Company of Flint, Michigan. Construction proceeded through the following months and finally the building was sufficiently near completion to hold the Dedication Ceremonies on October 24[th.]

Postmaster Dennis Kelleher planned to move the postal operation from the storefront on Leroy Street by the 1st of November. On "Dedication" day, the public assembled in front of the new Post office.

The Fenton High School band was present as were the Village President Harry Lemen and the Superintendent of Schools Clarence Heemstra. A small crowd gathered in the street as each of the dignitaries made some forgettable remarks

The talk around town was about how the town was growing. But did the census confirm this growth? The Census report issued in late June showed about a 6% population growth in the Village of Fenton and about 22.5% growth in Fenton Township over the ten-year period from 1930 to 1940.

	Year1930	Year 1940
Fenton Township	4887	5990
Village of Fenton	3171	3358

Scene Five…Clubs and Churches

There were no Caliphs or Rabbis in the Fenton Clergy fraternity as of 1940, but the Ministers, Pastors, Priests…the leaders of the community's Christian churches met the diverse spiritual needs of their congregations and also played a very influential role in all aspects of the life of the Village of Fenton. Fenton was a "church-going" town

While some may dispute the selection, the newspaper accounts of the church activities, indicated the six leading churches in the town were the: First Presbyterian, the Trinity Lutheran, First Baptist, Methodist Episcopal, St. Jude's Episcopal and St. John Roman Catholic.

Early in the year, the fraternity welcomed the Reverend Wesley J. Dudgeon as the new pastor at the Methodist Episcopal Church. The church had been without a minister since the transfer of the Reverend A.T. F Butt to a church in Algonac, Michigan in September 1939.

The Reverend Dr. J. Stanley Mitchell presided at the Presbyterian Church and had established himself as a fine speaker who seemed to deliver most of the Invocations or Benedictions at the many banquets and other public meetings.

The Trinity Lutheran Church's mentor was the Reverend Paul J. Mroch who not only led his flock at his church, but also was recognized as an outstanding bowler and softball player in the town leagues.

The Reverend William Thomas Smith of St. Jude's was a jewel of a man with many interests in and outside his church. He was active in the early days of organizing the activities of the Community Center, appeared before the Village Council as an advocate for a safe skating rink for the Village children of all ages, and was active as an actor in the Community Center's Dramatic club.

The Reverend Father Daniel P. Tighe was the Priest at St. John. He was an excellent golfer and had a passion for good cigars. His principal goal for his church community was the establishment of a church school. His dream would come to fruition, but years after his passing. He began the St. John Barbeque as an annual fundraiser for the church and its outreach activities. In his promotion of the event, he would always suggest one of his friends from the Detroit Tigers would "likely" make an appearance at the outing. As the date for the 1940 Barbeque approached, he happened to mention to the *Fenton Courier* that he thought Schoolboy Rowe might drop by..

The First Baptist church began the year with the Reverend Clare Whaley as their pastor. However, in late March, Reverend Whaley left Fenton for a new church in Wixom, Michigan. In late April the congregation of the First Baptist Church met and voted unanimously to "withdraw the ordination" of Clare Whaley. There was no public explanation for this action, but in the Baptist church, the congregation has the authority to bestow or remove the ordination of a person serving as the church pastor. In June, the Church accepted Russell Haggard as their new minister.

The Men's Fellowship, while based in the Methodist Episcopal Church, attracted members and participants from all the male population of Fenton and it's surrounding area.. The Fellowship generally planned a series of banquets for the "season" which began in October and met each month through the winter months and ending with the banquet in April. Each Banquet meeting had a different theme.

With Ray Cummings as Program Chairman, the January meeting featured Professor Howard Rather of Michigan State College. George W. Pellett introduced Dr. Rather. Mr. Pellett had been a classmate of the Professor at MSC before World War I and served with him during the war. Following the speech, The Village Players presented a one-act play. The banquet was held at the Community Center

Nathaniel "Than" Chestnut, who was the Chief Steward in charge of the food service for the affair, a meal that consisted of Corned Beef, Cabbage, Potatoes and Apple Pie, remarked that, in view of the total weight of the food prepared, "each of the diners should have gained an average of 2 ½ pounds at the banquet!"

The "Supper Squad" assisting Mr. Cummings with the banquet were: Ray Bradshaw, R.B. Renwick, W.R. Davis, S.M Wilson, Clare Lake, Donald Lake, Martin Parker, Arthur Heasnick, Ray Nichols, M.E. Hinkley, Y. C. Shine, B. G. McGarry, David Cox, Jack Klinger, John Hockett, Art Embury, Harry Falling, John Newton, Clarence Hall, George Kidder, Joe Bottecelli, Guy Gillem, Roy Wood, Angus Patterson, W.F. Close and Joseph Skinner.

The Men's Fellowship meeting for February was their annual Father-Son banquet. Frank Farry, Flint Boy Scout executive was the speaker. Those conducting the event warned that because of the increased membership, the initial ticket sales would be limited to the members and those fathers who had not yet purchased tickets for their sons may "be out of luck".

The Supper Squad for the February banquet was: Burton Street, Irving Gould, Ralph Winn, Raymond Hyde, E.E. Crane, R. G. Stoddard, Dr. M. B. Smith, Carl Holm, John Dery, Albert Welch, Hoyt Glaspie, Frank Collins, R. J. Buckley, Cornell Dexter, Robert Holtforth, Fred Williams, Julian Bristol, Harold Bristol, Grant Wright, Ralph Ellsworth, Elwood Ellsworth, Louis Kardatzki, Vernon Wright, Mark Gordon, Hollis Winn, John Turco, Vern Eaton, Murray Chase, W. F. Close, Angus Patterson, Daniel Wilcox, Peter Morea, Harold Schupbach, Leo Hall, Myron Churchill, Ralph E. Garrett, Claude Willover, T. Woodworth, Walter Lawson, Don Burdick and Ray Smith.

The March meeting of the Men's Fellowship was another "sell-out" with over 250 people attending. Some tickets were sold at the door "if any vacancies occurred". William J. Cameron, who was a noted speaker appearing on the radio program, "The Ford Sunday Evening Hour", was the guest speaker. Messrs. Leon Maxwell and Sidney Mitchell led the community singing and "Than" Chesnut continued as the "Steward" in charge of the food. As usual, the Methodist ladies prepared the supper for those attending in the Community Center main hall.

The *Fenton Courier*", commenting on Mr. Cameron's inspiring address, saying his speech could have been titled "Americanism". In the spring of 1940, as Americans watched the developments in Europe, the spirit of "Americanism" was sweeping across the nation.

The Men's Fellowship's last meeting for their season was in April and was their annual "Ladies Night". The year had seen the Men's Fellowship experience a new high in membership with over 250 men joining the organization.

The "Ladies Night" attendees at the Community Center were witness to one of the leading "pulpit orators, not only of Michigan, but of the United States" so proclaimed the *Fenton Courier*.

Dr. Henry Hill Crane's address was titled "Americanism" and was "somewhat different from the usual type and by his clever oratorical tricks kept his audience thoroughly alert from beginning to end", so reported the *Fenton Courier*. Dr. Crane was the pastor of the Central Methodist church in Detroit.

The Reverend Ira W. Cargo, who conceived and organized the Men's Fellowship when he was the pastor of the Fenton Methodist church, was visiting in Fenton and was present for the occasion. To the applause of his many friends and others in attendance, he expressed his deep satisfaction with the progress and success of the Fellowship

No sooner had the last banquet for the year been competed before the Fellowship's Executive Committee began planning the programs for the coming season. The program chairman for the upcoming season was the Reverend J. Stanley Mitchell.

The first meeting of the new season was held on October 7th at the Community Center, with the Methodist ladies preparing the food as usual. The speaker for this event was Agent John Biggs of the Detroit office of the Federal Bureau of Investigation. The event was very well attended, with capacity crowds of over 250 sitting for dinner.

The annual banquet honoring the Fenton High School football team was held in November and it featured the University of Michigan's assistant football coach Wally Weber. Wally Weber illustrated his talk with movies of selected plays from Michigan football games. Wally Weber was one of the most entertaining of football speakers. He was a very likeable person and a natural humorist. The overflow crowd of over 260 people were also entertained by Ford Dixie Eight, a "noted colored singing group" arranged with the Ford Motor Company by Theisen-Stein, the local Ford dealers.

. The planning was complete for the meetings scheduled for the first months in 1941. The themes selected for each of the meetings were as follows: January- Farmer's Night; February-Annual Father-Son Banquet; March-Appropriate Lenten Program; and the final program for the season- April-Ladies Night.

From the newspaper reports of 1940, it seems the other clubs in Fenton were enjoying a good year just like the Men's Fellowship. It appears that all the clubs continued to meet and many new clubs were organized. Club activity continued to be a major social activity.

Most of clubs meeting during the daylight hours were women's clubs, while the men's organizations met after working hours.

A few clubs, not mentioned in previous years, bore some very unusual, unexplainable names. For example, there was the "Green Dragons", whose motto was " To Treat Others As You Would Like to Be Treated". Shouldn't one ask why they didn't name themselves the "Golden Rule" Club? They started their year out with their Annual New Years Party at the home of Mr. and Mrs. Erwin Witherell

The "Glen Arbor Gleaners" had a Oyster Stew Supper at the home of Mrs. A. Swanebeck in early January.. Since the Swanebecks were farmer residents of Fenton Township, one can only assume the Gleaners had something to do with farming.

A veterans organization, the "Military Order of the Cooties" or M.O.C., had appeared in earlier newspaper reports, but in 1940 it emerged as a growing organization affiliated with the Veterans of Foreign Wars Curtis-Wolverton Post in Fenton. One of its first public activities was the sponsorship of a dance at the *Rainbow Gardens,* a dance hall/roller skating rink in Argentine. William "Bill" Harris was the Chairman for the event.

As they had done in the past couple of years, the James Dewitt Post of the American Legion sponsored three young men at the Wolverine Boys State encampment on the campus of Michigan State College. The Industrial Machine Tool Company, the F. & A.M. lodge and the XX Club provided the funds to send the boys to the three-week event. The boys selected were: Albert Turco, Charles McKeon and Richard Smale, all of the Senior class at Fenton High School.

The Fenton Music Club sponsored a very ambitious, but successful, program in mid April, called their "Spring Fest". The event attracted over 150 guests to the Community Center and was recognized as being "interesting and artistically performed" by the *Fenton Courier* reporter.

Following the welcome address by the Music Club's President, Mrs. D. C. Smale, the program opened with the Fenton Chorus singing "Welcome Sweet Springtime" by Rubenstein. The program included Soprano Solos by Mrs. Paul Bristol; a Violin Solo by Mrs. Verna Payne Moffatt of Flint; Piano Solos by Miss Alice VanAtta; a piano quartet composed of Miss Alice VanAtta, Miss Dorothy Giles, Mrs. H.K. Schaefer and Miss Gloria Reid; Soprano Solos by Mrs. Francis MaWhinney; a Violin Obbligato by Mrs. Moffatt; and a reading by Mrs. L.A. Wilson. The accompanists for the program were Miss Alice VanAtta and Miss Miriam Ryle. The *Fenton Courier* reported that "dainty refreshments" were served by. Mrs. W.H. Skillen and Mrs. C.B. Hamilton.

In mid-May, the Child Study Club sponsored a Mother-Daughter Banquet. The banquet was held at the Community Center and was a substantial success with over 300 attending. The Reverend Wesley Dudgeon, who had only recently arrived in Fenton, delivered the invocation. Mrs. Clarence Heemstra, the Club's President, welcomed the guests and introduced the Toastmistress for the evening, Mrs. L. Swanson. Mrs. Morgan, Misses Dorothy Austin and Dawn Hagerman made the customary exchanges of toasts to the Mothers and the Daughters

Magician David L. Norton, who excited the gathering with his different and interesting tricks, provided the principal entertainment. Miss Margreta Reid presented a violin solo and was accompanied on the piano by her sister, Gloria Reid.

Plants were presented as gifts to Mrs. Jessie Trowbridge, mother of Mrs. R.E. Silver, as being the oldest mother present; to Mrs. E. W. Silver for being the youngest mother present: and to Mrs. Fred Powers for having the most daughters, all eight of whom were present. The evening closed with the singing of "God Bless America".

One organization, the Fenton Welfare Association, headed by C. S. Rounds, was a group of volunteers concerned with meeting the needs of some of the more unfortunate families and people in the area. They depended on their funding from volunteer donations and an occasional fund raising activity.

For example, early in the year, the Association sponsored an "old-fashioned" box social at the Community Center and raised several hundred dollars for their effort. The *Fenton Independent* urged the "ladies to bring a box lunch fixed up pretty".

The church organizations such as the Cornerstone groups at the First Presbyterian Church continued to be active as they were in recent years. One group in particular received special notice in the community: The St. John Alter Society sponsored a "Mother-Son" banquet and had over 300 individuals attend. The banquet was held in the Community Center in February and was the first event of its kind in Fenton Following the opening prayer by the Reverend Father D.P. Tighe, Don J. Stein, who served as the Toastmaster introduced Mrs. Donald Dunn who gave a toast to the sons. A toast to the mothers by Maurice Foley followed. The speaker for the affair was Frank Farry, Flint Boy Scout Executive. Gerald Durand offered a trombone solo and an Instrumental Ensemble from Linden High School furnished the dinner music.

Most of the clubs were now well-established clubs, especially those like the Child Study Clubs, Bayview and Entre Nous. Their primary activities were almost exclusively social, and provided an opportunity for the women of the town to "get out of the house" and enjoy an afternoon with friends. A review of their activates over the years doesn't indicate much change from year to year. They all seemed to conduct similar activities and maintain the same membership year after year. The table below identifies some of the more active members of a few of the most active clubs in town.

Pro To Child Study Club	Pres. Mrs. William Gamble, Marie Stewart, Pauline Rockman, Mrs. Paul Shagne, Mrs. George Kidder: Mrs. Champ O'Heren, Mrs. Don Burdick, Mrs. R.B. Graham, Mrs. Brooks Kinne, Mrs. Pete Moorman
Junior Child Study Club	Pres. Mrs. Harry Alchin, Mrs. John Chapman, Mrs. Robert Lutz, Mrs. Earl Helmboldt, Mrs. Lynn Welch, Mrs. Ernest Hungerford, Mrs. John Millington, Mrs. Herman Wessendorf, Mrs. Gordon Bly,
Child Study Club	Pres. Mrs. C. R. Heemstra, Mrs. Charles Lea, Mrs. C.D. Arrand, Mrs. Harry T. Adams, Mrs. Don Alchin, Mrs. C.E. Trimmer, Mrs. Ray Hagerman, Mrs. Ed Morgan
The Music Club	Pres. Mrs. MaWhinney, Mrs. Lowell Swanson, Mrs. Clair Reid, Mrs. Leo Hall, Miss Mabel VanAtta, Miss Dorothy Giles, Mrs. H. Schaefer, Mrs. Thor Neilsen, Miss Alice VanAtta
Degree of Honor	Pres. Minnie Moore, Allie Parker, Ester Lord
Townsend Club	Pres. Elmer Ellsworth, Fred Clark
Isaac Walton League	Pres. Lloyd Kelly, Douglas Savage,: Henry Alchin
I.O.O.F. (Oddfellows)	NG: Clinton Kelly, Charles Truchan, John Millington, George L. Anglen
Rebekahs	NG: Miss Verna Eldred, Mrs. L. J. McGraw
XX Club	Pres. K.C Asman, Elton Austin, George W. Pellett, Clarence Heemstra, Robert Smith, Clifford Phillips

Entre Nous	Mrs. George Pellett, Mrs. S.F. Beach, Mrs. Harry Adams, Mrs. F.H. Hitchcock, Mrs. L.A. Riedel, Mrs. Walter Conrad, Mrs. Frank Mytinger
Bayview	Mrs. Charles Rolland, Mrs. Don McGuire, Mrs. Floyd Chapin, Mrs. Edith Hadley, Mrs. W.H. Skillen, Mrs. E.E Crane, Mrs. E.R. Sluyter, Mrs. Clifford Phillips, Mrs. A.E. Wolcott, Mrs. R.H. Hyde
F. & A. M. (Masons)	WM Albert Ives, Roy Polson, Ford Dormire,: D.R. Stiles, Hollis Winn, Charles Wastma, James Pasco, Fred Oritt, Jim Cooley, Ray Welch, John Martin, John A. Johnson
O.E.S. (Eastern Star)	WM: Mrs. Ray Welch, WP: Ray Welch, Mrs. George Pellett, Mrs. Harvey Swanebeck, Mrs. Maurice Matthews, Mrs. Roy Polson
Rainbow Girls	WA: Virginia Sluyter, Vada Ann Gordon, Joanne Smale, Clara Davis, Rosa Westman, Jean Pavey, Sheila Keddy, Dawn Hagerman, Patti Parker, Virginia Poppy, Esther Crawford, JoAnn Schaefer, Janet Piatt, Norma Lee Hoffman
American Legion	Cmdr: Jeddie C. White, Ray Storey, Sam Casazza, Hollis Winn, J.P. Francis, Frank Mytinger, Mark Gordon, Basil Bowman
American Legion Auxiliary	Pres. Louella Gould, Loretta Freeman, Maude Reed, Mrs. Charles VanAlstine, Ida, Gould, Lillian Goodrich, Mrs. Floyd Poppy, Mrs. Jed White, Mrs. Maurice Matthews
Veterans of Foreign Wars (VFW)	Cmdr I.A. Stiff, Fred Schleicher,.Jim Tribbey, William Harris, Harry Dobbs,: Sam Casazza,
V.F.W. Auxiliary	Edna Bly, Lelah Stiff, Fannie Schleicher, Naomi Bennett, Irene Tribbey, Myrtle Harris.
Women's Relief Corps	Pres. Martha Bender, Edith Collins, Clara French,
Daughters of Union Veterans	Pres. Dorothy Griswold, Ruth VanAlstine, Eva Boice

Early in the year, James Tribbey led the effort of the V.F.W. Curtis-Wolverton Post to obtain uniforms for the Fenton High School band. As Jim Tribbey rightfully pointed out, most all of the other high school bands in the area were properly uniformed, and our hometown high school band should have uniforms too.   Jim Tribbey conducted a vigorous campaign soliciting money from businesses, organizations and individuals, even obtaining a commitment from the Village Council in which they agreed to purchase the uniforms for the Drum Major and the Drum Majorette.

It was not an easy task, raising money in a community that only recently began emerging from a prolonged economic downturn. It took longer than expected, but in mid-May, the funds were in hand and the uniforms were delivered. VFW Post Commander Sam Casazza delivered the check for the uniforms to Superintendent Heemstra.

However, one question remains today after all the years since the Blue and Gold trimmed uniforms were delivered.   Why were the uniforms Blue with Gold trim when the school colors were, and still are, Orange and Black?

The Patriotic Council, representing the veterans organizations were the organizers of the Memorial Day Parade this year as they had been in the recent years.   It is interesting to read how the editor, Claude Cohoon, of the *Fenton Courier* commented on the parade.

"That was one fine parade the veterans organizations and the other patriotic societies put on for the benefit of Americans here Memorial Day. Of course most credit for the actual success of the parade is due to the two bands---the city and high school---in their marching regalia.   It wouldn't have been much of a parade without the bands, but it took some good organizing work on the part of the committees to get the various parts of the parade together so well. There was only one bad feature---the parade had to be held on Leroy street and the services at the Library park were right next to this through highway. Traffic kept worming its way north as the parade moved south and traffic from both ways disturbed the listeners at the park ceremonies. Perhaps next year traffic can be routed by some other streets during the affair."

202 The Village Players

The *Fenton Courier* ran Lemen's Food Market full page advertisement on May 23, 1940..

LEMEN'S FOOD MARKET

We deliver | Friday & Saturday Specials | ph. 9341

Pork Liver pound 10c

BUTTER
Linden or Hagedorn's
Fresh Churned
pound . . . 28c

Beef Liver pound . . . 19c

PINEAPPLE Fresh, 30 Size Each 10c

BACON SQUARES pound 9c

SUGAR 10 pounds 47c

ORANGES
Sunkist
126 Size
Dozen . . . 34c

PORK ROAST Lean pound 14c

A FULL LINE OF SEELY'S PURE EXTRACTS

Scene Six...Sports and Recreation

The skating season began with the Village Council directing the City Engineer John Bacon and the Fire Department to create a large skating rink on the High School's athletic field. As the *Fenton Courier* headlined "Skating Rink Now Open To Public, Safe, Free, Good". Their sub-headline continued with "Dangerous Mill Pond No Longer Need Be Used"

Councilman Nelson Curtis said "The rink was extremely large" and it was. The skating rink covered the entire area inside the running track that circled the football field. Skating was allowed until 10PM every night, after which the rink was flooded to create new ice for the following day.

The American Legion Post recognized an opportunity and announced they were sponsoring an "Ice Carnival" for Sunday, February 11th.

The Ice Carnival featured races for Boys and Girls, Men and Women of all ages. As the day of the race approached and the Legion members began to lay out the racecourse on the new skating rink, they encountered some unanticipated problems. They really needed more space for some of the longer races they had planned.

Mr. William J. Burkett, one of the Legionnaires working on the project, reported the ice on the millpond, above the dam, was 16 to 20 inches thick, and the area was more than sufficient to conduct the long distance races. When the weather warmed up a few days before race day, the ice on both the rink and the millpond began to deteriorate and the decision was made to conduct the races on the millpond.

On the day of the race, over 1000 people turned out to watch the races. Even though the ice was soft, the races went off without difficulty and some remarkable speeds were attained.

Harvey Walters won the mile event in the Open Division in a time of 3:33 minutes which was considered "pretty good" on soft ice.

There were four divisions for both Boys and Girls based on age: Early Elementary Ages 7-8-9; Later Elementary Ages 10-11-12; Junior Ages 13-14-15; and Senior Ages 16-17-18. There was also an Open Division for all ages. A total of 165 individuals registered to participate in the races in all divisions. The following table details the winners and runners-up for all races.

Boy's Ages 7-8-9
100 Yards   Billy Burkett, H. Eniex, W. Hungerford
220 Yards   Billy Burkett, G. Merrick, W. Hungerford

Girls Ages 7-8-9
100 Yards   M. Richmond, M. Paine, J. Duby
200 Yards   A. Normand

Boy's Ages 10-11-12
220 Yards   D. Townsend, J. Whitman, N. Lawless
440 Yards   D. Townsend, N. Lawless, R. Perry

Girls Ages 10-11-12
220 Yards   Irene Heemstra, M. Brown, E. Ehlers
440 Yards   Irene Heemstra, J. Paine, H. Armstrong

Boy's Ages 13-14-15
220 Yards   D. Lee, J.Law, J. McCormick
440 Yards   D. Lee, J. McCormick, J. Law

Girl's Ages 13-14-15
220 Yards   M. Churchill, D. Wilhoit,
440 Yards   D. Wilhoit

Boy's Ages 16-17-18
220 Yards   H. Smith, R. Wilson, J. Frew
440 Yards   K. Lawless, J. Frew
880 Yards   R. Perry, R. Bowles
1 Mile   K. Lawless, H. Daniels
2 Mile   R. Perry,

Girl's Ages 16-17-18
220 Yards   D. Gould, B. Burrows
440 Yards   D. Gould

Open Division
220 Yards   W. Wilcox, R. Hunt, L. Minor
440 Yards   W. Wilcox, K. Merrick, V. Hunt
880 Yards   H. Walters, W. Wilcox
1 Mile   H. Walters, D. Walters

As the New Year arrived, the town's bowling leagues were well underway at the New Fenton Recreation, now the only bowling palace in town. The "bowling world" now had three leagues competing: The Booster League; The Inter-City League; and the Ladies League.

The Booster League was composed of teams sponsored by: the Cobblestone; Merrick's; Hoffman's: Goodwill; Woodworth Brothers; Industrial Tool; Fisher; Shell Service; Michigan Bean; Mickey's Dairy; and Fenton Motors. At the end, the Cobblestone bowlers came out on top, followed by Merrick's and Hoffman's. Tom Woodworth with an average of 180 was the top bowler for the season.

The Inter City Bowling League had the following teams: Courier; Cutups, Fenton Recreation; Linden Lumber; Log Cabin Restaurant; Industrial Tool; Gould's Market' Lemen's Grocery; Frankenmuth Brewery; Theisen-Stein Ford; Joe's tavern; and Altes Lager Brewery.

The final standings found the Courier newspaper team in first followed by the "Cutups" and the Fenton Recreation. The individual top bowler was S. Parker with a 178 average.

The New Fenton Recreation Ladies League had these teams competing: Pin Pals; Dollens; Brooks; Smiths; Teachers; Woodworths. The final standings found the teams finishing in the order above. Jean Brooks continued to dominate women's bowling this year as she had in previous seasons. Jean Brooks held the season's high for three games (553), for a single game (235) and the highest individual average of 135.

Strange thing about bowlers, the long winter season had just ended and two summer leagues began a fifteen-week schedule of competition. The Reverend Paul Mroch of the Trinity Lutheran church was secretary for one of the leagues.

In early September, the call went out for starting the Bowling season all over again. The Inter-City league was the first to start answering the call of the league President Harvey Walters and Secretary Harold Fowler. The other two leagues were soon to follow.

Some new sponsors had replaced those of last year. We now had the Sanitary Market, Shoreacres Golf, Bobier Shoe Store and Harvey Walters Barber Shop with entries in the league.

In Fenton in 1940 and for years previously, the spring and summer meant softball! The league consisted of six teams and they played every third or forth day May through August on the high school diamond. The teams and their sponsors were: Lemen's Grocery; Mickey's Dairy; The Courier Newspaper; Matthews Law Office; Industrial Tool; and the Fenton Hardware. Mickey's team won the league and then embarrassed

206 The Village Players
themselves when they accepted Ed Gould's challenge to play his team
of "has-beens". The "Has-beens" beat the "cream of the league" 10-6.

The Fenton Merchants team was organized to represent the Village in
a county Baseball league. The team members were generally former
Fenton High School players with a wide range in ages.

In December, with the aid of the Community Center, George C.
Paine, Harold Fowler and others organized a six-team men's Basketball
league. The games were played at the high school gym on Wednesday
nights

Fenton High School in their new "Blue Uniforms with Gold Trim" marching in
northerly direction at intersection of Leroy and Caroline Streets

Scene Seven...Schools

As the New Year began for Fenton High School, the students and most of the townsfolk, were anxiously following the high school basketball team. The team started their season with a string of victories and everyone's hope and expectations were elevated.   The team, coached by Lester Miller, was composed of experienced players such as: Seniors Joe Craft, Gorton "Bud" Milliken, Ken Lawless, Howard Goodrich and Dave Dawson; Juniors Bob Zoll and Al Turco; and Sophomore Dave Bard.

As the season progressed, the league play became tougher and Fenton (5-2) ended up in third place in the County Conference behind Davison (7-0) and Mt. Morris (6-1).   In the District Class "B" Tournament, Fenton defeated Farmington and Detroit Redford, before falling to Walled Lake on the third consecutive night of play.

As the weather changed and Baseball and Track activities began, the hopes and expectations of winning teams once again were kindled by the number of returning lettermen for each sport.

Coach Roger Leestma had thirteen lettermen back from last year's squad that finished in second place in the County Conference. Farner and Milliken were returnees from the 1939 Championship 880 Relay quartet and Dave Dawson was expected to repeat as the best shot putter in the County. And the track team did not disappoint their fans. At the end of the season, the team placed high in the County meet and Dave Dawson placed third in the State meet. Those who won their varsity letters in 1940 were: David Bard, Carroll Butts, Marvin Carpenter, Joe Craft, Edward Daniels, David Dawson, Lawrence Farner, Kenneth Foust, James Gale, David Lathrop, Gorton Milliken, Deforest McKinley, Robert Perry, Robert Runyan, Harold Schleicher, Arnold Schutt, Wilbur Swartz, Ronald Wilson and Robert Zoll.

A veteran baseball team began a very successful season beating Grand Blanc High School on Bob Zoll's No-Hit, No-Run performance. Zoll continued his excellent pitching for the remainder of the season, always limiting the opponents to a few hits and fewer runs. Other hurlers did not have the same experience or results. At times, the number of errors exceeded the hits. The *Fenton Independent* reported on the loss to Brighton by a score of 9-4. The news report said, "Bob Harris started on the mound and was credited with the defeat although he allowed but one run and two hits." The team's success largely depended on the pitching of their star Bob Zoll. This was never better illustrated than in the game with Beecher High School that would determine whether Fenton ended in first or second place in the County Conference. Bob Zoll was suffering from a very sore arm on the day of the game, and while he attempted to pitch, he could not throw as well as he had in the past. Beecher won the game 3-0 and Fenton fell to second place.

The letter winners in baseball for 1940 were: George Bard, Pat Barkey, Joe Craft, Phillip Crane, Harry Daniels, Lee Gordon, Howard Goodrich, Robert Harris, Richard Hiscox, Donald Hunt, Gorton Milliken, Ernest Neely, Russell O'Berry, Leon Shelby, Albert Turco and Robert Zoll.

Following the season, the track and baseball teams selected Lawrence Farner and Gorton "Bud" Milliken as Captains of their respective teams.

In May, as the school year was coming to an end, the Fenton High School learned that Lester Miller, long time coach of football and basketball at the high school, was leaving Fenton, having accepted a position with the Bay City Schools. Lester Miller was not only a successful coach, but he was also highly respected as a teacher and as a genuine good person. Several years later, it was an even sadder day for his former students, friends and associates to learn that after he had returned to his home town of Buchanan, Michigan and after the loss of his wife he had committed suicide.

Fenton High School competed in Debate and other speech programs with considerable success. The Debating team participated in twenty-seven practice debates and won four of their six debates in league competition. The debate team was composed of the following: Kathryn Dode, Dawn Hagerman, Kenneth Lawless, Gloria Reid, Jack Schaefer and Harold Schupbach. Harold also won the district contest in extemporaneous speaking.

Soon it was graduation time again. On June 12th, the Class of 1940 had 53 members at their Community Center ceremonies Gloria Reid was the Valedictorian and Clara Davis was the Salutatorian. A list of names of all graduates is contained in Appendix One

For the third year in a row, Kindergarten teacher Lucille Miller held a "Graduation Ceremony" for her Class of 1952. There were 48 little people participating in the program. The Class elected their officers: President Dean Moore, VP Martin Piccinni, Secretary Patricia Meyer and Treasurer Connie Kostka. The program featured the reading of the Class Poem by Robert Strom and recognition of Gloria Jean Anible for perfect attendance.

The Alumni Association for Fenton High School scheduled their reunion banquet for June 21st at the Community Center. Nathaniel "Than" Chestnut and Ray Hunt were the co-chairman for the event and they actively worked a list of graduates encouraging each one to attend. Their efforts were rewarded when over 300 alumni were in attendance.

The toastmaster, Sheldon J. Latourette, introduced the guests of honor: W. J. Burkett, J. Dalrymple, and Clarence Heemstra, former and current Superintendents of the Fenton schools. Mrs. Harriet Toomey '22 and Burns Fuller '11 entertained the audience with their singing. Special honors were bestowed on Dan Jayne, former employee of the school system; John Jennings '79; the oldest graduate present; and the Lyons family who had ten members in attendance. As part of the meeting agenda, the Association elected Sidney C. Hay as President, Miss Edith Hadley as Secretary and John B. Hoffman as Treasurer.

Later in September, the Class of 1903 held a class reunion and seven members of the original twenty-two classmates assembled for their 37th anniversary. Those attending were: Mrs. Katherine (Curtis) Hinkley, Mrs. Cora (Peer) Billings, Mr. Roy Banks, Mr. Ward Gillett, Mrs. Bessie (Skidmore) Sugden, Mrs. Ada (Angell) McNeal and Mrs. Olive Louise Davies.

The banquet/dance season report is not complete without mentioning three of the annual affairs that were very important to the students and the faculty of the High School. There was the "All-Hi" banquet and dance in mid-April; the Junior-Senior Banquet in late May, a couple weeks before the Seniors were to graduate; and the "big" dance, the "J-Hop".

In 1940, the All-Hi Banquet was held in the Community Center and was attended by over 250 students and faculty members. Jack Schaefer served as Toastmaster and the speakers for their respective classes were: Freshman-Curt Schupbach, Sophomore- Maurice Foley, Junior- George Pellett and Senior- Joe Craft

The Junior-Senior banquet was held in the basement of the Methodist Church and over 100 students attended and enjoyed the dinner prepared by the ladies of the church. Group singing was conducted by Miss Thelma Barker, the vocal music teacher, and ended with a resounding rendition of "Stand Up and Cheer", the school's "fight song". The High School "Swing Band" played a couple popular tunes as their part of the entertainment program.

Ed Daniels gave the Welcome address for the Junior class and Kathryn Dode delivered the Senior Class response. Following the dinner, the group moved to the High School gym for dancing.

The J-Hop, an all-high "dress-up" dance sponsored by the Junior Class, had been a tradition at Fenton High School for several decades and was eagerly anticipated by the majority of the students. The young ladies wore formal dresses and the young men wore the best suit and tie they had in their generally limited wardrobe.

The Juniors engaged Frank Oviatt and his "Merry Musicians" to provide the music for the affair held at the Fenton Community Center. There were 110 couples at the ball and the Grand March was led by the Junior class President, Al Turco, and his guest Jane Walcott.

One of the last student productions for the year was the Junior-Class play, "Don't Take My Penny" which appeared to have the infamous cast "of thousands". The play was presented at the Community Center and the cast was composed of the following: Donna Austin, Ray Heemstra, Marilyn Miller, Don Hunt, John Hart, Helen Randolph, Mary Groll, Dave Lathrop, Maurice Foley, Mary Mitchell, Gerald Durand, Shirley Pavey, Phyllis Warner, Pat Luther, Tom Merrill, Jack Kean, Bob Morea, Jack Klinger and Deane Cox.

During the summer months, the Student Council debuted weekly "Dime Dances" at the school gymnasium. All high school age persons in the area for the summer were invited to attend. The price was right at 10cents. The "juke box" music was the usual fare, however, on occasion a band provided "live" music. One of the most popular bands from Flint was headed by Trumpeter *Extraordinaire* Jack Tobin and featured Ed Bryant at the piano.

For some time C. J. Furlong, longtime member of the Fenton School Board, had his eye on the vacant land directly south of the school's athletic field for use by the school. In mid-June, Mr. Furlong, who was then serving as the Board's secretary, learned that the owners, the heirs to the W.B Phillips estate, were about to put the land up for sale. He immediately arranged a meeting with the heirs, Mrs. Julia Hart and Mr. and Mrs. E.A. Phillips, and the administrator of the Phillips estate.

Mr. Furlong told the party of the schools interest in the land for use as an athletic field. He pointed out that the current field was overtaxed by the use of school athletes and the town recreational activities. He requested that the estate propose a sales price so he could take the proposal of purchasing the land to the School Board for their consideration and action.

Within a few days, the Phillips estate declined to sell the land to the schools, but wished to make a gift of this 6-¾ acre parcel to the schools. There were only two conditions for the gift: the land would be used for school athletics and be fenced. The Board accepted the gift and looked forward to improving the land for athletic use.   The field was not used for several years but was eventually dedicated as Phillips Field and became the "Home of the Tigers" for several decades to come.

In their annual financial statement the School Board reported the system had received $83,045 during the past twelve months and expended $62,006, which left $21,039 Cash on hand. The expenditures identified, as Instructional, including teachers' salaries, was $44,852, which was about 74% of the total expenditure budget. The practice in recent years of publishing the individual salaries of teachers and administrators, which had been discontinued, was not reestablished

In the fall, the Board of Education authorized the purchase of a new flagpole and had it erected in the front of the high school building. The school custodians, Odie Wilhoit and John Chapman were probably the most pleased with the Board's purchase. With the new flagpole in front of the building, Odie and John would no longer have to crawl through the school attic to raise the flag on the top of the building.

In August, the School Board announced the names of the new High School teachers for the coming year.   There was Olga Jones (Commercial), Elizabeth McIlvenna, (English & Speech) June Rothelesberger (English & Latin), Ormand Danford (Social Studies) and Ivan Williams (Biology, Physical Education & Coach).

Misses Jones, McIlvenna and Rothelesberger were "fresh" off the college campus and were only a few years older than many of their students. One should not have been surprised when Miss McIlvenna began surreptitiously dating one of her students, senior Howard Goodrich.   One would assume the administrators and the members of the school Board were not aware of this happening, since no action was taken. Soon after Howard's graduation and before he left for service in the U.S. Marine Corps and the battles in the Pacific, they were married. Mrs. Goodrich continued teaching at Fenton High School for many years thereafter.

Ivan Williams came to Fenton after a very successful, winning program at Flint's Hoover High School, a smaller school. Ivan Williams coached both football and basketball at Fenton until he retired many decades later. The present football complex at the high school bears his name. He had numerous championship teams, including a basketball team that in 1946 lost a close game to St. Joseph in the State Class "B" Championship finals.

As the school opened in September, a total of 975 students enrolled in the K-12 grades. The Kindergarten and the high school senior class had the largest enrollments with 68 and 84 respectively.

The building program for the Fenton Schools found the old North Ward School being demolished and a new modern shop building under construction. The new "shop" building was a one-story brick building, forty by fifty-two feet in dimensions, located directly behind the high school buildings. It faced the south with an array of windows on the west side. The new shop was designed to accommodate wood and metal shops and automotive programs, as they were developed .The old shop, a former outdoor lavatory, was relegated to storage.

Throughout the year the school conducted an excellent "assembly" program. Many of the assemblies were "in house" programs and a lot of "housekeeping" business was conducted at these meetings. The principal assemblies involved the appearance of some person who related his "thrilling " life experiences. In April of the year, one of the best speakers appeared. This was the "famous traveler" Jim Wilson who told of his "three-wheeling through Africa".

During the late thirties the students published a weekly newspaper entitled "Tiger Tales". Gloria Reid, Dorothy "Frilly" Milliken and Joyce Stein played leading roles as the editors in 1940 and the paper gained some favorable notices from other high schools. It was a common practice during this period for high schools to exchange their student newspapers. On one occasion, Dorothy Milliken received a request from the high school in Vicksburg, Michigan for permission to publish the column "Swing Studies", written by Robert Harris, in their student paper. "Swing Studies" consisted of biographical notes on the bandleaders of the day as well as comments on "swing" music and recordings.

As the classes resumed in the September, it was time for the new football coach, Ivan Williams to begin building a football team. Coach Williams was pleased to have 82 candidates turn out for the first practice. Many of these were returning lettermen from a team that was Co-Champions in the last season.

While the season record was nothing spectacular, the football team played exceptionally well in all of their games. Bob Zoll, playing both offense and defense, as did most of the players in that period, excelled as passer, punter, place kicker and defensive back. His play was exceptional in the first half of the season. During one of his last games he played, he suffered a broken nose, but the real tragedy was when Bob Zoll was diagnosed with Tuberculosis. His treatment required him to be placed in the Sanitarium located in Howell, Michigan for about a year. As a consequence, he did not graduate with his class who, previously, had elected him as their President.

Varsity Letter winners for the 1940 season were: Carroll Butts, Jim Gale, Dave Lathrop, Leon Shelby, Norman Crego, Dave Bard, Bob Zoll, Ed Daniels, Al Turco, Bob Harris, George Bard, Lee Gordon, Bob Runyan, Larry Sugden, Bill Rynearson, John Hart, Harold Schleicher, Ed White and Elmer Strom. Al Turco at end and Bob Harris at guard were selected for the All-County Conference first team.. Each was selected for first team honors in both their Junior and Senior years.

This is the 4th of July Parade in 1934.
The team of Sorrels with the white manes with first wagon owned by Tom McKinley. Second in line, Mr. J.A. Brabon is driving old gasoline delivery truck used by Standard Oil company until 1918. Note: Lady in white dress, upper right, standing on small balcony of the I.O.O.F. Building.

The corner of South Leroy Street and Shiawassee Avenue.
Mobil Gas Station on right advertises "7 Gals $1". Note angle
parking. The business with white front, three doors from
corner is office of Dr. John Book, Chiropractor. Dr. Book came
to Fenton in the mid Thirties and continued his practice until
age 96. Today, his son, Dr. Clark Book,, FHS graduate Class
of 1960, conducts his chiropractic practice in the same space

Fenton Hardware, owned by Lewis Gage, occupied the
building originally housing the Commercial State Saving Bank
that closed in 1937 and then merged with the State Savings
Bank. The building, located on the southwest corner of
Caroline and Leroy Streets has been occupied by
photographic business in the most recent years.

Scene Eight ...Business

Signs of the return to a normal economy were present almost everywhere. The automobile industry's production of cars and trucks was increasing and the nation's armament program was bringing new work into the area. In January there was a development in the Village that addressed a very special need. It would no longer be necessary to travel to Flint for a good "Coney Island"

Mr. and Mrs. Christopher T. Ghetsas opened the "Fenton Coney Island" restaurant in the store next to Grant Whitman's Grocery, just a couple doors down from the corner bar, the Virginia Tavern. Evidentially, business wasn't that good because when the snow began to fly, they closed shop for the winter!

The town gained a first class shoe store when Milton Bobier opened his store just north of Tamlyn's photo shop and just north of the intersection of Leroy and Caroline Streets. Within two months, Claude Kirkey added a new dimension to the store when he opened his shoe repair operation in the rear area of the store. Milt Bobier and his first assistant, Mrs. David Frew provided excellent service and quality products for years to come.

In August of the year, a Chiropractor opened his office in the first block of West Shiawassee Avenue and soon became a cornerstone in his profession. It was in August when Dr. J. A. Book came to Fenton and opened his practice in the Southside business district.

One of the younger Physicians in town, Dr. C.G. Walcott bought the building on East Caroline Street across from the new Post Office building. The one-story brick building had been built by the late Dr. A.G. Wright and later used by Dr. Jefferson Gould. Dr. Walcott would serve the community for many decades, returning to Fenton after a stint in the U.S. Navy in World War II.

The New Fenton Recreation opened and the Fenton Alleys (all two lanes of them) closed. Bud Edinger could not compete with this new modern bowling establishment. Subsequently, the storefront remained empty for almost a year, until William G. Draves, a Pharmacist from Detroit considered the town needed another drug store and rented the space. It was late in July when the Draves Drug Company opened for business. However, the long established Fenton Drug Company and L.M. O'Dell's Drug Store proved to be too much and Mr. Draves's enterprise folded soon thereafter.

The Michigan Bell...the only telephone company in town...had introduced the new dial telephone system in the area only a year or so before, but now the system needed to have additional capacity to meet the increasing demand for service. They increased the number of phones that could be serviced from 850 to 1000. When the Michigan Bell first came to Fenton in 1889 there were only 6 subscribers. Michigan Bell came to Fenton only four years after it had introduced telephone service in Detroit.

In early May, one of Fenton's young men about town, Ronald Butler, had some of the older folks asking "what will they think of next" when he introduced "milk in a paper carton" to the towns consumers.

Ron Butler, who had been active in most of the Community Center activities, served on its Executive Committee, Dramatics, Hiking and other clubs, was Vice President of the Junior Chamber of Commerce, had acquired the "Pure Seal" milk distributorship for the area.

Ron Butler emphasized the advantages of this new package for the delivery of milk as being the elimination of glass milk bottle washing, assurance of sanitary milk and ease of storage. The new method brought to the consumer, milk packaged, sealed and delivered in a single-service paper container.

In January of the year, General Motors Corporation held a banquet in Detroit celebrating the production of the first Buick. It was gala affair with the famous opera star Jan Pearce present and singing. GMC had invited several of the very early Buick workers to attend the banquet and one Fenton man, Jay. C. Davis attended. Mr. Davis had been employed at the Buick Company since 1905.

The Genesee Tool Company held their "gala" Christmas party for their employees at the Fenton Hotel. Over 90 employees and guests, including the manager Arthur M. Gruner, attended the party. The Master of Ceremonies for the party was Ron Butler. Ron had sold the Pure Seal Milk distributorship after a few months and accepted a position with the Genesee Tool Company as Production Manager.

At the time business was picking up rapidly at the Tool Company, who were producing machine-cutting tools for shipment to Great Britain. Because the German U-Boats were sinking so many ships, each order was made in triplicate and each order placed on a different ship, to better ensure the delivery of at least one order to Britain.

In general, the townsfolk were feeling a lot better about their hometown. So many positive developments had happened in the last few years, and the job situation had vastly improved. Some villagers felt so good about the way things were going they used the newspapers to spread the good word.

Julia Sweeney, full-time real estate broker and part-time Justice of Peace paid for a full-page ad in the *Fenton Independent* extolling the virtues of living in the Fenton area.

Reasons Why You Should Buy In Fenton Township

Village of Fenton and Linden –No Outstanding Bonds
Township of Fenton Out of Debt
Within the Township of Fenton You Will Find Fine Schools and
Churches, Public Libraries, Municipal Fire Protection, Good
Roads, Pure Water, Prosperous Farms, Ideal Resort Property With
Plenty of Boating, Bathing and Fishing
Active Civic Clubs and Fraternities

In a Word---Everything That Makes Life Really Worth Living

This is the street scene looking north on Leroy Street from the corner with Ellen Street in 1937 before the construction of the Fenton Community Center began. Six of the buildings on the left were razed to provide space for the new building. Beginning at the far left; the buildings removed were Woodworth Brothers Plumbing. This is the one story brick building with a sign hanging vertical to the building with the words "PLUMBING" visible. The white building to the right of the Plumbing business was the Wander Inn, a restaurant and beer parlor. The next building to the right, quite difficult to distinguish, but with three-second story windows with white trim and white door entrance below, was the Barber Shop of John Rohm. The contractors, the W.E. Wood Company, used this building as their office while the Community Center was under construction. The next building to the right is the Fire Hall with a large steeple and clock. The while two story building to the right of the Fire Hall was the Walcott's Mill. To the right of Walcott's Mill is another white wooden building, Foster's "Fenton Odorless Dry Cleaning" business. This property was the last to be acquired and razed. It provided needed parking space downtown which was reduced by the construction of the Fenton Community Center.

Scene Nine. …People, Characters and Events

Despite the public sentiment about staying out of "Europe's War", the people generally supported sending assistance to the British as they were defending their "island" from an intensive aerial attack and were facing the imminent threat of invasion by the Nazi forces.

They were also supportive of the buildup in the strength of the nation's military capabilities. As part of the military buildup, each of the branches of the armed forces was actively recruiting the young men of the country for military or naval service.

So, it was not unusual to read of one or two or three of our young fellows joining one of the services. There was Donald Clark of FHS '39 who enlisted in the Army Air Corps. Don traveled all the way to Chanute Field in Illinois, only to find their allotment for recruits was filled and he was directed to Selfridge Field in Michigan, not far from his hometown.

Lewellyn Crystal, FHS '38, had joined the Air Corps a few months earlier and the *Fenton Courier* proudly reported his graduation from the Airplane Mechanics School and his assignment to Hickham Field in Hawaii.

James Heffner, FHS '36, joined the Coast Guard in October, only a month after Robert "Junie" Atkins FHS '38, David Dawson FHS '40 and Roy Perry FHS '40 enlisted in the U.S. Marine Corps.

These and others were the forerunners of hundreds of others who would soon be found in the services and stationed in places throughout the world that no one in Fenton in 1940 ever knew existed.

The veterans of the First World War represented a fair share of Fenton's male population. They were witnesses to the horrors of war and were, for the most part, outspoken on the subject. On the other hand, these veterans were very strong proponents of "Americanism" and they defended our freedom with patriotic zeal.

However, the detrimental effect war has on some lives, was no better illustrated than when Jerry Aspel, a disabled combat veteran of the First World War, committed suicide.

Mr. Aspel had been "shell-shocked" during the war and had not been well for years. When his friend William Haybell came to his house to pick him up to go fishing, he found his friend had shot himself and was dead on the front room floor. They found his uniform laid out neatly on his bed.

About a month after this tragic event, three of Fenton's finest, were traveling to Florida via a commercial airliner. J.C. Peck, Horace H. Hitchcock and Clark Wilmot had boarded their plane and had taken their assigned seats. It was then when one of them recognized a woman sitting a few seats ahead of them. He told his companions of his discovery and they soon agreed the woman was who he thought she was; Mrs. Eleanor Roosevelt, the nation's First Lady.

J. C. Peck was the first to approach her and found she was traveling alone with only one female companion. (How different it would be today!). "Jayce" Peck visited with the First Lady for a while and was able to get Mrs. Roosevelt to address a postcard to his son Marc. All three of the men talked with her and obtained her autograph. The comment by the *Fenton Courier* about the chance meeting was "...have not heard whether all three of our townsmen are now converted New Dealers or not".

An unthinkable crime occurred in late March. Some thieves broke into the St. John church and stole three gold pieces from the church alter. One of the pieces was a Challis belonging to Father Tighe, the Priest at St. John, and was inscribed with his name. A few days later, the Challis was found in the Flint River, however the other two pieces were not recovered,

The crime wave relented for a few months, but in August, someone cut a hole in the plate glass display window at the Fenton Drug Company. As part of a sales promotion, Otter Watson, the owner had placed a display with three ten-dollar bills attached to a piece of cardboard in the store window. The thief, using a glasscutter, cut a circular hole in the glass, reached in and removed the three bills.

Late one night in October, two men from out of town stopped at Floyd Hartley's gas station, held a gun to Ron Longworth and took the contents of the cash register, $18 in all. As they were leaving the station, two of Fenton's youth, Gorton "Bud" Milliken and James Frew approached the station, where Ron Longworth quickly told them of what had just transpired. Milliken and Frew sped away from the station in "hot pursuit" of the robber's car. They sped through downtown Fenton and out Shiawassee Avenue trailing the thieves. As soon as they read the license number on the fleeing vehicle, they called off their chase and returned to town to inform Deputy Leon Durkee.

The climax of the affair came that night when one of the stick-up men, Russell Kehoe of Flint, committed suicide after visiting his girlfriend at her home and confessing his part in the robbery. Soon thereafter, the

Flint police apprehended Herman Dart of Flint, the driver of the criminal's car.

News of the robbery shocked the people in Fenton, who said they had not had a robbery, according to the *Fenton Courier*, "in the last dozen years". They had already forgotten the robbery of the State Savings Bank in 1937!

Not all of the bad things that happened were the result someone's misconduct. Nature came to call in early April as the spring thaw began with a vengeance. Again this year, the high waters in the millpond caused a rush of water over the dam, which threatened to tear away the riverbanks in Waterworks Park. Village employees prevented any damage to the park or the riverbanks by using sand bags, sand and hours of labor.

As previously mentioned, the Memorial Day Parade in Fenton was especially well received this year, probably because both the City Band and the Fenton High School Band participated in the event.

The parade started at the American Legion Hall, at the corner of Walnut and East Caroline Streets. It proceeded from there south on Leroy Street, pausing at the Shiawassee River bridge crossing, where the Womens Relief Corps members paid homage to those "who sailed away in ships" by placing a wreath on the river waters. The parade then moved to grounds of the A.J. Phillips Library, referred to as Library Park, for the major portion of the program.

Following the playing and singing of the Star Spangled Banner and a flag salute led by the Boy Scouts, Father Daniel Tighe of St. John church delivered the Innovational prayer. The remainder of the program included: Tribute to the G.A.R by D.U.V.; Gettysburg Address by Donna Morgan; Poem: In Flanders Field by Betty Simmons; and a Tribute to Gold Star Mothers by American Legion Auxiliary.

Father Tighe offered the Benediction, which was followed by the Fenton City Band playing "Sleep Soldier Sleep". As the comment by the *Fenton Courier* described, the automobile traffic on South Leroy Street not only caused concern along the parade route, but also was disturbing to those attending the ceremony.

At many of the Village Council meeting, citizens presented concerns and complaints to the members. On one occasion in August, Dan Haddon, who was the father of Russell Haddon, stated that the garage of one of his neighbors, a Mr. Schulte, was extending about 10 to 12 feet into Second Street. After an investigation, this encroachment was confirmed, and Mr. Schulte was given 60 days to move his garage. Mr.

Schulte said that sometime in the past, a village employee had given him permission to build his garage in that location.

Another interesting tidbit gleaned from the pages of the *Fenton Independent* was the report of an accident involving the Reverend Dr. J. Stanley Mitchell. It seems the Reverend Mitchell lost control of his vehicle and stuck a telephone pole and then veered into an Ed Mitt's greenhouse. The newspaper reported his friends said he was returning from hunting when this accident occurred.

The community Halloween celebration in 1940 was a "huge" event. There were over 300 children and adults in costume for the parade. Those in charge of refreshments at the school counted over 600 youngsters being served.

Prizes were awarded for the best costumes and makeup. Best All Around was presented to Arthur Bush with Barbara Ireland and Phyllis McCormick coming in second and third respectively. Other winners for a variety of classifications were: Edward Turner Jr., Gerald Palmer, Phyllis Loomis, Loretta Shelby, Betty Jean Hatherley, Helen Covert, Dave Gordon, Mary Mitchell, Carl Albert, Ryan Strom and Gerald Rawson,

One particular parade unit, which would be particularly contentious in today's cultural environment, was awarded a prize as a parade entry. Albert Grave's horse drawn wagon carried a "colored family" which the *Fenton Courier* reported, "...delighted the spectators with their singing and antics."

The Community Council organized the Halloween Celebration, with the most prominent working group being the American Legion and the three Child Study Groups. Mark Gordon was the general chairman.

A week after the Halloween affair, a large fire destroyed a good portion of the Fenton Lumber Company just east of the Michigan Bean Company elevator on Main Street. The loss was estimated at $16,000. The heat from the fire was so intense that it broke expensive beveled plate glass windows in the Main Street home of Fred Horrell. The cause of the fire was not determined although if it had occurred one week earlier, some wag would have certainly blamed it on the "trick and treat" youngsters.

Just a few months earlier the townsfolk were experiencing absolutely torrid weather. The August heat wave continued for weeks and air-conditioned homes in Fenton were as scarce as "hen's teeth". This prolonged heat spell resulted in two deaths in the Village.

Fred Horrell's sister, Mrs. Rose Patterson, lived on Main Street and Mr. Horrell had not heard from her that day, so he was on his way to visit her, when he saw neighbor Robert Goodfellow topple over on his porch. He immediately went to his assistance and carried him into his house to his family, before continuing on to his sister's residence. Mr. Goodfellow had gone to the porch to pick up his morning milk bottle and when reaching for the bottle he collapsed.

When Fred Horrell arrived at his sister's home, he found the door locked, so he proceeded to find an unlocked window to gain entry. Sadly, he found his sister lying dead on the floor. Her death was attributed to heat exhaustion. Mr.. Goodfellow also died that day from heat exhaustion.

Freddie Rolland, oldest son of Ivah Rolland, who was a civilian employee of the U.S.Army, had worked on Midway Island in the western Pacific Ocean for the past year, returned home to visit his mother. Fred Rolland, a Fenton High School graduate in 1935, was a part of a group of civilian and military engineers who went to Midway to blast a deep-water channel in the reef to provide better access to the U.S. Naval base on the island.

One of the residents of Fenton was Genesee County Deputy Sheriff Clark Thompson. Deputy Thompson first received notice in the press when he was shot during the riots at the Chevrolet plant associated with the infamous "sit-down" strike in 1937.

Before Christmas of 1940, Clark strained the ligaments in his back while chasing a fugitive. He had been hospitalized since then until mid February when he was taken home. Fitted with a form-fitting cast, which supported his back, he was restricted to a hospital bed, which had been set up in the living room of his house on North Leroy Street. This was his third long siege while recovering from injuries incurred in the line of duty.

The *Fenton Courier* editorialized in their news report about his situation that "When a man's healthy and strong he often thinks how wonderful it would be if he could just lie in bed of a morning instead of getting up and going to work." "But take it from Clark Thompson, when you've got to lie in bed it isn't such a pleasant thing"!

The year ended with on a high note with the *Rowena's* annual Christmas party for the town's children. The children were treated to a showing of "The Wizard of Oz" and free popcorn.

This is the Fenton High School during the decade of the thirties and beyond until it was demolished in 1990. Ellen Street was unpaved and ran along the south side of the school property. Note the "Twin Pines" that graced the front lawn of the school building at that time, hence the name of the 1938 school annual.

Scene Ten…The "Outside" World

It had been customary for many years for the U.S. Representative to Congress to provide the local newspapers with a weekly report on what he was doing for the common good and what was happening in Congress and the Federal Government in Washington.

Congressman William W. Blackney's weekly newsletter for the January 11ᵗʰ edition of the *Fenton Independent* contained the following statement:

> "I think that one of the most important functions of this session of Congress will be to protect America from participation in European wars. America has too many problems of her own to settle without adding to these problems new and European ones, with which we have no concern."

At his time, the Germans had invaded France, Belgium, Luxembourg, and the Netherlands and the British were mobilizing all species of water craft to cross the English Channel to Dunkirk in an effort to extricate their Army from the continent before it was destroyed by a seemingly indomitable German army, racing towards Paris.

In his letter of May 23ʳᵈ he speaks of this dire situation:

> "At the time that this letter is written the situation in Europe is particularly tense and acute. Germany's move to conquer western Europe has made the European situation very critical. Chamberlain has been replaced by Churchill and the English government is in the process of reorganization"

In July, Representative Blackney continued to "urge the nation to beware of war and talk of war". He said his mail contained an overwhelming number of letters "bitterly opposed to U.S. participation in the European conflict".

In early August the House of Representatives passed the National Defense Bill that provided $5 billion to build a two ocean Navy, equip an Army of 1,200,000 men and procure 19,000 airplanes.

Mr. Blackney continued to warn his constituents with the following message:

> " I have repeatedly stated in my letters that if the American people will stay sane and sensible and sober and not allow those propagandists in and out of Congress, who are urging us to war, there is no necessity or need for this nation embarking in a European conflict."

Earlier, in May 1940 Congress appropriated $2.5 billion for Franklin D. Roosevelt's program of rebuilding the military infrastructure, but Roosevelt did not feel the country was ready for a peacetime draft. However, on June 20th the Burke-Wadsworth Bill was brought before Congress

Some of the bills most salient provisions were:
1. Registration of all male citizens and aliens 18-64.
2. Men 21-45 liable for year's training in Army or Navy.
3. Men 18-21 and 45-64 liable for training and service in home defense units.
4. Any person subject to registration may enlist before being drafted.
5. In case of declaration of national emergency –subject to extension to indefinite service.

Representative Blackney wrote "The bill is entirely too drastic. It is un-American". Again he reported "thousands of letters pouring in opposing this legislation".

Franklin Roosevelt signed the Burke-Wadsworth Act into law in 1940, creating the first peacetime draft in United States history. This Selective Service Act required that men between the ages 21 and 30 register with local draft boards. The age range was later changed to 18-45. The government selected men through a lottery system. If drafted, a man served for twelve months. The office for the local draft board for the men of the Fenton area was in Flint's Dryden Building. Floyd Chapin had been appointed as a member of the board to represent the Fenton area.

On the "home front", the local people were becoming more aware of the war and the possibilty of America becoming involved. Mrs. Grace Rolland, wife of Charles, organized a group of women to knit sweaters and other clothing items for the refugees in Britain. A Mrs. Wright, who lived in Sussex, England, wrote several letters to the *Fenton*

Independent describing the horrible conditons of living under the constant threat of an air raid . Each week there was one or two articles in the local newspapers reporting on some local youth entereing the miliatry or naval service.

On August 27, 1940, the Congress approved the induction of the National Guard into active military service for a period of 12 consecutive months. The program would not be completed until October 1941. When completed, the induction of the nation's National Guardsmen brought over 300,000 men comprising 18 combat divisions and another 100,000 men in other separate units.

All units of the Michigan National Guard were inducted into federal service on October 15, 1940, February 24, 1941, and April 7, 1941, aggregating 527 officers, 8 Warrant Officers, and 7,673 enlisted men. Those mobilized would continue in Federal service throughout the war. Several young men in Fenton joined the National Guard, including some who dropped out of school to join. That fall, they found themselves conducting maneuevers at Camp Beaueguard, Lousiana.

In October, President Roosevelt ordered the embargo of all scrap iron sales to Japan. For years, most people thought this act was the "straw that broke the camel's back" so to speak. However, the Japanese government had been planning for the conflict for several years before the embargo and the attack on the U.S. military and naval bases in Hawaii.

The political climate in the summer of 1940 heated up quite early as both the Democrats and the Republicans held their National Conventions and nominated their candidates for the nation's highest offices. Franklin D. Roosevelt was nominated for a third term as President by the Democrats and Wendell L Wilke was tapped by the Republicans.

Wendell Wilkie, a lawyer and utilities executive, was from Indiana and although he campaigned vigorously, he lost the election to a very popluar President by a large margin. FDR received 27 million votes to Wilkie's 22 million. The electoral college results were 449 to 82.

However in Fenton Township, Wendell Wilkie led with 1,650 voted to Roosevlet's 1,062. The locals also voted for incumbernts U.S. Senator Arthur Vandenberg and Representaive William Blackney. The old acquantaince, Murray "Pat" Van Waggoner, who was frist encoutnerd as the State Highway Commissioner, was elected as the Governor of Michigan.

228 The Village Players

The people in the Fenton area had experienced a year that was much better economically then recent years. Most everyone believed that we were on the road to prosperity. Some thought that we were in danger of losing our focus on maintaining high values and living a good life.

Was a return to prosperity a threat to living a righteous life? Perhaps that is what S.F. Beach had in mind when he devoted the front page of the April 18th edition to the following list of "warning signs".

WARNING SIGNS ON THE ROAD TO PROSPERITY

You cannot bring about prosperity by discouraging others.

You cannot strengthen the weak by weakening the strong.

You cannot help small men up by tearing big men down.

You cannot help the poor by destroying the rich.

You cannot lift the wage-earner by pulling the wage-payer down

You cannot further the brotherhood of man by inciting class hatred

You cannot establish sound social security on borrowed money.

You cannot build character and courage by taking away a man's initiative and independence.

You cannot help men permanently by doing for them what they could and should do for themselves.

Act Five…The Year 1941

Scene One…Eight O'clock And All Is Well

If Fenton had had a "Town crier" in early 1941, the cry would have been, "Eight o'clock and all is Well". Little did they know that "12 o'clock–Midnight" was about to happen in early December.

It's been said that if one does not "loose his head" while all those around him are "loosing theirs", he just doesn't know the situation? Well, certainly, if one reads only the Fenton's weekly newspapers of early 1941, one could conclude the people of Fenton didn't know the situation!

Most of the townspeople kept up on national and international goings-on by reading the Flint Journal, Detroit Free Press or the Detroit News. Several AM radio stations from Detroit and Flint also had their evening news programs that carried headline news of the "world". Along with a movie "short", a cartoon and the "Coming Attractions", the *Rowena* generally had a "Movietone News" or "RKO-Pathe" newsreel. However, both the *Fenton Independent* and the *Fenton Courier* concentrated on the local news but did regularly publish the letters from Congressman William Blackney, who was decidedly opposed to the country entering the European war, but supportive of America's buildup of its defenses.

By the year 1941, most of the townsfolk were also supportive of the British in the European war. President Roosevelt and the majority in Congress had approved of Roosevelt's programs providing materiel support for the Allies, primarily Britain, especially after France surrendered to the Germans.

While some families of German heritage were rumored to be "pro-German" and some individuals were rumored to be members of the German-American Bund that is how it remained…. Rumors.

With the fall of France, the invasion of Great Britain was feared to be imminent. As the German began their air offensive against the British Isles, support of the British became even stronger. Many of the town's residents had relatives and friends in the British Isles with whom they exchanged correspondence. Occasionally one of the letters would appear in the *Fenton Independent*.

In February of 1941, Miss Patti Parker shared a letter from a friend in Middlesex, England. In his letter he tells of some "excitement " of a few weeks past when a whole block of buildings, housing textile factories and warehouses, were burned to the ground. But now he relates a more recent incident...

"Just after this fire there was a heavy bomb that fell on the "Bank" Underground station. This station is shaped like a well down in the booking hall with about six feet of concrete on top as a roof. The bomb crashed through the roof and exploded in the booking hall, the whole roof collapsed on the people in the hall, the blast went down the escalators and blew people on the platform in front of an incoming train. They think there were about two hundred people killed down there."

A few paragraphs later, the writer comments "...your views on Hitler are very much like most people's over here." However, the people in Fenton seemed to be more interested in attacking the "garbage" problem at home than the "garbage" mess in Europe.

Russell Haddon and Mrs. Sinclair, representing the Community Center's Community Council, appeared before the Village Council in early January to present a petition urging the development of a garbage disposal plan for the residents of the Fenton. The Community Council represented 45 organizations and over 1600 citizens signed their petition.

All Council members were in agreement that the village was in need of a garbage collection and disposal system. The sewage disposal plant was under construction at the time, but the citizens were "on their own" as to how they disposed of their garbage and trash. The "City" dump was south of town and would accept the refuse; however how one got the garbage and trash to the dump was the responsibility of the individual family.

The Council assigned the problem to their Health and Sanitation Committee, which had recently been appointed, to consider the problem and prepare a recommendation for the Council's deliberation. It is interesting to note that the City of Fenton did not establish a government-funded system until the mid-Forties, when then Councilman Russell Haddon spearheaded the action.

Mr. George Robinson of Clio, Michigan presented the Village Council with a proposal to collect the town's rubbish and garbage. Each resident would be asked to furnish "cans for the garbage and baskets and cartons for ashes and rubbish". *(Ashes? A coal-burning furnace heated most of the houses in town. The ashes resulting from the burning of the coal created a disposal problem for the residents, especially during the winter months.)* Mr. Robinson promised the cost of the service to the Village would "not exceed $100 per month."

It wasn't until mid-May before the Council accepted the proposal of the Robinson Garbage and Rubbish Company. However, only two weeks later, Mr. Robinson reported they could not keep up with the volume of garbage and trash, especially the amount being thrown into the alleys. So, the problem was only partially solved at the time.

In mid-June, it was reported the sewage disposal plant was completed and the plant was ready for operation. However, many problems were encountered and the operational date was extended until early September. Because of the numerous problems that occurred in the early months and the village announced there was a sizeable cost overrun. As the Village Council was deliberating about the tax mileage required to operate the new facility, the *Fenton Courier* opined, "...Indications are that the rate will be higher than last year. But, so are all other commodities and services, and since we'll be getting more for out tax dollar we should welcome it with a grin,"

For years many citizens of the town responded the "fire siren" as quickly as the volunteer firefighters. It was not uncommon to have a line of cars up to three blocks in length, following closely behind the fire truck as it sped to the fire. Since the truck often left the firehouse, before all the firemen had arrived, the late coming firemen had to contend with the "gawkers" as they made their way to the scene of the fire. Finally, at their January meeting, the Council took note of the situation and proclaimed, "Don't follow the fire truck ". Of course, the curious responded as always and when the siren sounded, out the door, into the car and follow the fire truck to the fire!. It seemed it was a hard to break the habit!

Early in the year, the Village Council had established a number of "commissions" to better address the various areas of governmental responsibility. The "Police Commission" was to establish the policies and administer the Village "police"...namely Leon Durkee and his principal assistant, Basil Chappelle. One of their first actions was to recommend that Leon Durkee be named the Chief of Police.

In June, Basil Chappelle resigned as a police officer and the Council provided a "police badge" for John Bacon.

In December, the Commission recommended and the Council approved the hiring of an additional "Deputy Marshall" at $1,600 per year. They also would provide this new officer a uniform, a $3,000 bond and insurance for his car.

The summer Band Concerts in the park on Shiawassee Avenue occasionally caused some parking and traffic problems, so the Council approved the closing of Parke Avenue between Elizabeth Street and Shiawassee Avenue and the placement of a "stop" sign on Parke as its intersection with Elizabeth from the south. It is unknown whether this street was actually ever closed but the stop sign remains as ordered

As citizens of the Village of Fenton, the townsfolk were also voters in the Fenton Township elections. The Township Board decided to abandon the caucus system for nominating candidates for office. The Board prescribed the primary election to make those determinations. However, the Village continued using the caucus system.

It was no surprise when the Citizen's party caucus nominated Harry Lemen without opposition. At the caucus, Ray Hunt topped incumbent Walter Conrad for the nomination for Village Clerk. Other nominations were: George Tamlyn over D.R. Stiles for Treasurer; Floyd Poppy over Harry Lowe for Trustee; and Charles Stein over Ray Welch for Trustee. Ray Welch resigned before the selection and chose to run against incumbent Nelson Curtis for the remaining Trustee opening.

The rival People's Party held their caucus and nominated Hoyt Glaspie to oppose Harry Lemen, however Mr. Glaspie withdrew before the election, and Harry Lemen continued his reign as Village President. Walter Conrad and D.R. Stiles, both incumbents, were nominated for Clerk and Treasurer, respectively. Nominations for Trustees were Willard Hatfield and Edward B. Mitts, both newcomers, and incumbent Nelson Curtis. Claude Cohoon was nominated for the office of Assessor.

As a result of the March election the following individuals were elected to serve:

President Harry Lemen,
Clerk Walter Conrad
Treasurer D.R. Stiles
Trustees: Ray Welch*, Charles Stein*, Gus Lutz,
    John Hoskins, William Burkett and Nelson Curtis*
*Newly Elected (Poppy, Hatfield and Mitts were defeated)

The Village Council became concerned about the increasing number of unregulated gaming devices being installed in many of the town's businesses. The "Pin Ball" machines were being played by people of all ages and the use of these devices for illegal gambling was more than a remote possibility. The Council decided to act and in January they approved an ordinance requiring the licensing of all amusement devices. The ordinance not only required licenses for "pin ball" machines but also included "music boxes", generally referred to as "Juke Boxes", and Gum Machines.

The New Fenton Recreation (Pinball), Mickey's Dairy (Pinball, Music box), Virginia Tavern (Music, Gum), John Turco's Central Tavern (Music, Pinball), Kelly's Ice Cream (Music, 2 Pinball), Joslyn's Pool Hall (Pinball), Robert's Pool Hall (Pinball) and Chris Gunis Ice Cream Parlor (Pinball) all paid their licenses fees.

The village leaders were also concerned about maintaining an abundance of water to accommodate the town's growth in population and/or industry. Consequently, in August, the drilling of a new well that flowed at 250 gallons per minute was a welcome augmentation to the Village's water supply. Even so, when summer arrived, the Council prescribed a policy on the watering of lawns. The town was divided with "on" and "off" days for watering.

The Council meeting of August 4th occurred during a "heat wave" and Editor/Publisher S.F Beach wrote in the *Fenton Independent* " full council was present, (we mean the whole bunch was there.)" …and "the usual bunch of newspaper men." It was at that meeting that Myron McGlynn reported he had "unintentionally placed (his) new garage …in the street". Mr. Bacon, the Village Engineer, stated Mr. McGlynn had "obligingly offered to move the building". That issue was resolved, but the discussion triggered the memory of Councilman Burkett and he asked about a similar situation of about a year ago, when Mr. H. Schulte was ordered to remove his garage from the street only to learn that the order had been delivered to Mr. Schulte, but the garage was still sitting in the street. Mr. Schulte was ordered to appear before the council at their next meeting.

The hot weather didn't seem to speed up the meeting as a discussion about a proposed strict dog ordinance triggered a response from Treasurer D.R. Stiles. According to Mr. Beach, "Treasurer Stiles don't love dogs, I guess, for at this time, having kept still as long as he could, he opened up with a flow of oratory which would have done credit to William Jennings Bryant, the boy orator of the Platte." He continued,

234 The Village Players

"Both he and the Treasurer was and are Democrats, but Bryant confined his oratory to political issues, while Mr. Stiles spoke on the subject of dogs. Anyway, Stiles has a way of presenting the dog question which leaves no doubt, but that, ordinance or no ordinance, dogs had better keep a long way from his home on South Leroy Street."

At the conclusion of the fiscal year, the Village Treasurer presented a report that evidenced the Village had received $38,864 in the past year and limited its expenditures to $35,687. Independently, the City Band reported that of the $1,794 provided by the Village, they had only expended $1,463. Not surprisingly, those responsible for the public funds were imbued with the notion of "living within the budget". An ethic much admired, but seldom practiced by many public officials of the present day.

Dr. William J. Rynearson, who was serving as the Village's Health Officer, reported to the Village Council in February and announced the past year had been the "healthiest" year of his eight years of service. He announced there had been no cases of Polio this past year whereas there had been five cases in the previous year.

From the newspaper reports, it seemed there was an unusual number of individuals undergoing appendectomies. Parents were still quite fearful of the Polio disease, and the number of young people being diagnosed with Tuberculosis, TB, was also very worrisome. .

In mid May, the students in the 10th, 11th and 12th grades were given TB X-Ray examinations. There were seven retakes required out of the more than 100 examinations.

The results of a study was published in the *Fenton Courier* late in the year that provided some very sobering information concerning Tuberculosis as a "killer". The report stated that TB remained the greatest health obstacle among working men ages 25 to 45. TB killed 88 out of every 100,000 workingmen in that age range. Following TB was Heart Disease with 70, Pneumonia with 52, Suicides with 29, Cancer with 26, Kidney Disease with 25 and Accidents with 24.

Several young people, notably outstanding high school athlete Robert Zoll was confined to the Howell Sanitarium for treatment of the disease. When a person was diagnosed with Tuberculosis, a very contagious disease, they were generally placed in a State Sanitarium for treatment. Those ordered to go to the Sanitarium went either voluntarily, or they were forcibly taken to the facility.

Traveling by automobile to Howell and other points south along US 23 had slightly improved over the past several years. The pavement now extended north from Brighton through Hartland and to the outskirts of town. The unpaved section was "treated" and "blacktop" was rumored to be coming in the near future.

The new US 23 prompted the "naming" of the sections of the old US 23, which was now a County Road. The promise was that those old section would also be "blacktopped" in the near future. At the suggestion of the residents of Tyrone Township "old US 23" was named Hartland Road in Tyrone Township and State Road in Fenton.

The July 4, 1940 edition of the *Fenton Courier* included a "Tourist's and Sportsmen's" Map of Fenton and Surrounding Territory". A portion of the map is shown below. Note that Route 23 is an "improved road" as it approaches Fenton from the south until it reaches the Village limits.

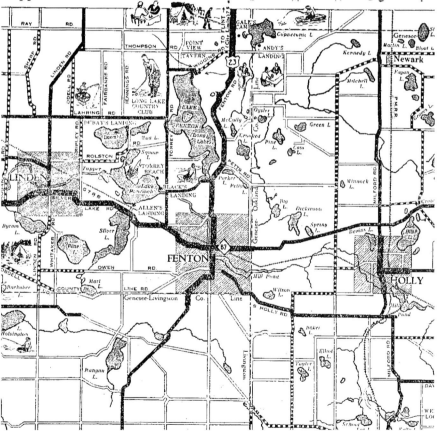

Scene Two...It's Show Time!

The first stage production of the year was a very ambitious undertaking by the Fenton Chorus under the direction Frances Hicks. The group selected to perform Gilbert and Sullivan's classic operetta, "The H.M.S. Pinafore".

Thor Neilsen very capably played the lead role of "The Right Honorable Sir Joseph Porter, first Lord of the Admiralty". Burton MaWhinney sang the part of Captain Corcoran, the Captain of the H.M.S. Pinafore. Others in the cast were: Mrs. Claude Cohoon, Lyle Davis of Linden, Henry Alchin, Mrs. Robert Black, Eileen Freeman, Grant Wright and Joe Woodworth.

Mrs. Dorothy V. Aman, the art director, Roger Leestma for lighting and Richmond Browne, the pianist received exceptional praise, as did the Director Miss Frances Hicks and the Stage Director Claude Cohoon. The stage was hardly empty before another show was ready.

The cast of the "H.M.S. Pinafore" presented at the Fenton Community Center. Thor Neilsen is pictured in his Admiral's uniform surrounded by other cast members Grant Wright and Mrs. Robert Black. Two men in rear unidentified.

The next show at the Community Center was one that would not be considered or presented in today's social environment.

The Minstrel Show was "Comin' to Town"! In view of the tremendously successful Minstrel Show of last year, the Mimes Club joined with the "Minstrel Men" to present this year's version of the "Minstrel", a classic form of the American Theater of the time.

While the 1940 Minstrel show featured an all Male cast, this year's production would have men and women, boys and girls, some forty performers all in "black face".

The ad to the right was placed in the *Fenton Courier's* March 6th edition. The majority tolerated its representation of "colored people" in 1941.

Grant Wright directed the show for the second time. Others were: Thelma Barker-Vocal music, Harvey Thomsen-Instrumental music, and Leon Jolly- Dancing.

WHO IS AH ??

I'se Hambone, a Cullud Gen'men Wif' mo' talent dan ambition
See me at de
ANNUAL MINSTREL SHOW

Thursday and Friday, March 20 and 21. Community Center, "

Mixed cast of 45. Hear our color-Ful Blues Singer.
See the traditional Minstrel Citcle
Laughs Drama Music
All-Fenton Folks In Blackface

The Mimes Club continued the effort to produce a real professional play. The play selected was "Petticoat Fever" that had only recently completed a long run on Broadway and which many in town would remember as a recent motion picture.

Claude Cohoon, fresh from the successful direction of the "Pinafore" directed the new venture. Ryan Strom played the lead male role, a gentleman afflicted with a "strange malady"-"Petticoat Fever". Madeline Wessendorf was the female lead and Walter Conrad, Miss Ethelyn Burrows, Wilbur Strom, Miss Ramona Burrows, Miss Geraldine Stedman, Mrs. Ernest Hungerford, Richard Bigelow and Russell Haddon completed the cast.

The productions of the first part of the year were hardly over when the Mimes Club met to reorganize and plan for the next "season" which was scheduled to start on September 16th.

At their annual meeting in October, the club re-elected Willard Hatfield as their President. Other elected to serve for the 1941-1942 season were: VP Ryan Strom, Secretary Helen Hockett and Treasurer Madeline Wessendorf.   Emile Gauthereau and Walter Conrad were elected to meet with the officers as the Executive Committee.

Apparently, it was time for a name change again. This time the group, who has been known as the Drama Club, Village Players, Mime Club and perhaps others, this time selected the name "The Fenton Players". They proclaimed that "…from hence for they will be known…" as such…(until the next time?).

The "Mimes" set their membership goal at 250 men and women and planned to produce three plays during the season.

For the first time, the club decided to engage a professional theater person to direct their activities. Mrs. Phyllis Blanchard Wright of Ann Arbor was selected because of her extensive experience as a director. Mrs. Wright began immediately casting for the first of the three plays for the season; "You Can't Take It With You". The play was presented at the Fenton Community Center on December 11th, only four days after the "day that will live in infamy"…December 7, 1941.

This lively three act play written by theater giants Moss Hart and George Kaufman, was well know to the townsfolk mostly from the movie version of the play, eve though the play did have a very long run on Broadway. The cast, with Mrs. Jane Wilson as the female lead, included: Juanita Weirich, Ramona Burrows, Paul Conde, Ras Cole, Emile Gauthereau, Jim Denhart, Ryan Strom, Roger Leestma, Yvonne Stein, Wilbur Strom, Done Weirich, Lynn Burrows, Earl Silver, Pauline McNeil, Jane Bonnell, Russell Haddon, Walter Conrad and Willard Hatfield.

Not all of the stage activity at the Community Center was done by the "grownups". Fenton School's annual Variety Show played for a full house at the Center in March. The cooperative venture involved students and faculty from Fenton High School. About one hundred grade and high school students performed or were active in the production.

A "Swing Group" led by Mr. Thomsen, Music Teacher, provided most of the music for the show. The group was composed of: Robert Perry, Jean Brooks, Dick Smale, Gerald "Meatball" Durand, Leone Hagerman, Tommy Merrill, Dick Hiscox, Murray Stanley, Lee Gordon, Dave Gordon, Maurice Foley, George Steward, Wayne Young, Dale Hagerman and Marvin Youker

Some of the featured acts were: Exhibition Tap with Murray Bell, Lois Searight, Nancy Bly, Elaine Ireland and Barbara Ireland, all students of Leon Jolly, tap dance instructor.

The trio of Patsy Hagerman, Annie Burgstaller and Mary Mitchell sang several numbers with the "Swing Group" as did "The Concessionaries" (Sid hay Jr., Fred Harper, Ray Heemstra, Leon Shelby, Bruce Sinclair, Junior Lutz, Wilbur Swartz and Mr. Ormand Danford.

The whole ensemble closed the program singing "The Star Spangled Banner"

The funds raised by this production were used to support the School Assembly program, allowing the students to bring speakers and presenters to the school throughout the school year.

The Christmas season was the occasion for another play performance at the Community Center. It was "The Other Shepherd" by Dorothy Wilson Clark, hardly as well known as the playwrights of the earlier productions, but much appreciated by the actors and those in attendance.

Mrs. J. Stanley Mitchell representing the Presbyterian Church and Mrs. Henry Alchin of the Methodist Church joined together to produce this Biblical story. Mrs. Phyllis Wright of Ann Arbor and the Mimes Club directed the play. Many of the local people portrayed the Biblical Characters in the play. They included: Lynn Welch, Madeline Wessendorf, Sybil Haddon, Ilene Edinger, Mrs. Shull Woolworth, Peter Browne, Walter Conrad, Ormand Danford, Clement Dibble and Don Bell.

It was now becoming an annual event with the Fenton Chorus joining with the Hartland Chorus in the presentation of the "Messiah" in both Hartland and Fenton. On December 19th, the "Messiah" appeared at the Fenton Community Center under the direction of Miss Frances Hicks. A small orchestra led by Richmond Browne accompanied Mrs. W.T. MaWhinney –Soprano, Marie Warren-Contralto, Lester McCoy-Tenor and Vernon Syring-Bass during the performance. As in the past, the public filled the auditorium and expressed their appreciation with a standing ovation at the end of the performance.

As it had been for many years, some of the best shows in town were the performances of the City Band. Before the building of the Fenton Community Center, the Band's major activity was limited to the series of summer concerts…"Music in the park"… with an occasional concert in one of the community's churches. In recent years, the band "season" was extended into the winter months, with several concerts at the Community Center. And so it was for the year 1941.

As in the past, the Band met in early February to elect their officers for the upcoming year. They decided to continue keep the leadership in position as they re-elected Fred Parker as President, Henry L. Willing as Secretary and Charles A. Simmons as Manager. The Director was Henry H. Stanton,

The summer concerts began on June 11th and were held every Wednesday evening through July. The site was the bandstand in a park on Shiawassee Avenue, hence the location of the concert was often said to be "on the Avenue". On August 6 and 7, the Band played at the St. John Church annual Barbeque. Incidentally, the newspapers printed the upcoming Band programs and added "Motorists are requested not to blow their horns".

The opening "winter" concert at the Fenton Community Center on October 12th was an exceptional program. The Pontiac Motor Division Male Chorus, under the direction of Mr. Edward Osslo, appeared with the City Band, which had been augmented with some excellent musicians from the Fenton High School Band. The overflow crowd at the Center rated the performance "outstanding".

The final appearance of the Band for the year was at the Community "Yule Carol Sing" program on December 22nd. It's fitting that the last number for the band in this wartime year was the National Anthem.

Military Order Of Cooties of the Veterans of Foreign Wars .
Front Row L-R Emanuel "Dick" Boilore, John Hauitz, Joe Rosbury, Sam
Casazza, Isaac Stiff, Walter Stiff. Back Row L-R Harold Butcher, Webb
Kelleher, Harry Pokorny, William Harris, William Husted

V.F.W. Auxiliary. Seated L-R Lelah Stiff,
Lillian Goodrich, Marcella Bowman, Gerry
Carlson. Standing L-R Hazel Crystal, Bessie
Taylor, Nethal Walters, Fannie Schleicher,
Marguerite Petts, Myrtle Harris, Violet Harley,
Irene Boilore, Leda Hanby

Scene Three...The Gift That Keeps On Giving!

The Fenton Community Center was into its third year of operation and the community's enthusiasm in support of the Center and its multitude of programs had not waned. Morning and Night, seven days a week, the Center was the site of meetings, dances, lectures, church services, classes on a variety of subjects, bridge clubs and club meetings, Girl Scouts and Boy Scouts and the operation of a community employment service. Director Russell Haddon, with the help of a large number of volunteers was making the dream of the Rackhams a reality.

The activities started with an "old-time" dance on January 2nd and kept on going at a steady pace throughout the year. The "Turkey in the Straw" dance featured Schottische, Quadrilles and the "Grapevine Twist". It was reported over 200 dancers enjoyed the evening.

Modern dancing was featured in February at the Valentine's Day Ball and in March when Art Strom chaired a committee assisted by Mella Williams and June Bigelow in producing the "Buttercup Ball". Mella and June were responsible for the decorations at both the Valentine and Buttercup dances, and received many kudos for their efforts.

Other dance parties occurred during the year, but the next special affair was the "Cabaret Party". As in the past years, the main room of the Center was transformed into a "night club" with tables surrounding the dance floor. Magician David Norton was featured in the "floor show" and he thrilled the partygoers with his slight-of-hand tricks.

The Young Ladies of Fenton had planned their annual Semi-Formal Christmas Ball for months, but with the nation now plunged in war, the met to discuss what they should do in view of the recent events. They decided to have their Christmas Ball as planned, but to donate the proceeds of the party to the American Red Cross. Miss Theresa Vincent, President of Sodality, had appointed Miss Marie Dery as Chairman of the Ball and Miss Dery selected the following members as her committee: Elizabeth McKeon, Helen Weigant, Frances Senecal and Florence Botticelli. Bob Conklin and his Orchestra was engaged for this annual dance at the Fenton Community Center

The executive committee for the Center, who worked closely with Director Haddon in developing the Center's programs and setting policy governing its activities, met in May and reappointed the members of the Planning Committee. The members were: June Hartley, George C.

Paine, Barbara Barnes, Arthur Strom (who had earlier replaced Ron Butler on the Executive Committee), C.D. Arrand, Mrs. Marjorie Lee and Mella Williams. Mrs. Lee and Miss Williams replaced former members Charles Groover and Faye Olmstead.

The annual election of officers of the Fenton Community Council in July, named C.D. Arrand as their President, N.H. Chesnut as Vice President and Barbara Barnes as the Secretary. The Council expressed their gratitude for the service of the retiring President, C.R. Heemstra.

The new committee proposed establishing the following new programs for the Center: Bridge, Boxing and Wresting, Public Speaking, Salesmanship, Youth Games Night, Youth University of Life, Men and Womens Gym classes, Camera Club, Art classes, Mechanical Training and Citizenship Classes. Several of these activities, such as the Youth University of Life had previously been conducted on a trial basis.

In the fall, the Center joined the Fenton Merchants in a program to promote and sell Defense Bonds and Stamps.

The Community Center conducted its second annual "Open House" in September. The "open house" was held at the beginning of a new season of activities, to announce the programs and literally open the doors to the public. The evening program began with a selection by the Fenton City Band, greetings from the Village President Harry Lemen and Community singing led by Miss Frances Hicks. Russell Haddon, the Center's Director, followed with an announcement of the Center's 1941-42 programs. Vocal selections by baritone Charles Melvin Gregor completed the formal program. The attendees were then invited to visit the various booths and tables and register for the activities of their choice.

The Center's Lecture program began in early January and continued throughout the year. Dr. Dennis Glen Cooper, a Professor of Political Science with the Detroit Public Schools delivered the "kickoff" lecture. His topic was not "political", but was an entertaining talk of travel from Detroit to the Isle Royale.

Only a couple weeks later, the Center presented Alvin F. Zandler, a research assistant at the University of Michigan, whose subject of discussion was the Michigan Community Councils

Entertaining and predictable Ben East returned to Fenton in February, this time under the sponsorship of the Isaac Walton League of Fenton. Ben East, a columnist for a Grand Rapids newspaper, had established himself as an authority on the wildlife and wildernesses of

Michigan. He was a prolific writer and an inexhaustible speaker at events in Michigan and the nation.

A large crowd of over 150 attended a very timely presentation by Dr. H. J. Henneman, an Associate Professor of Political Science at the University of Michigan in early October. The Professor spoke on "Current World Affairs" which at the time were in great turmoil.

Dr. Henneman returned in November for his second lecture on "Russia". Again his topic was of great interest to those attending, since Russia was heavily engaged in the European conflict.

Ten days after Japan had attacked the United States, the Isaac Walton League sponsored an address by Dr. Lawrence Preuss of the Political Science Department at the University of Michigan, about the US-Japanese war. As one would expect, with interest running high, the presentation was very well attended.

The University of Life program was a church based agenda supported by four of the local churches. It was promoted as a "fun, fellowship, devotion" program for high school Juniors and Seniors. Charles D. Arrand, the high school principal, was a leader in the program and Beulah Keddy ably assisted him. Students like Mary Mitchell, the daughter of the Presbyterian minister, were also leaders in the group. The "University" was supported by the Center, but after a month or so, the "University" expired for lack of interest of the target age group. The church people substituted a "Bible Lecture" for Sunday evenings at the Center, and it too, was discontinued after a couple of months. C.D. Arrand, who was a "no nonsense" high school principal, became very active in church ministry following his retirement from public education.

Most of the clubs operating out of the Center continued to be very active. These clubs served a wide-ranging range of interests. William "Bill" Marshall, barber and erstwhile politician, continued to do what he loved best, showing others how to "tie flies" in his classes at the Center. At the other extreme, the more vigorous Hiking Club continued to be very active.,

When they weren't hiking or partying, they were sponsoring a dance at the Center. They engaged Fred Oates' "Arcadians" for a public dance in January. Art Strom and Adelaide Neininger were chairmen for the event and Ellwood Ellsworth and Dorothy Aman did the decorations that included several hilarious "cutouts" of a hiker

Not all the hikes were of the "over hill and dale" type, especially the "Hare" hike. "Follow the Hare" involved tracking the signs…bits of confetti, odd tracks, etc…to the end of the trail. The last hike of the season was a "cross-country" trudge that when completed would make a total of 90 miles hiked during the past season. Don Chase led this hike and was accompanied by 17 hikers, all of whom completed their 90 miles.

The tennis courts were flooded again this year to provide a skating rink for the "little folks". With lighting available the rink, with a coin operated meter, the rink was well used into the early evenings.

Once the warmer weather arrived, the Center's recreational activities swung into "high gear" with a very ambitious summer recreational program. The new high school coach, Ivan Williams was hired to run the program and he was assisted by 12 adult volunteers. The swimming program at Silver Lake was returned from the previous summer and there were fun and games for children of all ages, either at the Community Center or on the playing fields of the high school.

For the second year, the Flower Show was held for two days in June. The show, sponsored by Fenton's Garden Club, featured exhibitors who were both amateurs and "professionals" showing "specimen blooms". The exhibits filled the main hall of the Community Center and the exhibits included: Roses, House plants, Cacti and Succulents, Peonies and flowers from shrubs, and a large assortment of other flowers and plants.

The Farm Festival also returned in November for the third year. Many of the Fenton Merchants were the sponsors of the Festival and provided the prizes for the various competitions. Those merchants supporting the Festival were: Michigan Bean Company, Winglemire's Furniture, Pelletts, McGuire Hardware, Fenton Hardware, Rolland Dry Goods Company, Beckers, Hinkley Jewelry, Bobier's Shoes, Don Alchin Grocery, Byerly's Grocery, Lutz and Son, and Lea Kerton Lumber. The Festival attracted over 1500 people during the two-day event.

The Community Center's Employment Service, which was established by Russ Haddon and the Fenton Community Council in 1939, was finding a "shortage of job seekers". The summary activity report for the past year, issued in July, showed over the past twelve months 375 adults employables registered with the service. During the period the service averaged one placement per day. However, now the present file was almost exhausted. There remained a shortage of persons for employment in domestic, clerical and farm labor.

Scene Four…Kiwanis Joins the Club Scene

The big news in the club world was the organizing of a Kiwanis Club. On June 17th several members of the Flint Kiwanis Club met with a group of Fenton men for the purpose of discussing the formation of a Kiwanis Club in Fenton. Mssrs. Charles O'Neil and Walter Orr of the Flint Club met with the Fenton businessmen who had expressed an interest in forming a Fenton Club and explained the process of organizing a club.

Some credit for the developing an interest in forming a club in Fenton should be credited to the Kiwanians of South Lyons, who first came to Fenton and kindled the interest of the Fenton Men, and sparked the Flint Kiwanis into taking a more active role in forming the new club.

A temporary organization was formed and Wilfred Hunt was chosen as its temporary chairman, Paul Stedman became the temporary Secretary and Treasurer and D. A. O'Dell the Sergeant at Arms. The organizing group attended a meeting of the Flint Kiwanis at the Durant Hotel the following week. Soon thereafter they began to seriously recruit members to meet the charter requirements of Kiwanis Intentional

The organizing committee for the Charter Night for the new Fenton Kiwanis was set for. September 30th. The organizing committee was Charter Night was composed of Chairman Hoyt Glaspie, William R. Davis, Don Alchin, Arthur Gruner and Eric Sjogren.

The Charter Night festivities found Flint Kiwanian Russell C. Roberts presiding and the Kiwanis District Governor Dr. Bert Parish presented the Charter to the Fenton Club President Wilfred L. Hunt. Other Fenton Club officers present were: VP Reverend W. Thomas Smith, Secretary Paul Stedman and Treasurer R. B. Graham

In October the Kiwanians elected their officer for the upcoming year: Rev. W. Thomas Smith-President, Deke Miller-VP, Paul Stedman-Secretary and R. B. Graham-Treasurer.

The Club set up a committee on "entertainment" headed by Eric Sjogren and with members: Carl Tisch, Ron Butler, Howard Hunt, Raymond Hunt, Howard Heinz and Elmer Westman.

It is interesting to note that the centerpiece for the speakers' table was a present of the XX Club and was accompanied by a congratulatory message from their President, Elton Austin.

The Masonic organizations continued to be one of the more active in the community. In early March, the Fellowship Club sponsored a Father-Son Banquet in the Temple. Ray Welch was the Chairman of the event.

The Fenton Masonic Lodge held their annual elections in December and elected Roy E. Polson, Worshipful Master. Other officers elected were Ray A. Cummings, Charles L. Thornton, D.R. Stiles, M.G. Sanders, Nolan M. Cartwright, Jack W. Bush, Clinton A. Leetch and E.A. Lockwood. Earlier in the year, the Fenton Commandery observed their 75th Anniversary

The Order of the Eastern Star met in early December and elected their officers for the coming year: Worthy Matron-Carolyn Pellett, and Worthy Patron-Harvey Swanebeck. Others selected were: Mattie Hiscox, Ray Cummings, Mary Matthews, Marion Bristol, Zella White, Myrtle Swanebeck and Minnie Winn.

The Rainbow Girls elected Sheila Keddy as their Worthy Advisor. Other to serve were: Jean Woodworth, Esther Crawford, Janet Piatt and Norma Lee Hoffman.

The I.O.O.F, the Oddfellows, another very active men's organization elected their new leaders in June and selected: Don Burdick as their Noble Grand, John Millington as the Vice NG, William Stocken as their Secretary and George Anglen as their Treasurer.

The Favorite Rebekahs named their officers in January with the election of NG Verna Eldred, Vice NG Thelma McGraw and Secretary Violet Vandercook.

As they had for over a half a century, the Bay View and the Entre Nous Clubs continued to maintain their viability and leadership among the many women's clubs in the Village.

The Fenton Music Club's Annual Spring Festival in March attracted over 200 people to the Community Center program. Pianist Miss Alice Van Atta accompanied Soloist Mrs. Ralph E. Talcott. Featured on the program was an instrumental trio, including Mrs. Kenneth Klingbiel, cellist; Mrs. Fred Hill, violinist and Miss Dorothy Seider pianist. They played Haydn's "Minuet" and Saint Saens' "The Swan". Representatives of the Flint Symphony participated in the program.

Mrs. Lowell Swanson, Mrs. E.C. Reid, Miss Mabel Van Atta, Miss Dorothy Giles and Mrs. Leo Hall assisted Mrs. W.T. MaWhinney, President of the club

Other club members who assisted were: Mrs. Don Smale, Mrs. J.J. Cell, Mrs. Elsie Skillen, Mrs., Harry Bush, Mrs. Earl Bell, Mrs. Anson Wolcott, Mrs. H.K. Shaefer and Mrs. Lloyd Bell.

The patriotic organizations were very active, perhaps stimulated by the community's spirit of Americanism, which was evidenced by their outspoken support of increasing the military and naval forces of the nation. For years, the American Legion and the Veterans of Foreign Wars Fenton Posts had been promoting "Americanism" and patriotism.

The Patriotic Council again as in recent years conducted the Memorial Day Parade. And again, the townsfolk were praising the efforts of the bands and the organizations…"best ever" was being heard again! The President of the Patriotic Council was William G. Harris of the V.F.W.. Mr. Harris was the Master of Ceremonies at the ceremonies conducted at the Library Park where he read the order by General Logan establishing the day as one to memorialize the veterans of our wars.

The parade began at the American Legion hall at the corner of Walnut and Eat Caroline Streets. With the Officer of the Day James Tribbey of the V.F.W. supervising, the units marched in this order: City Band, W.R.C., D.U.V., VFW, VFW Auxiliary, Gold Star Mothers, American Legion, American Legion Auxiliary, FHS Band, Boy Scouts, Girls Scouts followed by school children of all ages.

Members of the Ladies Auxiliary of the American Legion James Dewitt Post had been visiting the Veterans in the VA Hospital in Bay City distributing toilet items, candy and pastries for several years, but now the visits seemed to carry more of the message of carrying for our wounded veterans. Mrs. Zella White was the leader of the group responsible for these visits.

The membership of the Auxiliary had reached 68 members and the leaders of the various committees had many volunteers to conduct the many activities. Some of the committee chairmen were: Mrs. Emma Curtis, Mrs. Ruth Van Alstine, Mrs. Lillian Goodrich, Mrs. Ida Gould, Mrs. Maybelle Reid, and Mrs. Rosetta Trimmer.

In September, the Auxiliary installed their officers for the coming year: President Gladys Dobbs, 1st VP Ida Gould, 2nd VP Eleanor Patten, Secretary Maud Reed and Treasurer Emma Curtis.

The Post members elected their officers in September. Those elected were: Commander Basil Bowman, Senior Vice Cmdr.Sam Casazza, Junior Vice Cmdr. Hoyt Glaspie and Adjutant Harry Reed.

The Veterans of Foreign Wars Curtis-Wolverton Post held their election in March and selected the following officers: Commander Fred

250 The Village Players

Slover, Senior Vice Cmdr. Fred Schleicher, Junior Vice Cmdr. James Tribbey and Quartermaster William G Harris. It is interesting to note that Schleicher, Tribbey and Harris represented the "new blood" in the organization who were moving into leadership positions. William G. Harris was later to be elected as Post Commander on three separate occasions. He is the only member of the Curtis –Wolverton Post to have had that distinct honor.

One of the commitments made by the members of the V.F.W. Post was to visit the veterans in the Grand Rapids soldiers home. Joe Botticelli, the Post's Poppy Day chairman, reported the "poppies" to be sold for Memorial Day were made by the veterans at the Grand Rapids home.

The V.F.W. Auxiliary elected their officers in April and selected Fannie Schleicher as President, Naomi Bennett as Senior Vice President and Irene Tribbey as their Junior Vice President.

The two older Womens' clubs, the Bay View Club and the Entre Nous, exhibited a very accommodating attitude in the early months of the year. The Bay View club attended the lecture by Roger Gleason, Special Agent of the Federal Bureau of Investigation, at the Community Center in late January. The lecture was sponsored by the Entre Nous.. Earlier in the afternoon, the Bay View held their regular meeting at the home of Mrs. G.L. Whittier. Mrs. Don Smale was accepted as a new member during the meeting.

The two clubs met for a "social" at the home of Mrs. E. C. Reid a few weeks later. The cooperative mood continued as the clubs joined to sponsor a talk at the Community Center by Mr. Joseph Joseph of Flint. The subject of Mr. Joseph's address was "Hitler and His Consular Activities in the United States".

Those in charge of the lecture were: Mrs. A.G. Becker, Mrs. E.R. Sluyter, Mrs. Don C. Smale and Mrs. C.E. Rolland.

The Entre Nous club traveled as a group to the Cranbrook Institute in late October to view the art exhibit. Mss. Lowe, Pavey, Morgan and Merrick were in charge of this "outreach" program.

For many years, especially before the building of the Fenton Community Center, the Methodist Episcopal Church was the venue for many events not related to the church. It was the scene of banquets, lectures, music programs and other events The Methodist women provided the food service for many banquets in their hall and even after the Community Center came on the scene, they continued to serve dinners at both the church and the Community Center.

In March the Methodist Episcopal church offered a style show for the fourth consecutive year. With support of Pellett's Departments Store, Rolland's Dry Goods, Becker Federated, Suzanne Hat Shop and the Stella Shop, the Women's Society for Christian Service of the M.E. Church put on a first class presentation at the Community Center. The tables were scattered throughout the auditorium for the guests. The models came down from the stage and mingled with the audience, giving people an opportunity to see the styles close up. The program also included entertainment, musical numbers and tap dancing. Mrs. Frank Wiggins was the chairman for the event.

About a month late the congregation at St. John held their annual Mother-Son Banquet. Mrs. Phillip Foley chaired the event and was assisted by Mrs. John McCann. Duane Theisen did the obligatory toasts for the sons and Mrs. Robert C. Brown for the mothers. State Representative Robert J. McDonald was the speaker for the evening.

Father Tighe led the parishioners in producing the annual St. John Barbeque in early August. As in past years, the major attraction, besides the excellent barbequed meats, was the concert by the Fenton City Band. Dinner was served from 5PM to 8PM, and this was followed by Bingo and Dancing. As usual, the crowd was large and happy!

Fenton Kiwanis-Post War:: 1st Row L-R Wm. Daniels, O. Stanstill, W. Roberts, E. Austin, L. Snyder, Art Howard, Al Callahan, M.S. Kline, Beck, E.C. Reid, Curt Schupbach 2nd Row L-R H. Craft, Bill Early, Joe Parker, Dr. Ambler, Clay Hurd, A.C. Locke, Bill Ruckel, Milt Bobier, B. Robinson, Art Sorenson, C. White, Ed Lee, Murray Chase, L. Herrick, C. Sheriff. Back Row L-R: Ken Harris, Ed Stiles, L. Reidel, P. Williams, Bill Davis, C. Tisch, Bob Beach, H. Hitchcock, Joe Essex, Bob Nieresher, Terry Rosa, Hal Sanford, North Townsend, Kline Sprague, P. Bottecelli, Fred Bostick, Al Carlson, Curly Ennis, Austin Howard, Bob Lutz.

This picture of Post-War Kiwanis is included because it includes many of the men who were "village players" during the period 1937-1941.

252 The Village Players

Minstrel Show of 1942 with cast of Men and Women, all ages.
Location: Fenton Community Center. A photo of the original All
Male Minstrel Show of 1941 is not available.

Old Time Dance at Community Center
with Lew Gage on the Violin during the late Thirties.

Scene Five…Fenton High School…Pre-War

The leaders of the school recognized the nee to expand the curriculum as the world was changing about them. In January of the year they announced the addition of three new courses to the high school curriculum: Solid Geometry, Economics and Commercial Law.

Solid Geometry was to be taught by August Arndt, an outstanding Mathematics teacher. Mr. Arndt was a pleasant quiet man; with a smile on his round face almost all of the time. His round face went well with round body. He rarely raised his voice above a conversational level, but maintained discipline and order in his classroom. He commanded the respect of all of the students. After the war, Mr. Arndt followed Mr. C.D. Arrand as the High School principal. Mr. Arrand was considered to be a strict disciplinarian, who many students feared to cross. The contrast in styles between Messrs. Arrand and Arndt could not have been more dissimilar!

Charles D. Arrand

The Economics course was to be taught by Mr. Ormand Danford. Mr. Danford educated in Economics and he may have been the first member of the faculty qualified to teach this subject. Mr. Danford in later years became a Judge in a northern Michigan community. He was a man of small stature, and an excellent classroom teacher who maintained a friendly positive relationship with his student.

Miss Olga Jones taught a first year teacher the Commercial Law course. Miss Bessie Cramer, essentially the one woman Business education department, received some help when Miss Jones joined the faculty. While Miss Jones taught Typing, but her availability permitted adding Commercial Law to the curriculum. Miss Jones left FHS within a few years, but Bessie Cramer continued to teach until she retired at age 60. Miss Cramer graduated from Fenton High School in 1910 and after a short teaching stint in a rural school in Argentine she attended Cleary College to study business. In 1917 she joined the faculty at FHS and remained until her retirement in 1951

Vocational Education received a real boost in the Fenton schools with the building of a workable "shop" building. Mr. Wilford Crissman, the shop instructor, pridefully told of how students and other volunteers helped build the new building and used material salvaged from the old North Road School that was recently torn down.

As the New Year began, Fenton High School's basketball team was well underway. A new cast of players was now representing the school on the court. The starting team members were Center Ray Heemstra; Forwards "Wilbur "Bib" Swartz and Al Turco; Guards Don Hunt and Bob Runyan. The ready and able substitutes were: Larry Sugden, Dick Hiscox, Jack Kean, John Hart, David Lathrop, Bob Gould, Dwight Lee and Curt Schupbach. It was Ivan Williams first of many seasons as FHS basketball coach.

The team experienced a winning season, highlighted by two wins over archrival

FHS 1940-41 Basketball 1ˢᵗ Row L-R Ray Heemstra, Jack Kean, Al Turco, "Bib" Swartz, Dick Hiscox. 2ⁿᵈ Row L-R: Coach Williams, Curt Schupbach, Don Hunt, John Hart, Dave Lathrop, and Mgr. Bob Turco.

Holly. The team faltered in the District Tournament at Farmington and even their new "Black and Gold" uniforms couldn't produce a win!

Some very interesting Assembly programs were presented during the 1940-41 school year. A tumbling group, "The Three Leonards" led the lineup, followed by the "Kitty Trumpeters" a quartet of young ladies all expert instrumentalists playing music of all kinds. The first assembly in January featured G.W. Strauss of General Motors. Mr. Strauss created some "Scientific Wonders" on the stage at Fenton High School. His program featured "Ultra Violet" light exhibits and a demonstration of some new synthetic products from chemistry.

In April, the Student Council announced the assembly program for the next school year. They had arranged for the appearance of the dance team of Sybil Shearer and Allison Choate. They also scheduled Walter Morgan who will speak of his experiences as a Page in the U.S. House of Representatives. The finale of the assemblies would have Robert M. Zimmerman, the noted swimmer and deep sea diver, who would describe his adventures on the ocean's floor.

The big social event of the school year, the J-Hop, was held at the Community Center on May 2ⁿᵈ. The theme for this year's extravaganza was "nautical". The eleven-piece band, the Borst Brothers, provided the music for dancing. While most of the members of the Junior class were actively involved in preparing the hall, providing refreshments, selling tickets (at $1.25 per couple), decorating and making all the other arrangements the following are the chairman and their primary assistants: Decorations: Marilyn Miller and Donna Austin; Favors: Helen Randolph and Marie Durant; Refreshments: Mary Groll and Pat Luther; Orchestra: Gerald Durand and Shirley Pavey; Advertising: Dave Lathrop and Russ O'Berry; Tickets: Maurice Foley and Sid hay.

Another traditional event, the All-Hi Banquet was held at the Fenton Community Center in mid-April and attended by more than 250 students from all four class years. The Toastmaster for the banquet was Ed Daniels and the individual classes were represented by the following speakers; Freshmen-Dave Gordon, Sophomore-Bob Dery, Junior-Maurice Foley and Senior-Murray Bell. The *Fenton Courier* reported the Methodist Church women were kept busy serving ham, tuna, beets, salad, coffee and Lemon pie. The "Modernaires", a group of student musicians playing "swing" music, provided the music. While there is no record of the names of the players, the group was certain to include Dick Smale, Gerald "Meatball" Durand and Tommy Merrill, all of whom were active in the swing bands in the area.

Sports was a big part of "high school" life for many of the students, but many other activities attracted many of the students as participants and were equally enjoyed by all, students and many parents and citizens.

In February, the students of all the grades presented their Annual "Fun-Fest". High school junior, David D. Lathrop acted as Master of Ceremonies for the event that offered the following program:
1.   Pantomime by the Dramatics Club
2.   A patriotic skit presented by grade school students
3.   Toe, Tap and acrobatic dancing by Leon Jolly's students.
4.   "Uncle" David Lathrop's "bed-time story"
5.   The "Gay Nineties Sextet"
6.   Burlesque of the "Concert in the Park".
7.   "Swing " by Gerald Durand, Dick Smale, Jean Brooks, Leone Hagerman, Tommy Merrill and "Maestro" Harvey Thomsen leading the band.

According to the *Fenton Courier,* "Uncle" David's bedtime story was the same one that " earlier kept 320 grade school youngsters breathless' and "rolled the high school boys beneath the tables" at earlier performances.

About a month after the "Funfest", the High School band, under the direction of Mr. Harvey Thomsen, presented it's second annual concert at the Community Center. The Girls Glee Club under the direction of Miss Thelma Barker also participated in the concert The FHS band played well and looked splendid in their "Blue uniforms with the gold trim". In the fall, the student writer for the *Fenton Courier* reporting on the high school football games undoubtedly was taken in by the color of the band uniforms. He began referring to the team as the "blue and gold". Only goes to show that a clothes makes the band, or something like that!

The last "banquet" of the year was traditionally the Junior-Senior Banquet. The Junior class hosted the Seniors at this annual banquet that was held at the First Presbyterian church parlors in early June. The event was designed as a gesture of congratulations to the graduating class. The Junior class speaker was Gerald "Meatball" Durand and Bill Brown spoke for the Seniors. David Lathrop, who was becoming a "pro" at toast mastering, performed the M.C duties. Junior Mary Mitchell delivered a reading entitled "Too Late for the Train".

The traditional spring sports found a "newcomer" had arrived. For the first time, FHS would field a golf team. Mr. August Arndt coached the team and its members were: Bobby Bachus, George Pellett, Wilbur Swartz, Nathan Woodward, Don Hunt, Pat Vandercook, Dave Nelson and Clair Cheseboro. In their first match versus Bendle High School, Cheseboro was the low man with a "brilliant" (according to the *Fenton Courier*) score of 44 for nine holes. Bachus-55, Swartz-56 and Pellett-66 followed him. They defeated Bendle by 21 strokes

The Track team had one of the best records in the history of the school. The team won the State Championship in their class, Class "B". Nate Woodward "scampered to glory" as he won the low and high hurdles in the State Championship meet. Bob Perry won the 440 in fifty-five seconds, while Jim Gale tied for first in the Pole Vault. Bob Runyan came in second in the 440 and Carroll Butts came in fourth and fifth in the high hurdles and broad jump respectively. The students enjoyed viewing the mahogany and bronze trophy on display in the study hall.

Baseball season started with a new coach, Ivan Williams, and a major void in its pitching staff because of the absence of last years "star" Bob Zoll, who was now residing in the Howell TB Sanitarium. The team members for this 1941 season were: Bill Rynearson, Harold Schleicher, Wayne Townsend, Charles McKeon, Ray Heemstra, Dwight Lee, Dick

Hiscox, Lee Gordon, Leon Shelby, Al Turco, Curt Schupbach, Ernie Neely, Ed Daniels, Tom Becker, Bob Runyan and Don Hunt.

It wasn't always "fun and games" for the members of the Junior Class. When the school closed to allow the teachers to attend a meeting in Ann Arbor, the Junior Class used the day to assist homeowners in their "spring cleaning". The village was divided into four sections with a "trash Lieutenant" in charge of each section. The "trash Captain" was class President Jack Kean and he directed the whole operation. The class members picked up newspapers, magazines and debris from the Fenton households in their section. The money made from the sale of the newspapers and magazines, was placed in a fund to help defray their anticipated "Senior Trip" for the next year. The "trash Lieutenants" were Don Hunt, Dave Lathrop, Mary Mitchell and Sid Hay. It is interesting to note that in later years Mary and Sid would become husband and wife!

The Valedictorian and Salutatorian for the Class of 1941 were Evelyn Graham and Margaret Chesnut respectively. The next eight students by grade average were: Virginia Joslin, Ray Barnes, Ed Daniels, June Hartley, Shielah Keddy, Joyce Stein, Murray Bell and Neil Walker The list of graduates in the class is to be found in Appendix One.

The graduation ceremonies were held at the Fenton Community Center on June 18th and featured a group of speakers from the class addressing the topic "We look to the future", little knowing that powerful forces were in motion that would greatly affect their future. The class speakers were: Evelyn Graham, Edward Daniels, Marvin Youker, Virginia Joslin, Joyce Stein and Margaret Chesnut.

Miss Lucille Miller finished her teaching career in Fenton with the Graduation ceremonies for her Kindergarten students, just as she did when she originated the practice for the Class of 1950, in June of 1938. The Class of 1953 graduated 78 little people. Soon after the close of school, Miss Miller married educator Derby Dustin.

In July, the Fenton Schools issued their annual financial statement. Again, as in recent years, the Schools elected to not include the individual salaries paid to the school personnel in the statement. They did report the Superintendent C.R. Heemstra was paid $1,302 for the year and the Mr. C.D. Arrand $650 for his services as Principal. Both individuals received additional compensation for their teaching duties. The total payrolls for the school divisions were: Elementary- $19,134, Junior High School-$7, 575 and Senior High School-$15,068.

At about the same time, the Superintendent announced all teachers were returning for the next year except Miss Lucille Miller and Miss Thelma Barker. Misses Miller and Barker had been exceptional teachers during their tenure and been very active in the community. All those associated with the school and the Community Center was especially saddened with the prospect of not having them involved.

The Board of Education held a special election for approval to develop the Phillips field for football, track and baseball. The old athletic fields would be used for physical education activities and summer playground and recreational programs.

In December, elder citizen J. H. Jennings visited with Superintendent Heemstra and delivered several items of historical interest. Mr. Jennings presented the original Diploma presented to his sister Lizzie M. Jennings in 1872. He class, the Class of 1872, was the first to graduate from Fenton High School. He also presented Mr. Heemstra with two sepia pictures the Class of 1879 as Juniors and Seniors.

The school enrollment at the beginning of the 1941-1942 year was the highest in the history of the school. A total of 1,025 students were enrolled. The distribution of High School students by grade was: as follows: 12th –67; 11th –76; 10th –80 and 9th – 101.

Coach Ivan Williams, starting his second year as the football coach, experienced several injuries to several of his players in the early part of the season. First string Fullback Leon Shelby injured his leg and was lost for his Senior year. The season ended with a record of 4 wins, 3 losses and 2 ties, just barely a winning season. However, the "Tigers" trounced the Holly in their Thanksgiving Day classic, 12-0, where running backs Dave Bard, Dwight "Baldy" Lee and Curt Schupbach each gained more yards than the Holly team. Members of the 1941 team were: Ray Heemstra, Bob Perry, Harold Schleicher, Richard Smith, Tommy Merrill, Ed White, Norman "Beanie" Crego, Richard Black, John Hart, Jim Gale, Bob Dery, Ralph Crawford, Kenny Schultz, Carroll Butts, Dave Lathrop, Curt Schupbach, Dave Bard, Dwight Lee, Cedric Whitman, George Lathrop, Wallace Bronson and Albert Cape

The Fenton XX Club hosted the Football Banquet, as it had in past years, however things were different this year. For the first time the banquet was not a small, all men's affair. Tickets were sold to all comers, men and women, fathers and mothers, girlfriends and the general public. As a result over 250 people attended the banquet at the Community Center on December 8th. Charley Bachman, football coach at Michigan State College was the guest speaker and as an extra bonus,

Michigan State's Athletic Director Ralph Young attended and made some remarks. The guests presented Technicolor movies of some of the Michigan State football games of the past season.

Many of the young men who played in these games, would soon find themselves playing in a much larger game…and several would find it a matter of life and death.

The men and women of Fenton, for the most part, continued their interest and support for Fenton High School long after they left the "hallowed halls" on Adelaide Street.

The Alumni organization continued their recent practice of holding an all-class reunion every year. The 1941 Reunion was held on Friday, June 13th and, in spite of the superstition surrounding the date, over 400 attended the banquet. The entire space in the main hall of the Community Center was occupied with diners and the overflow crowd extended the seating to the stage and the hallway outside the hall. The officers for the coming year were elected at the meeting and J.C. Peck was elected President. The 1st Vice President elected was Mrs. George Paine. Others elected were: 2nd VP Russell Haddon, Secretary Catherine Cronk, Assistant Secretaries Edith Hadley and Thelma Clement and Treasurer Raymond Hunt. Sidney Hay was the Immediate Past President.

The Toastmaster was Burns Fuller. Special recognition was given to Miss Sue Kelly who traveled from Los Angles to attend the reunion and Earl Husted who traveled from Everett, Washington.

Abner E. Larned and Brson D. Horton delivered brief addresses. Fenton's songbird, Mrs. Harriet Mortimore Toomey, was " at her best in two vocals" according to the *Fenton Courier.*

J Hop 1941- Identifiable Dancers: On Left, Facing and leaning left is Jim Frew; Middle Dick Hiscox, next right Ken Lawless to right is Hope Hamilton & Norm Reed. Marie Durant & Bob Harris are behind and between Lawless and Hamilton Front right , back only is Leon Becker

Alumni Association Reunion Banquet-June 1938 at Fenton Community Center

Scene Six...Town Sports and The Movies!

The "out-of-school" crowd favorite sports, year after year, were Bowling and Softball. Only in recent years has the Merchants Baseball team attracted "younger" older fellows to compete in the sport.. Until the New Fenton Recreation opened in 1940, the town only had two bowling alleys. Having only two alleys severely restricted the number of teams and the number of participants, and was especially difficult for women bowlers.

But now in 1941, the leagues enjoyed their best years ever. There were two men's and one women's league bowling during the season. The men's leagues were The Boosters and the Inter-City Bowling Leagues. The Women's was the Fenton Recreation Ladies Bowling League.

With twelve teams in each league, mostly all of them sponsored by Fenton businesses, there was amble opportunity for the men and women of the community to participate in the sport.

Soon after the bowling balls stopped rolling in the Spring, the "softball people" were meeting to organize their league, picking the players and preparing the schedule. The interest in softball was high and eight teams entered the summer competition. In the end, the playoff teams: Genesee Tool, Industrial Tool, Alchins Market and Matthew's "Lawmakers" competed for the championship. Elmer Hunt, Captained the Industrial team to finish at the top. The *Fenton Independent* credited much of his success to his "little brother Rapid Robert". Bob Hunt excelled in any sport he played. When asked why he did not compete while at Fenton High School, he replied, " I was a farm boy...after school I had chores to do...there was no time to play".

More tennis was being played in the Village, as the tennis courts at the Community Center were available beyond the daylight hours. The meter controlled lights allowed night play on both of the courts. The coin meters required 20 cents for 32 minutes of lighting.

The Fenton Merchants opened their Genesee County League season in the first week of May with a 8-3 victory over Burton. Verne Hunt pitched for the Merchants and Art Brown had three of the team's nine hits. And so it went throughout the season, the Fenton baseball team dominated the league.

The team manager was Rolland Sewell. He was experience in managing in the amateur leagues, such as the Genesee County League and contributed substantially to the success of the team.

Verne Hunt was a stellar performer on the mound and Lyle Neely, Pete Burnside, Jack Hartley, Tom Chappelle and Nicky Williams joined Brown with many timely hits. Neely's batting average was .450, exceptional in any league.

The Fenton Merchants had eleven players from Fenton, three players from Linden, one from Flint and one from Grand Blanc.

Another star pitcher emerged with Joe Ethier of Flint. Joe Ethier was injured late in the season, but came back in time to materially contribute to a championship season. The season ended with a 10-4 record.

The followers of the team, of which there were many, supported a fund-raiser dance with Lewis Gage providing the music. The dance was in recognition of their championship season and to raise funds for equipment and expenses for the next year.

During the golfing season, the prime supporter of a golf league was the Industrial Tool Company. The supported a league at the Shoreacres Golf Club, located on Torrey Road to the west of Lake Fenton. At the end of the season they also sponsored a tournament.

After a three-year absence, the City Basketball League was revived. Six teams were organized to play a round robin schedule at the Fenton High School gymnasium. Two games were played each Wednesday evening at 7 PM and 8 PM. The teams were named the Industrial "Eagles", Hunt's, Fenton Recreation, Genesee Tool, Moffett's and Industrial. Bill Terwilliger and Al Turco were engaged to referee the league games. Jud Phillips was a playing manager for the Moffett's team and Bob Hunt played and managed his Hunt's team.

At the seasons end, the Industrial team gained the championship. The Industrial team experienced only one loss during the entire season. Over fifty men were involved in the league during the season.

The bowlers began their season in early September and the teams from a year ago were present and raring to give it another "go". Chet Hillis was the League President and A. Guy Simmons served as Secretary. The Team Captains were: Alex Anderson, George Tamlyn, Bill Halls, Chet Hillis, A. Guy Simmons, Herb McKinley, Myron Richmond, Jack Temming, Wilbur Strom, Joe Chene, James Pasco and Tom Woodworth.

In June, the "old" Fenton Recreation opened again, under the management of Al Gray. The old alleys were located at 117 South Leroy Street next door to the old Post Office location. This time there was "Billiard-Pool-Cards" available and "Free Smokes Saturday".

For those who weren't spending their afternoons and evenings on the ball diamond or the high school gymnasium or the bowling alley, there was always a good movie at the *Rowena*. All the great stars of the 30's were still making movies and some new faces were beginning to establish themselves as "Stars" in the Hollywood heaven.

Those attending the movie shows at the *Rowena* were thoroughly enjoying the expanded seating, and the new lounge. The theater's external appearance on Leroy Street brought a sparking new look to the downtown where most of the buildings were built in the 1800s. The theatre was air-conditioned in the summer months and had good comfortable seats. Perhaps too comfortable for some!

Paul Bottecelli tells of the time his two younger brothers, then of early elementary school age, went to the movies together. Long after the movie theater had closed, they had not returned home and their family began searching for them. After a time, it occurred to them that they might have been locked in the theater when it closed. They contacted Harold O'Grady, who was the theater manager, and asked if he would look inside the theater for the two young boys. A quick search of the theater found the two young lads; sound asleep in their seats. Both Jim and Max Bottecelli were rescued! In later life each pursued careers in medicine and distinguished themselves as Medical Doctors.

While the physical facilities were "first class" they were surpassed by many of the movies,. J.C. Peck brought to the theater. He continued to present three different pictures each week, with matinees and evening . Most of the weeks, had one "double feature" day and the shows always include Coming Attractions, a Cartoon or short feature (or both) and a newsreel such as Movietone News. The prices remained at 25 cents for adults and 10 cents for children as in the past years.

"Gone with the Wind", the blockbuster movie of 1940, didn't appear on the *Rowena* screen until late February of this year. However, the price was right! No increase in admission and no reserved seating. For the three days it was showing.

For those who attended the matinee at the *Rowena* on Sunday afternoon, December 7, 1941 and upon returning to their homes only to find the United States was at war with Japan, they should know the movie they viewed that fateful afternoon. The movie was "International Squadron" starring Ronald Reagan.

The following list of movies and the starring actors is a sample of the 200 odd movies that graced the screen at the *Rowena* in 1941.

Mark of Zorro	Tyrone Power
Bitter Sweet	Nelson Eddy & Jeannette McDonald
Santa Fe Trail	Errol Flynn
Northwest Mounted Police	Gary Cooper
Tin Pan Alley	Alice Faye, Betty Grable
Go West	The Marx Brothers
Strike up the band	Mickey Rooney, Judy Garland
Kitty Foyle	Ginger Rogers
High Sierra	Humphrey Bogart, Ida Lupino
Hudson's Bay	Paul Muni
The Philadelphia Story	Cary Grant, Katherine Hepburn
Come Live with Me	James Stewart, Hedy Lamarr
Dr. Kildare's Crisis	Lew Ayres
Mr. and Mrs. Smith	Carole Lombard & Robt Montgomery
Tobacco Road	Marjorie Rambeau
Topper Returns	Roland Young, Joan Blondell
Western Union	Robt Young, Randolph Scott
The Lady Eve	Barbara Stanwyck, Henry Fonda
Road to Zanzibar	B. Hope, B. Crosby, Dorothy Lamour
The Great Dictator	Charlie Chaplin
Zeigfeld Girl	James Stewart, Judy Garland
Harmon of Michigan	Tom Harmon, Anita Louise
Sun Valley Serenade	Sonja Henie, John Payne,
Kiss the Boys Goodbye	Don Ameche, Mary Martin

Scene Seven…Individuals and Events…*potpourri!*

In the first weeks of the year, Claude Cohoon, the editor and publisher of the *Fenton Courier* sold his newspaper to Mr. Jay Miller from the Detroit area. Under the tutelage of Mr. Cohoon, the *Courier* was published in "tabloid" size and included a column entitled "Courier Comments" which provided Claude with an opportunity to express his personal biases. He was very insightful in most instances, even though on occasion his remarks were a bit brusque. Claude Cohoon's *Courier* provided an interesting contrast to S.F. Beach's *Fenton Independent.*

Soon after Mr. Jay Miller assumed control, the *Courier* abandoned the "tabloid" size in favor of the large sheet, similar to the sheet size used by the *Independent.* Unfortunately, the "Courier Comments" was discontinued and the only editorial expression was what crept into the news articles.

During the late Thirties, the Federal Government had established the Civilian Conservation Corps, better known as the "CCC". The CCC was organized along military lines and in many instances, set up their camps on military bases or installations. Several young men from the Fenton area signed up for the CCC and were assigned to units in the northern part of Michigan. One such camp was Camp Luzerne, north of the town of West Branch, Michigan.

On July 29 at Camp Luzerne, the rain began to fall and a thunderstorm was imminent. Jerry Cheney of Fenton was one a group of fellows, who made a dash to the camp's flagpole with the intention of lowering the nation's flag before the storm arrived.

As the group approached the flagpole, with Jerry Cheney in the lead, yelling to the others, "Don't let the flag touch the ground", there was a flash of lightening and Jerry Cheney was thrown several feet in the air. All efforts to revive him failed.

Jerry Cheney's funeral was held at the First Presbyterian Church in Fenton with several CCC boys serving as honorary pallbearers. Two truckloads of CCC boys drove to Fenton to attend his funeral.

Jerry's death was only a few days before he was to celebrate his 18th Birthday. His mother had planned to bake a large cake and take it to Camp Luzerne so her son could celebrate his birthday by sharing his cake with his friends. On his birthday, Mrs. Cheney with Jerry's brother Laverne and sister Joyce made the trip to the Camp, carrying a large cake and plenty of ice cream, and held the party with Jerry's friends

Not all of the stories found in the newspapers were as tragic as the one about Jerry Cheney. One of the heartwarming stories that appeared in the *Courier* was about the return of Howard Stocken, a petty officer in the U.S. Navy, to visit his parents Mr. and Mrs. William G. Stocken. Chief Yeoman Howard Stocken joined the U.S. navy at age 17 and had not been home since 1927...14 years ago. The Christmas visit was the best gift for all concerned.

Elton Austin

The A & P Company recognized the 15 years of service by Elton B. Austin, the manager of their Fenton Store. Mr. Austin became the manager of the A & P store in January 1926 when the store was located in the building just south of Pellett's Department Store on South Leroy Street. When the Post Office moved in next door, the A & P moved across the Street. Elton Austin was very well respected by all the townsfolk and served the community in many capacities.

The A & P Company announced their new personnel policy, a "first in the retail food industry" in July. Henceforth, no A & P employee would work more than five days a wee, even though they would continue to have their stores open for six days a week, closed only on Sunday. The weekly salary of A & P employees would not be reduced while working only five days instead of the six days under the old policy.

Harold Schupbach, a FHS graduate in 1940, beginning his second year at Michigan State College, was awarded a full four-year college scholarship. Harold had competed with over 300 young men and women graduating in 1940, for the Genesee County scholarship. His examination score placed him in second place, so Harold accepted another scholarship he had been offered and enrolled at Michigan State College. The first place winner was unable to accept the Genesee County scholarship, and the four-year scholarship was then awarded to Harold Schupbach. Later Harold was selected by the U.S. Army to pursue a medical education and became a Medical Doctor.

The Fenton newspapers were pleased to report one of the town's favorite sons, Garwood Marshall, had been elected as President of his fraternity at Hillsdale College. It was obvious that Garwood "Fuzz" Marshall, the son of William Marshall, was a natural leader. Alton

Garwood Marshall was a 1938 graduate of FHS. Later in life, Garwood was the Secretary to Nelson A. Rockefeller when he was Governor of the State of New York. He held many important positions in the Rockefeller organizations, including the Director of the Rockefeller Center. He was selected to the Fenton High School Hall of Fame in 1996.

One of Garwood's closest friends was Donald "Bud" Lemen who died in 1939. As one will recall, Bud Lemen's death was one of the more emotional times during this period. . It was a small town tragedy that affected many who knew him and many who wished they had known him.

. Bud's mother, Ila Lemen, was deeply affected by her son's death, and for years following his death, she would compose a poem for publication in the *Fenton Independent* on the anniversary of his death. The poem appearing in 1941 is printed below:

"Bud"
Two years of memories are
sweeter than one
Two years of love thoughts for
our dear young son
Two years he's been there…
alone on that hill
Everything peaceful, saintly and still
No one disturbs him, he's alone
'neath the flowers
The sun shines upon him and
Oft time the showers
Snow softly falls…the birds chirp
"Hello"
Stars shine their brightest
On "Bud" here below

In Memoriam
May 22, 1939---------May 22, 1941
"Bus" Lemen's family

Many of the Villagers had mixed emotions concerning Dr. Carl H. White's decision to leave his practice in Fenton to open a Eye, Ears, Nose and Throat practice in nearby Flint, Michigan. For several years

Dr. White had been studying the EENT specialty while conducting a general practice in Fenton. Dr. White first came to Fenton in 1922. The Whites would continue to reside in Fenton

Dr. William Fremont "Buck" Buchanan, whose tenure in Fenton was to be interrupted by a tour as an Army Doctor during World War II, came to Fenton and assumed Dr. White's practice.

Dorothy McBroom, wife of "Mickey" McBroom, had already distinguished herself as a Champion caliber Skeet Shooter over the past decade and in I 1941 she was named as an All-American by the National Skeet Shooting Association.

Another young man, Donald Rounds, a graduate of Fenton High School in 1933 and the University of Michigan in February 1940, was reported to be undergoing flight training in Pensacola, Florida as a Naval Aviation Cadet. Don Rounds earned his wings in April and became a Naval Aviator. In 1943, then Lt. j.g. Rounds lost his life while flying to Grosse Isle Naval Station from Washington, D.C.. During a severe winter storm his plane crashed into a mountain in Pennsylvania.

Roy Perry was one of the fastest runners who ever participated in sports at Fenton High School. Roy graduated in 1940 and joined the U.S. Marines soon after graduation. The *Fenton Courier* reported that Roy had ruptured a leg muscle and was hospitalized in Quantanamo Bay, Cuba.

The Ice Carnival was held in January for the second time and again it was held on the millpond. The crowd was not as large as turned out for the first carnival, however over 300 braved the cold to witness the races on the ice. The day was very clear, but very crisp…ideal for ice-skating

This year the racing classes were restricted to boys and girls in the following classes: **3rd & 4th Grades**; 5th grade; 6th Grade; Novelty and Figures skating. The races were for 100, 50 and 25 yards. The winners were: 3rd & 4th Grades: Girls- Denise Watson (Three 1st Places,), Glenna Wright (Three 2nd Places). Boys-Pat Pinckney (.Three 1st Places).John Wright.(Three 2nd Places). **5th Grade**: Girls-Loretta Shelby (Three 1st Places), Donna (Three 2nd Places), Virginia Swartz (Two 3rd Places), Rosemary Jacobs)One 3rd Place). Boys- Maurice Neeley (One 1st Place), Billy Burkett (one 1st Place, One 2nd Place), James Gillem (One 3rd Place, one 2nd Place), Alvin Ross (One 3rd Place). **6th Grade:** Girls: Janice Paine (three 1st Places), Jean Thorp (Two 2nd Places) Marie Morman (Two 3rd, One 2nd Place). Boys- James Thompson (Four 1st Places) and Ernest Burke (Four 2nd Places) . **Novelty:** 1st-Billy Burkett, 2nd-Maurice Neeley and 3rd- James Gillem. **Figure:** 1st-Loretta Shelby, 2nd- Janice Paine and 3rd- Phyllis Loomis.

While Homogenized Milk had been available in some parts of the country, generally in limited amounts, it finally came "big" to Fenton in 1941. Mickey's Dairy began advertising they were producing Homogenized milk. Mickey's announced their milk was available at Dubord's Grocery, Sanitary Market, Kroger's, A & P, Lemen's Grocery, Whitman's Grocery, Gould's Market, Hagedorn's Dairy, Locke's Service Station, Matthews market and Mickey's Dairy Bar. With the advent of homogenized milk, many youngsters would be deprived of their winter "treat" when the frozen milk would pop the paper plug out of the glass milk bottle and push up an inch or so of frozen cream. Ummmmm!!

In July there was the usual "bumper crop" of picnics. Family picnics galore and the local industry did them even bigger and better. The Genesee Tool Company was working around the clock producing cutting tools for Great Britain and now, with the increasing federal expenditures on defense material, the United States industrial market. So when it came time to "party" the Genesee Tool picnic was the time and place for its employees to take time out and play.

The Genesee Tool picnic was held at the Pleasant Valley Country Club off US 23. There were horses to ride, at least until one of the horses kicked a hole in the side of Walter Burke's truck which had only recently been painted. The "boss" Art Gruner pulled a tendon in a race (which the other "boss" Eric Sjogren won!) and later teenage Art Barnard tap-danced for the enthralled gathering. All in all, a good time was had by all!

The Industrial Tool folks held their annual picnic at the Davisburg Park. All were concerned by the threat of rain, but the sun came out and stayed bright all day and the picnic was on! The activities program kicked off with a golf tournament for both men and women. The winners for the men were: Carl Holm, Bud Welker, Emil Strom, Johnny Martin and Bruce Runyan. The ladies were lead by: Mrs. Ted Nelson, Mrs. Carl Holm and Mrs. James McKinley.

Harry Lemen, Village President, led the list of guests. A group of young ladies were also guests. Those so honored were: Mary Mitchell, Jane Walcott, Phyllis Warner, June Boilore, Martha McCann, Joanne Hitchcock, Evelyn Swartz, Mary Groll and Jean Collette.

Another picnic, which had become an annual occurrence, was the "Florida" picnic. Each year in late July, the "Snow Birds" in the area would gather for an outing. This year the location was at Torrey Beach on Lake Ponemah (which the old-timers still called "Mud Lake"). The families represented this year were: Wolverton, Lang, Bush, Bedan, Inghram, Hitchcock, Rosenkram, D.C. Haddon and Miller.

Many years earlier, the cement plants near Silver Lake and Mud Lake (now called Lake Ponemah), were flourishing businesses. The marl dug from the lakes was used in the making of the cement. However, in the mid thirties, the cement industry took a drastic turn when materials other than marl were found to provide a more efficient and economical source for the basic element of cement, Limestone. Consequently the Fenton area cement plants were abandoned.

In May of 1941, it was announced that the Aetna plant at Silver Lake would be reopened. The increased industrial activity sparked by the defense buildup resulted in an increased demand for cement and the Aetna cement company decided to reopen their old plant.

However, in July the plant suffered two terrible accidents when several high-pressure steam lines ruptured within one week. John Longworth was badly burned in the first incident and Alfred Brown and Joseph Lawrence were burned a few days later. The plant was immediately closed for repairs after the second incident. Soon thereafter, the plant closed…permanently. The hulking concrete skeleton of the two plants remained for more than 50 years as a reminder of the once booming industry.

There was a "new " grocery store in town. Don Alchin, a longtime employee of Moffett's and manager of their Fenton store, purchased the store from his company. So now, the Moffett's sign came down and "Alchin's" went up! Curtis Nelson continued to operate his meat market in the store.

In July, three Fenton boys entered the Soap Box Derby that was held in Flint. Harold Downer, the winner of two heats, with his best speed clocked at 28 MPH had the best showing of the Fenton lads. Harold had built his car in the new Fenton High School vocational building.

Last years Halloween parade and costume contest was an outstanding success with over 300 participants. Consequently, the planning for this year's Halloween was intense in an effort to be "bigger and better" than last year. On the day of the event, the rain was falling with "cats and dogs" and that certainly dampened the enthusiasm for the event. However, over 500 people attended the event despite the inclement conditions.

Scene Eight…The War

.

Proclamation

Our country is now engaged in war and as our village is situated in an industrial and defense area, I do hereby proclaim an emergency exists and call upon our people to unite and join a united front to help preserve the lives and property in this community.

Our water system and other important units in the village must be protected and I urge that the people be on the alert and watch for suspicious persons and movements and report same to your police at the earliest moment.

The members of our Veterans organizations have offered their services for this defense program for which we are most grateful. We are in need of many more people to carry on this work and I ask all those who are able and desire to lend some service, both men, women and children to register at the Firehall, Saturday, December 13 from 9-12 and 2-8 and on Monday, December 15 from 9-23 and 3-8.

Let us all prove that we are true-blooded Americans and work toward our goal. UNITY.

HARRY G. LEMEN
Pres. Village of Fenton

The front page of the December 11th edition of the *Fenton Independent* displayed Village President Harry G. Lemen's Proclamation as seen above. It was only four days after the Japanese attack on our naval base in Pearl Harbor. Probably most of the people were still in shock from learning of the surprise attack, but others were already making decisions as to what they were going to do to defend our country and strike back at those who had attacked us. On Monday, December 6th, the recruiting stations found crowds of young men waiting for their doors to open. A few wondered how it was we found ourselves at war with not only Japan, but also Germany and Italy. However, an observer of the events of the recent past would have known that our participation in a war against tyranny was inevitable.

In December of 1940, President Franklin D. Roosevelt addressed the nation. The subject of his address was the proposed legislation entitled the "Lend Lease" act…. a far reaching proposal to give the President the authority to sell, transfer, exchange, lend equipment to any country to help it defend against the Axis powers. In his speech the President expressed his position on the legislation:

"In the present world situation of course there is absolutely no doubt in the mind of a very overwhelming number of Americans that the best immediate defense of the United States is the success of Great Britain in defending itself; and that, therefore, quite aside from our historic and current interest in the survival of democracy in the world as a whole, it is equally important, from a selfish point of view of American defense, that we should do everything to help the British Empire to defend itself."

It was predictable that Congressman William Blackney would be opposed to the proposal. While Representative Blackney was supportive of the defense buildup, he was unalterably opposed to any action that might lead to the nation's participation in the "European" conflict. He held that if the Lend Lease Act became law, the Neutrality Act would be "virtually wiped off the statute books." Whie Mr. Blackney was still opposed, the National Veterans of Foreign Wars leadership asked for "all out" aid to Great Britain.

The Congress passed the Lend Lease Act on March 11, 1941. A sum of $50 billion was appropriated and the money went to 38 different countries with Great Britain receiving $31 billion. This was a huge step toward the United States becoming the "Arsenal of Democracy".

Mr. Blackney's letter to his constituency in late February reported on the increasing naval strength of the nation. He reported that 183 fighting ships were built between 1933 and 1940 and another 313 were under contract. The Navy enlisted strength had increased by 130,000 men to 209,667 over the same period. Mr. Blackney wrote, "…Building up of our defenses is not for the purpose of attacking any nation, but for the purpose of discouraging any nation from attacking us."

In April, Mr. Blackney expressed his suspicion that the President and his spokesman were not "leveling" with the Congress. He reports that during the consideration of an appropriation bill, the Secretaries of War and Navy and representatives of the administration, the Congress was told "…any munitions or implements of war to be used by democracies in Europe would not be sent in American ships or convoyed by American ships". However, in the testimony of Colonel William J. Donovan, the Administration's unofficial observer in Europe, he stated, "…goods being sent to Europe should be protected by American convoys". Colonel "Wild Bill" Donovan was the organizer of the Office of Strategic Services, the OSS…the forerunner of the CIA, the Central Intelligence Agency.

In July, Mr. Blackney wrote very prophetically in his weekly newsletter in the *Fenton Independent.* He wrote "We still sell oil to Japan…this oil, at the very moment when Great Britain and the U.S. both need the supplies, is being stored in Japan for the day when she may use it against the United States".

In September, the Representative said he was "…receiving lots of letters expressing loyalty to the U.S., but opposed to sending boys to war in Europe".

During the year, Mr. Blackney and the world had witnessed the Nazi Germany's conquest of all of Western Europe, the German invasion of the Soviet Union, the German conquest of Yugoslavia and Greece and the continuation of massive air raids against London and cities of Great Britain.

The killing of thousands of Jews by the Germans was not common public knowledge. Whether Mr. Blackney, as a member of Congress, knew of the Nazi "final solution" is not known. What is known is that he did not waver in his opposition to America's participation in this "European war".

In his letter of October 16th, he wrote, "There are those who preach the fatalistic doctrine that America depends for it is existence and its safety on the good fortune or the good intention of some European or Asiatic power." He continues, "But what are the facts? Is America in danger of invasion, come what will across the seas? Are the American defeatists accurate when they would push this country into the war with the argument that we had better fight when others do because we cannot protect ourselves?"

To substantiate his position, he quotes the highly respected Military Analyst for the New York Times, Mr., Hanson W. Baldwin, saying " (he) does not know a single responsible Military or Naval officer or government official who believe that this Nation is threatened by direct invasion, even if Germany wins".

Only ten days before the attack on Pearl Harbor, Mr. Blackney announced the Army Air Force was to be doubled to 400,000 enlisted by June 30, 1942 and that the present $60 Billion arms program was being raised to $108 Billion. In the same newsletter, Mr. Blackney used some wording that may have suggested a change in his attitude about the "European war". He wrote, "…(the Arms program). is to take on any size the Army may feel is necessary to accomplish the defeat of Hitler." (The underlining is the author's).

On December 15th, our representative in Congress spoke to the Men's Fellowship at the Fenton Community Center where he told of the advantages of having bases in the Caribbean, where he had recently visited on an inspection tour. (…and the result of the Lend Lease legislation which he opposed.) He spoke of the growing strength of our Navy and the armed services in general, and offered encouragement for our impending struggle to victory over Japan.

The United States was a war and the nation began to mobilize for a long and difficult struggle. The leaders in the Village of Fenton were also in the same mode of operation and the *Fenton Independent* newspaper carried a special notice on their front page on December 18th.

In his newsletter of December 18th he wrote in a statesmanlike manner, " We must have a united people and political differences must cease. The welfare of the United States is above politics; it is above the whim and caprice of any faction or any group of men." He further wrote, "This war should not be fought as a means of revenge; it should be fought to preserve American institutions and to preserve the rights of democracy for those nations that desire them." After a joint session of Congress addressed by President Roosevelt, the Declaration of War was passed by a vote of 388 to 1 in the House of Representatives and 82 to 0 in the Senate.

Back on the "home front", the village leaders moved swiftly to prepare the community for possible enemy action. While most everyone realized an attack on Fenton was not imminent, there was this fear of the unknown and the urge " to do something" at the time. The following announcement appeared on the front page of the *Fenton Independent*.

Please Cut This Out and Place Where It Can Be Used for Reference

For weeks the Fenton Police Commission have been working on the formation of the Fenton Home Guard, its personnel and activities in case of emergency. It is not the intention of the Commission to cause the people of this community unjust fear. However, the recent events prove that we are in great need of an emergency organization. With that in mind we have formed under the direct supervision of the Commission an organization dealing with the numerous phases of such an emergency. Every citizen is urged to read carefully all instructions and be ready to comply with same The most important and deadly of all enemy actions is the air raid and we have built our plan on that basis

NOTICE OF RAID of threatened danger.
  The Fenton Fire Horn will sound continually (no variations of tone) for a long period.
INSTRUCTIONS to Citizens
  Over 150 men of the organization will go immediately to designated stations.
  People at home should not show lights in buildings.
  Flashlights, axes, pails of water or sand, ladders should be placed in readiness.
  Keep off the streets, as cars will not show lights.
  Report to Fire hall any fire or other important thing.
  All Registered Guards will wear arm bands –trust them.
  Don't drive downtown-that section will be blocked off.
  The key men in the organization and their duties:
  General Chairman-Harry Lemen
  Co-ordinator- N.H. Chesnut
  Assistant Co-ordinators-William Marshall & Sidney Hay
  John Brown-Streets & Blockades, Cleaning Obstacles, etc
  Jim Ryan-Water Works, Hydrants, Valves, Repair to same.
  Karl Asman-Maintenance of light, power, gas, telephone.
  Howard Craft-In charge of trained force of men Fire Fighting
  Dr. Walcott-Medical and First Aid work.
  Mark Gordon, J.H. Tribbey and Hoyt Glaspie-Armed Home Guards
  Clifford Phillips-Girl Scouts, Boy Scouts, Communication
  Chas. E. Rolland-Red Cross
  H.W. Hitchcock-Public Relations

Specific duties have been given to a great number of citizens. We know they will not fail in an emergency. We ask the people of the Village again to post the instructions and follow them. Some other signals may be added later. More instructions will follow. We believe we have a complete organization capable and willing to help. Men will be on duty at the Fire Hall, Consumer Power Co. and other places to receive telephone calls for help. We wish to than the people of Fenton for the interest shown in making this a success. We have had a great many organizations and are expecting many more. The Council Rooms will be open from 9 to 12 and 1:30 to 4:30 each day until December 21st for those who wish to register.

N.H. CHESNUT, Co-ordinator

Many of the area's men were either volunteering or being "drafted" for military service. Some of the young men mentioned in this writings were not called to service until early 1943 when men under 21 were called in the draft. On one occasion, Mr. Elmer Westman, the "boss" of Industrial Tool Company feted a group of local young men who were to report to the their draft board for induction on the following day. The group was treated to dinner at the Fenton Hotel at which time the following photograph was taken.

L-R Seated: Jack Kean, Jim Buckingham, Al Turco, Al Bacon, Murray Bell, and Jack Soper. L-R Standing: Bob Gould, Tom Merrill, Gerald "Meatball" Durand, Earnest Neely, Deke Shively and Wallace Bronson

Scene Nine ...War or No War, Life Goes On

The year of 1941 began much like the years in the recent past. War or the threat of war, life must go on. Julia Sweeney ran an advertisement announcing she would give $41 in Defense Bonds to the first Fenton area child born in the New Year.

While the majority of the citizenry probably paid only scant attention to the report, the significance of the announcement would have great consequences for them...or at least their children and grandchildren and the people in Michigan for generations to come.

The Michigan Mirror column in the *Fenton Independent* addressed the St. Lawrence Waterway project. The writer reported the State of Michigan had approved the plan proposed by President Roosevelt and his administration   Roosevelt's plan was to open the Great lakes to ocean shipping and thereby improve the economic situation for the nation, especially the Midwestern states and the states surrounding the Great Lakes.

The plan however was not without opposition. The Association of American Railroads were especially opposed to the plan and called it "unsound economically and dangerous politically". Eastern and Southern states were also cool to the idea.

As more and more of the local men entered the armed services, the *Fenton Independent* recognized the need to provide them special attention. In mid-march, the *Fenton Independent* initiated a column headed "Our Boys...Following the Flag". Needless to say, Mr. Beach had no trouble filling the column space each week for the many months to come.

In mid-year, the nation witnessed the birth of the United Service Organization, which all learned to call the "USO" in short order. The Federal government announced it had set in motion a united effort to provide service for "selectees" that it cannot offer. In Fenton, Russell Haddon, assisted by Rose Whittle and Otis Furman as secretary and treasurer respectively, headed the USO organization.

The local plan was to conduct a house-to-house canvass for funds to support the activities of the organization. Chairman Mark Gordon, W. C. Lawson, Mrs. J.A. Johnson, Horace Hitchcock and J.C. Peck were in charge of these fund-raising efforts. One week later, Otis Furman reported the drive had exceeded its $500 goal by $152, with some donations exceeding $50.

Many of those activities associated with assisting the defense and, later, the war effort happened in Fenton as it did in most of the cities and towns across the nation. There was the drive for scrap iron and steel, that resulted in some farmers losing yards of old fencing, the aluminum drive, the Red Cross drive for both blood and money and the sale of Defense stamps (in 10cent and 25 cent denominations) and Defense Bonds.

Other fund drives, in support of many local activities were undertaken during the year as in recent years.   The Community Fund set their goal at $1500 and completed their fund raising campaign in mid-December. The drive was supported by the businesses in the town and was capped off with a door-to-door solicitation that pushed the campaign "over the top". As in the past the money raised by the Community Fund was used to support many organizations and in particular, the summer recreation program conducted by the Fenton Community Center. Chester Hillis and Mrs. Cleber Merrick led the campaign and were assisted by Russell Haddon and Horace Hitchcock

In many ways, everyday life continued in the Fenton area during the war years. The people had to work with the rationing of selected commodities, most notably gasoline and meat rationing…. and most annoying to the women…. nylon hose! Both the Industrial Tool and Genesee Tool companies expanded their facilities and their work force, which for the first time included a substantial number of women.

A large number of the young men were serving their country in all corners of the world. When they returned they would bring many new ideas to their old hometown. Many would not return to Fenton, but having experienced other locales and met new people, would choose to relocate and pursue ventures not available to them in their hometown.

One young veteran returned to Fenton and opened a small restaurant featuring "Mexican" food. Tacos and Burritos were now on the menu in Fenton! However, within a few months the restaurant closed…. the general reaction of the townsfolk was "tacos…burritos…we don't eat that stuff!". He was a bit ahead of the curve. The townsfolk were still of the "meat and potato" class. The introduction of pizza was a little more successful as the returning veterans were already addicted having experienced the culinary treat during their tours of duty.

During the early days of the war, many of the local youth aspired to becoming pilots, and many realized their goal. For a period, the Army Air Force allowed their pilots to "borrow" an airplane and take a "weekend jaunt". Many made it home for the weekend. One of the first to arrive was Lt. Donald Clark. He made his arrival in grand style as he flew his B-25 twin-engine bomber the length of Leroy Street only a few hundred feet about the town. Don may have been the first to "buzz" the town, but others such as Dwight "Baldy" Lee and Carroll Butts did the same thing. Carroll flew all the way from his base in Mississippi in a single engine trainer to spend a few hours at home.

After the war many found the village had changed. The men and women, who had served in the armed forces or worked in the defense plants, were now much more sophisticated and demanding. The Village became a City in more ways than one, many of the citizens had seen "the other side of the mountain" and their innocence was lost.

Dr C. G. Walcott and family are welcomed home by Horace Hitchcock (Sword upraised), J.C. Peck on right with sword upraised and "high-hatter" Les "Duke" Whittle

Dr. Carver Walcott was highly decorated for his courageous efforts in treating wounded and burned men during naval battles at sea. After the war he returned to his practice in Fenton, with offices at the north east corner of E. Caroline and Walnut Streets.

Epilogue

The peace of heaven is theirs that lift their swords, in such a just and charitable war.

William Shakespeare

This play is over. The players now move on to a multitude of new stages. Each has many more parts to play before the curtain falls on the final act. Some will find their new play ending long before anyone would have anticipated; many will find their new stage located thousands of miles from their hometown. Most all of them will find a new cast of players in their new plays. Some of these new cast members would stay for the long run; others would fall out and move on to other stages. As time passed, and our players were older, they would have to play different roles, no longer would they play the bright new ingénue. But, these new roles would be even more challenging. With the passage of time, younger actors would arrive on their stage and require their care and support.

Yes, this play is over! It's time to move on to another stage!

Of all the stages available after 1941, the World War II provided the biggest ones. Hundreds of the Village's young men, and some young women, would enter the service in America's armed forces and within months find themselves in all corners of the globe. Others would find their work at home directly supporting America's war effort.

It wasn't until November 11, 1943, that the community dedicated a large "billboard" sign listing the names of most of the area's men who were serving in the Armed Forces. The community's Patriotic Council led the effort to erect the sign containing the names of the 438 men who were known to be serving at that time. The names were been painted in black on a white wooden sign. Each of the names was individually hand painted by Grant Wright. The sign was placed on the front lawn of the Community Center just north of the Industrial Tool Company building.

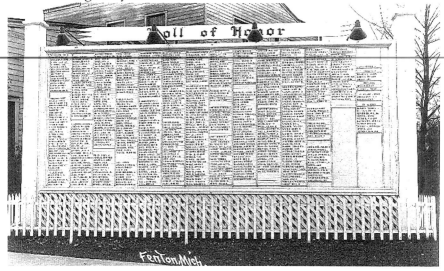

The Dedication Ceremony was held on Armistice Day, November 11, 1943 at 7 PM. Mrs. Myrtle Harris, in her capacity as President of the Patriotic Council opened the program and introduced Mrs. J. B. Obenshain as Mistress of Ceremonies Both the Fenton High School and City Bands were present and played the National Anthem and other patriotic songs during the proceedings. The Reverend Wesley J. Dudgeon offered the Invocation and the Reverend J. Stanley Mitchell was the main speaker. The Reverend Bell offered the Benediction.

Mrs. J. B. Obenshain was an excellent Mistress of Ceremonies, especially when one understands the circumstances in which she found herself. The Dedication occurred only a day or so after the Obvershains learned of the death of their son, Major J.B. Obenshain, U.S. Marine Corps. He had lost his life in combat in the South Pacific.

The Honor Roll sign was modified several times during the next few years as additional names were added. After the war, the sign was removed and destroyed. In spite of the efforts of the Fenton Museum and its Director Ken Seger, only a few photos of the sign are evidence of its existence.

The original Honor Roll listed the following as serving:

Clifford Abbey	Jack Brooks	Dominie Conklin
William Abbott	James Brown	Walter Conrad
Garl Alber Jr.	William Brown	Robert Cooper
Earl Alberts	Kenneth Bump	Bruce Cox
Don Alexander	Max Bump	Harold Covert
Gerald Alexander	A.D. Burdick	Claude Covert
Ben Alger Jr.	**Keith Burdick**	Roland Covert
Harry Amsink	Wesley Burgess	Dean Cox
Harold Annis	William Burkett	Roy Cox
Robert Atkins	Walter Burow	Joseph Craft
Lloyd Ayliffe	Ronald Butler	Earl Crane
Wilbur Bachus	Carroll Butts	Phillip Crane
James Bachus	Robert Carlson	Ralph Crane
Almarion Bacon	W.M. Carlson	Ralph Crawford
+Joseph Bacon	Earl Carmer	Norman Crego
David Bard	William Carmer	Stewart Crego
George Bard	Don Carpenter	George Crocker
Earl Barden	Marvin Carpenter	Richard Cronk
Ross Baxter	Raleigh Carpenter	Kenneth Crumer
Robert Beach	Ross Carrick	Woodrow Crump
Thomas Becker	Wilbur Case	Clifford Crystal
Murray Bell	Joe Casazza	Llelwyn Crystal
Harry Bender	John Chapman	Kenneth Cummings
Max Bennett	Eugene Chappelle	Norman Cutler
Jack Bidelman	Thomas Chappelle	John Dagan
Donald Biggs	Clair Cheesebro	Edward Covert
Robert Biggs	Arthur Cheesebrough	Harry Daniels
Robert Black	John Christman	Jack Davies
Edward Black	Carter Churchill	James Davis
Warren Boilore	Robert Clark	Lyle Davis
Paul Bottecelli	Donald Clark	David Dawson
Ralph Bower	Dwayne Clark	Kenneth Day
Thomas Bowman	Harvey Clement	William Dean
Lewis Brabon	Harvey Clement	Eugene
Harold Bradley	Maurice Coates	Walter Denker
Max Bretzke	Luther Cobb Jr.	Clyde Dean
William Brewer	Ras Cole	Conrad Dery
Harold Bristol	Vincent Collins	Claude Dery

Robert Devereaux
Theodore Diott
Willis Doan
Leo Doan
Loren Doan
William Dode
Donald Dormire
Donald Edwards
Joseph Edy
Lowell Ellsworth
Ralph Ellsworth
Kenneth Faust
Ted Filkins
James Foley
Harold Fowler
Earl Fredenburg
Donald Freeman
Lee Freeman
Robert Freeman
James Frew
Glen Gale
Charles Gannon
Phillip Garvey
Robert Gearhart
Fred Gilbird
Glen Gilbird
William Giles
Howard Goodrich
Roy Goodrich
Floyd Gordon
Howard Gordon
Lee Gordon Jr
Gene Goss
Robert Gould
Earl Granger
William Gray Jr.
Ralph Gray Jr.
Clifford Green
Charles Groover
Ross Hagerman

Eugene Hall
Clifford Harding
Roswell Harding
Fred Harper
Robert Harris
John Hart
John Hartley
Paul Haskell
William Hathaway
Sydney Hay Jr
Byron John
James Heffner
Walter Hill
Richard Hiscox
Samuel Hobbs Jr.
Harold Hoffman
William Holdsworth
Crane Horrell
Frank Howes
Gerald Hoyle
Carl Hudson
Junior Huff
Orrin Huffman
Kenneth Hulet
Clarence Hull
Glen Hull
Arthur Hull
Verne Hunt
William Irish
Johndean Jacobs
Gordon Jennison
Edward Johnson
George Judson
John Kean
Arthur Keeling
William Keist
Edward Kelleher
Jack Kimball
Howard Kirschman
James Klein

Jack Klinger
Jack Koeger
Louis Kordatzky
Max James
Burton Harris
Bruce Langley
Dave Lathrop
George Lathrop
Kenneth Lawless
Orville Lawson
Cassius Lea
Jack Lea
Joseph Leeper
Edward Leeper
Jack Legg
Harry Lewis
Orville Lewis
William Lewis
John Longworth
Ronald Longworth
Duane Loomis
Jack Looze
Edward Love
Harold Lyons
Robert Lyons
C.M. Lyons
Clifford Macmillan
Don Macmillan
George MacNeal
James Madden
Harold Madden
DeForest Marshall
Garwood Marshall
John Martin
M.W. Marwede
Robert Matkin
Dana MaWhinney
Lester McAllister
Robert McArthur

Ralph McAvoy
John McCann
Virgil McDowell
Burton McGarry
Myron McGlynn
Fred McKenzie
Charles McKeon
DeForest McKinley
Norman McNeil
Earnest Meadows
Richard Measles
Thomas Merrill
William Merrill
Robert Mertz
James Meslo
Stephen Milewiki
Jack Miller
Noel Miller
Gorton Milliken
Charles Mills
Leo Miner
Arthur Miner
H.J. Miner
Jack Mitchell
Robert Moffett
Julian Moore
John Moore
Robert Morea
Roy Morris
Charles Morton
Matthew Morton
L. Mossholder
Malcolm Murray
Anton Nakovic
Ernest Neely
Gerald Neil
James Nierscher
J.G. Obenshain
Robert Obenshain
Russell O'Berry

Pat O'Connell
George O'Neil
Wilbur Orthner
Robert Page
Glen Palmer
Stanley Parker
Charles Parker
James Pasco
Gerald Pasco
Douglas Patton
William Payne
Charles Pearsall
Dudley Pease
George Pellett
Robert Perry
Oliver Perry
Theodore Perry
Clare Pettis
Kenneth Pettis
George Phile
Charles Pinkston
Dallas Powell
Lisle Pratt
Chet Przewciznik
Donald Randolph
Don Rasmussen
Julius Rasmussen
Jack Reardon
George Reardon
Jack Reed
Norman Reed
Norman Reed
Gerald Reed
Cleon Reedy
William Renwick
Frank Rertaino
George Reynolds
Lyman Reynolds
John Rhodes
Douglas Ridholls

Richard Riedel
Ronald Riegle
Jack Riegle
Marvin Roberts
Elvin Robinson
Harold Robinson
Albert Rogers
Burnette Rogers
Jack Rolland
Ted Rolls
Donald Rounds
Gerald Rounds
Evart Runyan
Robert Runyan
Walter Runyan
Edward Rusinski
George Rusinski
Gerald Russell
Lazarre Russell
William Rynearson
Claude Sansam
John Schaefer
Harold Schaefer
Richard Schaefer
Arnold Schutt
Ralph Schillinger
Fred Schleicher
Robert Schleicher
Leo Schleicher
Kenneth Schultz
Curtis Schupbach
Harold Schupbach
William Searight
Leon Shelby Jr.
J. B. Shinnabarger
Clifford Sifford
Earl Silvers
Donald Sinclair
Bruce Sinclair
Joseph Skinner

Delmar Skutt	Robert Trimmer	Dr. C.H. White
Richard Smale	Vincent Truchan	Cedric Whitman
Sidney Smale	Albert Turco	Chester Willing
Don Smedley	Donald Vincent	Ronald Wilson
Millard Smith	John Vincent	Stanley Wilson
Leo Smith	Charles Vining	Russell Wilson
Lester Smith	Earnest Vining	Hollis Winn
Richard Smith	Grover Vorhies	Arthur Wolverton
Robert Smith	Howard Vosburg	Lloyd Wolverton
William Solomon	Tholund Vreeland	Ray Wolverton
Jack Soper	Dr. C.G. Walcott	R.R.
John Sortman	Walter Walker	Rex Woods
Donald Stehle	Neil Walker	Robert Woodward
Emerson Stiles	Herbert Walters	Neil Woodward
Howard Stocken	Verne Walters	Leslie Wright
Jack Stork	Harvey Walters	Max Wright
Howard Sutherby	Fred Walters	Carl Wyckoff
Stan Swartz	Glenn Ward	Earl Wyckoff
Stafford Swarz	Don Watters	Howard Yager
Robert Taylor	Rod Watters	Marvin Youker
W.M. Terwilliger	Herbert Watts	Austin Young
Leonard Thompson	Percy Way	Michael Zabich
J.K. Tippler	Robert Weise	Walter Zabich
Glen Townsend	William Wermuth	**Melvin Zabich**
Wayne Townsend	Arnold Westman	Russell Zoll
Francis Trimmer	Edwin White	Frank Zowilanski

Those names printed in **bold** are the names of the deceased.

From the information provided by Mr. Kenneth Seger, Curator of the Fenton Museum, 23 men from the Fenton community died during World War II. Mr. Seger has devoted several years to assembling the photos and personal information about those who gave their lives and all others who served during the most horrific war in the history of the world. The information published in these pages was derived from the material he has collected.

In the following pages, we have attempted to capsulate into a short paragraph each man's story of life and sacrifice. The effort admittedly falls far short of the true measure of their being. Their willingness to serve and face the uncertainties and tribulations of war is the reason the United States and western civilization has survived. May God bless their souls.

Photo Not
Available

Staff Sergeant Thomas E. Bowman was killed in action in Italy in July 1944, while serving with the 88th "Blue Devil" Division, Fifth Army. He was awarded the Bonze Star posthumously for heroic achievement in action. He was the son of Marcella G. Bowman of Fenton. He attended high school in his native Springfield, Illinois before moving to Fenton. He served as assistant Manager of the A & P store in 1940 before joining the U.S. Army.

Yeoman Second Class E. Keith Burdick died on October 10, 1944 when his ship, the destroyer USS Buck was torpedoed and sunk in the Tyrrhenian Sea south of the Isle of Capri. His ship had been engaged in anti-submarine activities prior to being torpedoed. The severity of the explosion caused the ship to sink rapidly and the  destroyer's own depth charges, having been set to explode at a prescribed depth, contributed to the casualties as they exploded as the ship sank, with some survivors still in the water. Keith was a 1939 graduate of Fenton High School.

 Corporal Roy Goodrich, United States Marine Corps was killed in action in the South Pacific in December 1943. Roy was a 1938 graduate of Fenton High School and had worked at the Industrial Tool Company prior to enlisting in the Marine Corps. Roy was the son of Roy and Lillian Goodrich of Fenton. His brother Howard also served with the U.S. Marines in combat in the South Pacific.

Private Duane Gruner of the U.S. Army died of wounds he received in combat in France in November 1944. Duane was a 1943 graduate of Fenton High School. After high school graduation Duane attended Michigan State College until inducted in the Army in November 1943. He was the son of Mr. and Mrs. Arthur Gruner of Fenton. Mr. Gruner was the Superintendent of the Genesee Tool Company in Fenton.

Private First Class Donald Hunt died of wounds he received in combat in France in November 1944. He was with the infantry and had been sent overseas in August 1944. Don Hunt was a 1942 graduate of Fenton High School and attended Massachusetts Institute of Technology before entering the service in June 1943. His parents were Mr. and Mrs. Floyd Hunt of Fenton.

Motor Machinists Mate Second Class William C. Merrill, U. S. N. died in action on June 9, 1944 after first being reported as missing in action. William Merrill graduated from Fenton High School in 1934. He served as a merchant sailor on the Great Lakes for a period after graduation. He joined the Navy in 1942 and served overseas since October 1943. He was the son of Mr. and Mrs. Lowell Merrill of Fenton.

Major James G. Obenshain, U.S. Marine Corps was killed in action in the South Pacific on June 22, 1943. The Marine aviator had been promoted to Major only weeks before his demise. He was an honor graduate of Georgetown (Kentucky) High School and College. He received his Naval aviator wings and commission as a Second Lieutenant of Marines at Pensacola, Florida in June 1941. He was the son of Mr. and Mrs. J. B. Obenshain of Fenton.

Lieutenant j.g. Donald L. Rounds USN was killed in an airplane crash in 1942. At the time of his death he was serving as a flight instructor at the Naval Facility at Grosse Isle, Michigan. He crashed on a return trip to Grosse Isle from Washington, D.C. when his plane struck a mountain near Somerset, Pennsylvania during a severe snowstorm. Don Rounds graduated from Fenton High School in 1933 and the University of Michigan in 1940. He was the son of Mr. and Mrs. C.S. Rounds of Fenton.

Corporal Jack T. Rolland was killed in action in France on February 9, 1944 while serving as a paratrooper with the 508th Airborne. Jack had spent twenty days in Fenton in September 1943 before returning overseas. He attended Fenton High School. He enlisted in the Army in July 1941 and after training went overseas for the first time in December 1942. Later he returned to the States for training before being transferred overseas for the second time in March 1944. He served in Italy, France, Belgium and Germany. He is buried in France. He was the son of Ivah Rolland of Fenton.

Private Lazare E. Russell, Army paratrooper, died in action in France on June 7, 1944. He attended Fenton High School but left school to join the Army in September 1941. He began training in Fort Beauregard, Louisiana and attained the rank of Sergeant. When he transferred to the Paratroops in October 1943, he was reduced to the rank of Private. Lazare was the son of Mr. and Mrs. Lazare Russell of Holly Road, Fenton, Michigan.

Private Francis R. "Bob" Runyan, U.S. Marine Corps, was killed in action in the Pacific theater on October 1943. The month before his death, he had written of being with two friends, Pvt. Rod Bowles of Linden and Pvt. Don Sinclair of Fenton. Bob Runyan was a 1941 graduate of Fenton High School. He enlisted in the Marines in September 1942. He was the son of Mrs. Thelma Norton of Fenton. He married high school classmate Esther Crawford on April 11, 1942 and went overseas on February 21, 1943.

Technician Julius E. Rasmussen, U.S. Army was killed in action on August 19, 1944 in the European theater. Julius Rasmussen enlisted in March of 1942 and went overseas in July 1944. He served with a reconnaissance unit of a Mechanized Cavalry Division. Julius attended Fenton High School. He was the son of Mr. and Mrs. Jens Rasmussen.

Private First Class Donald R. Sinclair, U.S. Marine Corps was killed in action on Guam on July 21, 1944. Don enlisted in the Marines in 1942 and after training in San Diego and Camp Pendleton, California went to the Pacific theater. Pfc. Sinclair participated in Marine combat operations on Guadalcanal and Bougainville. Don Sinclair was a graduate of Fenton High School in 1938. Don was the son of Mr. and Mrs. Claude F. Sinclair.

Private First Class Kenneth A. Schultz, U.S. Marine Corps was killed on the Island of Tinian on August 1, 1944. Kenny attended Fenton High School before enlisting in the Marines in 1941. At the age of 15 and 16 he participated in the Golden Gloves tournament in Flint, Michigan. He volunteered to go into the caves in search of the Japanese soldiers who were hiding there. He had entered a cave in the dark hours of the morning, encountered the enemy and when he emerged from the cave, apparently wounded and  staggering, he was thought to be an enemy soldier and other Marines shot and killed him. He was the son of Mr. and Mrs. Arthur F. Schultz of Fenton.

 Sergeant William H. Terwilliger, Royal Canadian Air Force was shot down over London, England while engaged in combat with German bombers. Sergeant Terwilliger enlisted in the RCAF in February 1941 and was awaiting transfer to the U.S. Air Corps when he was killed in combat. His parents were former residents of Fenton.

Private First Class Robert Weigant was a paratrooper in the U.S. Army. Robert Weigant was killed in action in Belgium on January 30, 1945. Robert graduated from Fenton High School in 1943 and enlisted in the Army on March 9, 1944. He served in France and Belgium. He was the son of Mr. and Mrs. William J. Weigant.

Private Melvin J. Zabitch U.S. Army was taken prisoner by the Japanese in The Philippines on May 6, 1942 when Bataan was overrun. He died when a U.S. submarine off the Island of Mindanao sank the Japanese prison ship Shinyo Maru, on which he was aboard, en route to Japan. Melvin was in the Class of 1942 at Fenton High School, He enlisted in the Army on July 11, 1941. He was one of four brothers who served in the armed forces during the war. Melvin and two of his brothers lived with their foster parents, Mr. and Mrs. L. M. O'Dell of Fenton, for seven years

There were three other servicemen from Fenton who died in World War II, however there is no information available to further describe them, or their service. They are the following:
Harry Coblentz, Edward J. Heble, Julian Moore and Leo Smith

Our revels now are ended. These our actors,
As I foretold you, were all spirits, and
Are melted into air, into thin air
And, like the baseless fabric of this vision,
This cloud-capp'd towers, the gorgeous palaces,
The solemn temples, the great globe itself,
Yea, all which it inherit, shall dissolve,
And, like this insubstantial pageant faded,
Leave not a rack behind. We are such stuff
As dreams are made on; and our little life
Is rounded with a sleep.
William Shakespeare

Appendix One... Graduates of Fenton High School

Class of 1937	
A	**M**
MARJORIE E ABBEY BURGER	JOYCE MINOCK FLICK
EARL L ALBERTS	EILEEN MINOCK HUGHES
BENJAMIN T ALGER Jr.	GERALDINE MOREA
ETHEL M ANNIS	**N**
MAXINE ARMSTRONG	LYLE ROBERT NEELY
B	EDWIN NORTON
JAMES BACHUS	**O**
ROBERT BAKER	ROSE O'DELL HATCH
VIRGINIA BARNARD CUMMINGS	GERALDINE OGDEN
ROBERT BURGESS	**P**
C	VIVIAN J PARKER BORKOWSKI
LUTHER COBB Jr.	AGNES PETTS PARK
HELEN L COMSTOCK ALDRICH	HELEN PINKSTON MC LAUGHLIN
JANET CONARD ELLSWORTH	**R**
D	JEAN RIEDEL WESTMAN
CLAUDE DERY	RUTH ROUNDS CRIDER
JEANETTE M DERY DOWLING	DONALD ROWLEY
WILLIAM DODE	GEORGE RUSINSKI RUSINAKI
JUNE DUBY	**S**
G	SHIRLEY SHAW CUMMINGS
JANE GOULD CLARK	JOANNE SMALE LAWRENCE
H	PETER STERN
ELWOOD HAGERMAN	**T**
ROSWELL S [ROS] HARDING	FRANCES MUNSON SINCLAIR
GLEN HULL	THOMPSON
J	**W**
JOHNDEAN JACOBS	DONALD WALTERS
GORDON JENISON	KENNETH WEAGE
WILLIAM [BILL] JOSLYN Sr.	HAZEL WHITE
L	KENNETH W WILHOIT
EDWARD P LEMKE	DONNA WILLIAMS MARWEDE
	BEATRICE WOODRUFF
	NEIL WOODWARD

Class of 1938

A-B	L-M
HARRIETT ABBEY OWEN	JACK LEA
MARGARET ADAMS WENDT	MARGUERITE LEE FRASE
PEARL ALPAUGH KLUG	DONALD LEMEN
ROBERT JUNIE ATKINS	CHAUNCIE J LUCKE
RICHARD AVERY	ALTON G MARSHALL
VIOLET BACHUS RODGERS	ALICE MATHEWS MCGARRY
DAVID BLACK	BURTON MC GARRY
ROBERT BLACK	BRUCE MC LENNA
HAROLD W BRADLEY	EILEEN MCKEON FOUS
HAROLD BRISTOL	BLANCHE MCLENNA
KENNETH BUMP	BETTY MERRILL O'GRADY
C-D	WINIFRED MILLIKEN STROM
NORENE CARPENTER LEE	MARION MORGAN BARTON
WALTER M CONARD	N-O-P
BRUCE B COX	ROSE JUNE NAKOVIC CANTOR
FLOYD E CRIPPS	HAROLD P O'GRADY
THOMAS CRONK	SUSAN PICCINNI KING
LLEWELLYN CRYSTAL	DOROTHY POLSON FAULL
RAY CUMMINGS	R-S
NELLIE DAVIS GOULD	JACQUELINE REED STEFFEY
IRENE DENNIS DETWILER	JEAN RICHMOND SCHLEEDE
MARIE I DERY RITTER	BRUCE RUNYAN
LEONA DOAN CHANDLER	PATRICIA RYNEARSON
ROBERT DODE	FAIRBANKS
JEAN DURANT LOUCKS	RALPH SCHILLINGER
RUTH DURKEE HELMBOLDT	IRENE SCHOEMACKER HUNT
E-G	ROBERT SEARIGHT
RALPH ELLSWORTH	GERALDINE STEDMAN BELL
MARIANNA GARNER SENKINE	YVONNE STEIN AUDETTE
RAYMOND GLEASON	PAULINE STIFF MC NEIL
ROY GOODRICH	WILBUR [BILL] STROM
GENEVIEVE GRANGER VACLAVIK	MARJORIE SWARTZ RUCKEL
WILMA E GREEN UNGER	JEANETTE SZEKERES BOWLES
H-I-K	T-W
GENEVIEVE HALL HASKELL	DI DAMIA TERWILLIGER CORNISH
JOHN R HARTLEY	MARY THOMPSON
DON HERMAN	MAY THOMPSON HARRIS
JOYCE HINKLEY THOMSON	KATHRYN TROLLMAN BRADY
JOHN HOSKINS	VERNAL WEEKS BELL
DORIS M HUBERT HUFF	HELEN WEIGANT COX
FRANCES IRVIN EVERT	MARGARET WHITE GANSHAW
JACK KEUTHAN	REX WOOD
CECELIA KUCHARSKI	WALTER WOOD

Class of 1939

A
JACK ABBOTT
RICHARD ALEXANDER
BETTY ALEXANDER REID
LOIS ATHERTON SCHRAEDER
B
NORMAN BAILEY
 ARTHUR BARNARD
DONALD K BELL
PAUL BOTTECELLI
GERALDINE BROWN CARLSON
ONNOLEE BROWN SHUMWAY
KEITH BURDICK
MILDRED BURGESS NETTLETON
ETHELYN BURROWS WINTER
C-D-E-F-G
BARBARA CHESNUT RIEDEL
DONALD L CLARK
AGNES COLLETTE DUMANOIS
JEANNE COPP TOMLINSON
ROLAN COVERT
JOANNE COX DIMLER
JOSIE DAVIES ATCHINSON
MARION EVART
JAMES FOLEY
 ELIZABETH JEAN GORDON
WEIGANT
H
HELEN HAGER DUFFIELD
GLADA HERMAN BATTLES
HELEN HOCKETT HILL
 BRADLEY HOFFMAN
K
VERNA KEUHN WYNE
GILBERT KLEIN
FLORENCE KRAMER
 L
MARION LAWSON LEECE
JEAN LEE FASHBOUGH
LORA LEWIS DOLE

L
LAURA LEWIS HUDSON
DORIS LOBDELL COLE
RONALD LONGWORTH
CAROL LUTZ DENNIS
M-N-O-P
BLANCHE MC LENNA FINK
 ESTHER MCDOWELL WILES
JUSTIN RUCKEL MEACHAM
NEVA NEELY GAINEY
MARY L O'BERRY SUTHERBY
PATRICK H O'CONNELL
ROBERT PARTRIDGE
 DONALD W PETERSON
KENNETH PETTIS
MAXINE POWLISON WALCOTT
R
JAMES [JIM] RASH
RICHARD L [DICK] RIEDEL
ELVIN ROBINSON
DOUGLAS ROGERS
EDWARD A RUSINSKI RUSIN
S
LORIMER SAROSKY
MILDRED E [BETH] SCHILLINGER
ALBERTS
JEANETTE SCHULTZ MC CREADY
RUTH SHELDON DRAKE
MARY SIMMONS MCDEVITT
DONALD SINCLAIR
SIDNEY SMALE
THOMAS J SMITH
JEAN SWARTZ FREEMAN
V-W-Y
ERNEST VINING
YVONNE VOSBURGH
CHURCHMAN
ANNIE WALTERS WHITE
MARJORIE WILLIAMS WATTERS
DOROTHY WOOD SUCIU
GRACE YOUNG LICHT

Class of 1940

A
THERESA ALLEN BOUR
ZELMA ALPAUGH VAN WAGONER
ONALEE ARMSTRONG WINDSOR
DOROTHY AUSTIN SMALE
B
VIRGINIA BOTTECELLI
MCKENNEY
JEAN BROOKS TIGHE
EUGENIA BUCKINGHAM SADLER

ROSE ANNA BUFFMYER POWELL
ARLENE BURROWS PETTIS
C
JOSEPH CRAFT
D
HARRY DANIELS
CLARA DAVIS KILLIN
DAVID W DAWSON
AGNES DLUGOSE
KATHRYN DODE HELMBOLDT
E
ARLOA ELLSWORTH SAWER
F
LAWRENCE F FARNER
ILA FOUST SKEMAN
EILEEN FREEMAN HETCHLER
JAMES R FREW
G
ALICE GILLEM NISSLE
BETTY GLASPIE CLARK
VADA GORDON WHALEN
BERNICE GREEN LONG
H
DAWN HAGERMAN SPEED
CLARA V HALSTEAD
WANDA L HAMMEL PIPES
LOREEN HARDING MACNEIL
BETTY HARTMAN MORRIS
MARJORIE HINKLEY
        BREITENSTEIN

J
JOYCE JOHNSON RUSSELL
K
HAZEL KARSHNER ROBERTS
YVONNE KEDDY FOX
VIOLET M KLINGLER NEIL
L
KENNETH LAWLESS
CATHERINE LUKE
M
MARY MCELROY GEARHART
DE FOREST MCKINLEY
JACOB G MILLIKEN
DOROTHY ELIZABETH MILLIKEN
WINNARD
CHARLOTTE M MINER KELLER
N
FELIX F NAKOVIC
HELEN LOUISE NEELY CRANE
P
PATTI PARKER SAROSKY
ROY PERRY
CHARLES B PINKSTON
VIRGINIA POPPY SEARIGHT
R
GLORIA REID GILKEY
LUCILLE R REYNOLDS WRIGHT
S
JOHN SCHAEFER
ROBERT SCHLEICHER
 HAROLD SCHUPBACH
VIRGENE SLUYTER TAYLOR
MILDRED SMITH DREISBACH
T
ELIZABETH THORNTON HIPPE
FRANCIS TRIMMER
W
RUSSELL WILSON

Class of 1941

B
JOSEPH H BACON
GEORGE BARD
RAYMOND W BARNES
LEON F BECKER
MURRAY F BELL
WILLIAM J BROWN
BEATRICE BUCKINGHAM ALBURTUS
DONALD M BUMP
ANNA BURGSTALLER TRACY
C
MARVIN CARPENTER
MARGARET CHESNUT PHILLIPS
SARAH CRANE ANDERSEN
RALPH CRAWFORD
ESTHER CRAWFORD STIENER
D
EDWARD DANIELS
BETTY DOBBS COHEE
DONALD D DORMIRE
F
FLORENCE FOLEY NAGY
G
ROBERT GEARHEART
BETTY GILLEM OLIVER
JOANNE GOODFELLOW WARE
HOWARD C GOODRICH
LEE E GORDON
ROBERT W GOULD
DOROTHY GOULD WEST
EVELYN GRAHAM WILSON
H
LEONE HAGERMAN MEIER
HOPE V HAMILTON REED
ROBERT G HARRIS
JUNE HARTLEY ATKINSON
ANNA HAURITZ SCOTT
JUNIOR HUFF
DORIS HUNT MOTT
J-K
WILLENE JENISON TAYLOR
VIRGINIA JOSLIN PRATT
SHEILA KEDDY
JUNE KEUHN RICHARDSON

M
ARLENE MARSHALL REDDY
CHARLES MC KEON
SHIRLEY METCALF
ARTHUR J MINER
ROBERT W MOREA
BETH ANN MOREHOUSE PUGH
GERALDINE MORTON COBDRA
LAWRANCE B MYTINGER
N-O-P-R
MARILYN NORTHRUP HAYNOR
RUSSELL O'BERRY
JEAN M PAVEY HERMAN
GEORGE PELLETT
CARL R PINKSTON
ARLENE POWERS PINKSTON
DONALD J RASMUSSEN
MARY JEAN ROWLEY ARMSTRONG
ROBERT RUNYAN
WILLIAM J RYNEARSON
S-T
RAYMOND E SCHULTZ
ARNOLD W SCHUTT
ELMER D SCHUTT
MARGARET SHAW ROMINE
RICHARD SMALE
JACK SOPER
MURRAY STANLEY
JOYCE STEIN GIERYN
ROBERTA JANE STODDARD MCDOWELL
LAWRENCE SUGDEN
ALBERT P TURCO
W-Y
NEIL WALKER
GERALDINE WARNER RODGERS
JOYCE WEAKS HARMON
ROSE E [PEGGY] WESSEL
ROSA WESTMAN MARCHESE
PAULINE WILHOIT LOOMIS
RONALD C WILSON
JEAN WOODWORTH SCHLEICHER
HILDA WORTMAN BROOKS
MARVIN YOUKER

Appendix Two...List of Contents in Cornerstone

In its April 28, 1938 edition of *The Fenton Independent,* the paper printed the list of material deposited in the cornerstone of the new Municipal Building, aka the "new" Fire Hall. The following is the list as reported:

American Legion membership, history and officers of the post.
   Women's Auxiliary, membership, history and officers of post.
   V.F.W. membership, history and officers of the post.
   Daughters of Union Veterans, membership, history and officers.
   Fenton Lodge No. 109 F. & A. M. pamphlet.
   Genesee Chapter No. 29 R.A.M. pamphlet.
   Fenton Commandery, No. 14, Knights Templar pamphlet.
   Eastern Star No. 248, pamphlet.
   Fenton Lodge I.O. O. F. No. 125 pamphlet.
   Favorite Rebekah Lodge, No. 47 pamphlet.
   Fenton Telephone Directory.
   Fenton Directory, Village and rural.
   Fireman's List, 4 pictures.
   St. John's 92nd anniversary Book and Paper.
   Girl Scouts
   Boy Scouts
 Christian Science Journal.
 .
	Grand Trunk pamphlet
	 Consumers Power letter.
	 Entre Nous Club Pamphlet.
	 Bay View Club Pamphlet.
	 W.C.T.U. pamphlet.
	 XX Club pamphlet.
	 Junior Child Study Club letter.
	 Isaac Walton League letter.
	 Men's Fellowship letter.
	 Flint Journal dated April 23, 1938.
	 Detroit News dated April 23, 1938.
	 Pictures of Fenton Churches.
	 High School students list.
	 High school faculty.
	 Village list of officers, Council, Water Board, Board of Education, Police officers, Firemen.
	 Township officers.
	 Tamlyn Studio pictures of all sorts, Centennial pictures, street scenes, Paper money and Centennial Book of the history of Fenton.
	   Several other articles such as old papers, coins, records, arrow heads and old pictures.
	 Registration list.

The Registration List was placed in the office of *The Fenton Independent* where those interested could sign the list. It is estimated about 500 to 600 person signed the list, which was about half of the number attending the Cornerstone dedication ceremony.

Appendix Three…The Supporting Cast and Crew

Interviews were conducted with the following persons:
Name and Fenton High School Class if appropriate:

Marge Johnson Kelley	1931
Russell D. Haddon	1932
Paul Bottecelli	1939
George D. Pellett	1941
Duane Theisen	1943
Robert J. Dery	1943
Lee E. Gordon	1941
Jean Gordon Weigant	1939
Albert P. Turco	1941
Nathaniel J.Woodward	1942
Barbara Barnes Syring	1935
Marie Durant Harris	1942
Raymond D. Durant	1950
Kenneth Seger	1954
Sidney Smale	1939
Dorothy Austin Smale	1940
Carroll G. Butts	1942

Newspapers
The Fenton Independent, Weekly editions 1936-1937 inclusive
The Fenton Courier, Weekly editions 1937-1941 inclusive

Books and Family Histories

But, That's Another Story	Robert G. Harris
Fenton Remembers When	Leo Weigant
Burns Fuller Remembers…	
…Fenton-My Home Town	Burns Fuller
Bottecelli Family History	Max Botticelli
A Time to Remember	Mrs. Ruth Anne Silbar

The Fenton Museum
Various documents, Biographies, Bibliographies, Newspapers,
Obituaries, Photos and Timelines from On Line Sources.